D0216895

EX LIBRIS
NEW YORK INSTITUTE
OF TECHNOLOGY

The
Unfinished
Revolution

Other Titles of Interest

The Letters of Rosa Luxemburg, edited and with an Introduction by Stephen Eric Bronner

An Infantile Disorder?: The Crisis and Decline of the New Left, Nigel Young

Radicalism in the Contemporary Age. Volume 1: *Sources of Contemporary Radicalism,* edited by Seweryn Bialer and Sophia Sluzar

Radicalism in the Contemporary Age. Volume 2: *Radical Visions of the Future,* edited by Seweryn Bialer and Sophia Sluzar

Radicalism in the Contemporary Age. Volume 3: *Strategies and Impact of Contemporary Radicalism,* edited by Seweryn Bialer and Sophia Sluzar

The Unfinished Revolution: Marxism and Communism in the Modern World
revised edition

Adam B. Ulam

Marxism has been the most pervasive and widespread ideological phenomenon of our times, but seldom, if ever, has it been found in its "pure" form. Whenever the Marxist ideology has been historically significant, it has been so as a beneficiary and associate of another set of political beliefs and passions. As a contender for power it seeks to express the dreams and yearnings of societies caught in the painful process of modernization and industrialization. In power it tends to pay lip service to its lofty goals, but associates them with old-fashioned nationalism. Practice does not reflect theory. Ruling elites and parties surpass traditional capitalism in their dedication to political centralization and industrialism at all costs.

This revised edition of Adam Ulam's standard work retains the author's summary and critique of Marx's historical, economic, and political arguments. Ulam then examines the relationship of Marxism to other schools of contemporary socialism and to other radical and revolutionary theories. He traces the development of Marxian thought, explains why it has been the potent force in certain societies—while in other societies its influence has been insignificant—and analyzes how Marxism and Leninism have affected the shaping of Russian Communism. Finally Ulam looks at Marxism in the future: the role it will play in the development of the Soviet Union, and how it will affect the contemporary crisis of liberal institutions in the West.

Adam B. Ulam, one of this country's most eminent authorities on Marxism and the Soviet Union, has been a member of the faculty at Harvard University since 1946, where he is now professor of government. He is also associated with Harvard's Russian Research Center as a research fellow and member of the executive committee.

Adam B. Ulam

The Unfinished Revolution

Marxism and Communism in the Modern World

revised edition

Westview Press / Boulder, Colorado

Copyright © 1979 by Westview Press, Inc.

Published in 1979 in the United States of America by
Westview Press, Inc.
5500 Central Avenue
Boulder, Colorado 80301
Frederick A. Praeger, Publisher

Library of Congress Cataloging in Publication Data
Ulam, Adam Bruno, 1922-
The unfinished revolution.
Includes bibliographical references.
1. Socialism—History. 2. Communism—History. I. Title.
HX37.U42 1979   355'.009   79-700
ISBN 0-89158-485-4
ISBN 0-89158-496-X pbk.

Printed and bound in the United States of America

Contents

Preface to the Revised Edition

It is difficult to assess the role of ideologies in this fast-changing world. This book appeared originally in 1960, but I have found little reason to change my original conclusions about the nature of Marxism and why it has been the most pervasive and widespread ideological phenomenon of our times. Where the work needed emendation, in view of our experience of the last twenty years, was in the assessing the current status and prospects of Marxism in the Soviet Union, as well as in evaluating the influence of Marxian socialism and its relationship to the contemporary crisis of liberal institutions in the West.

One of the main theses presented here is that one seldom, if ever, finds political Marxism in its "pure" form; that is to say, whenever this ideology has been historically significant, it has been so as a beneficiary and associate of another set of political beliefs and passions. As a contender for power, Marxism derives its popular appeal from the basically anarchist feelings exuded by societies undergoing the painful process of industrialization and modernization. Once in power, as in the Russia of the 1920's and 1930's, the Marxist party quickly sheds its semi-anarchist and libertarian vestments and matches and surpasses early capitalism in its ruthless dedication to industrialism and political centralization.

When the main task of political and economic modernization has been completed, Marxism in our experience has been relegated to the status of official cult of the authoritarian state.

The Soviet Union is the most vivid, but far from being the only, example of a Communist country where whatever significance the ideology still retains is due to its symbiosis with nationalism.

In fact, what has proved to be the most vulnerable tenet of the doctrine has been its self-proclaimed role as the solvent of national and racial conflicts and the harbinger of universal peace. Workers have no country, Karl Marx asserted. But today every Communist regime, including those which depend on the power of the USSR, couches its appeal for popular support and acceptance in the nationalist idiom. The one undoubted advantage of Communism has been its ability to preserve the national state from those forces which everywhere else have eroded the bases of political and traditional authority. And it is difficult to resist the conclusion that it is because the rulers on both sides are Communist that the Sino-Soviet conflict has become sharp and remains basically intractable.

But even though Communism has shown little promise that it can satisfy the most urgent need of the age and become the foundation of a peaceful international community, its ideology remains a potent force in the non-Communist world. Parties professing allegiance to the ideas of Marx, Engels, and Lenin exist in practically every country of the world. Revolutionary movements in the Third World and the sects of terrorist fanatics in the West, while rejecting any ideological orthodoxy, still employ the idiom of Marxism. Even those who consider Communism to be an authoritarian and bureaucratic excrescence upon the doctrine and who repudiate violence often seek in Marxian socialism a guide to a more just and effective social order.

Do all these developments attest to the strength and correctness of the theory of history and society first propounded by Karl Marx? Or do they reflect the ever deepening condition of social and international anarchy consequent upon the decline of liberalism and other creeds and ideologies, representing in their sum Western civilization? Or does the power of Marxism "proceed out of the mouth of the gun," reflecting the growth of power of the USSR rather than the inherent political and intellectual strength and attractiveness of the doctrine?

It is to such questions that this inquiry is addressed. I have tried, as well, to see the problem in its historical setting.

Cambridge, Massachusetts
September, 1978

Preface to the First Edition

This book is not a genealogy of political ideas. My main interest has been to find out what makes Marxism alive and relevant in certain societies, while elsewhere socialism and Communism remain the creeds of insignificant sects or intellectual coteries.

It would take me much too long to list all the people to whom I am indebted in connection with this book. But I should certainly mention with gratitude Mr. Charles D. Lieber of Random House, Miss Mary Towle, my secretary, and Mr. Gabriel Grasberg, my assistant during one phase of this work.

It is perhaps appropriate, in view of one of the main themes of the book, that this study of socialism should have been assisted by Guggenheim, Rockefeller, and Carnegie, the names being those of the foundations which have been very generous. The Russian Research Center at Harvard has provided me with leisure not usually available to a college teacher. I am grateful to its personnel and to my colleagues on its staff, and particularly to its first director, Mr. Clyde Kluckhohn.

Eliot House
Cambridge, Massachusetts
April 1960

— 1 —
The Problem

What Marxism is and is not is a question that has occupied and divided scholars and politicians for a long time. The difficulty is obvious. Here is a doctrine of enormous intricacy and subtlety addressed not to the intellectuals but to the masses; a philosophy of liberation and freedom that in our day has given fruit in two of the most despotic and bureaucratized states history has seen. The earliest Marxists assumed that their doctrine would triumph in fully industrialized and modernized society: by contrast, history has shown Marxism victorious and influential mainly in societies groping their way toward industrialization and modernity, and not in the cradle of the doctrine, the industrialized West. Such is a small sample of the paradoxes of Marxism, which may well convince the average American or Englishman that life is difficult enough and sufficiently complicated by the visible results of the doctrine— Soviet Russia and China and their satellites—without the additional trouble of comprehending the intricate system of thought that is somehow behind it all. Furthermore, the doctrine is not only intricate but elusive. The mutual relationship of the elements of the triad Marxism-socialism-Communism is far from simple. An academician may look condescendingly at the obtuseness of the people who do not understand how *Communist* Russia can proclaim itself to be a *socialist* state, yet obviously the Soviets themselves are confused on the subject. Witness the declaration made in 1961 by Nikita Khrushchev that in 1978 the Soviet state and society would enter the era of Communism. Well, Nikita Khrushchev is long gone, 1980 is around the corner, and nothing has been heard about the dramatic transformation the year was supposed to bring. There is a suspicion among both statesmen and academicians in the West that "serious people," in this case the rulers of international Communism, cannot really be motivated by theories and analyses devised a century ago by two German thinkers. The ideology is relegated to the realm of propaganda; or, conversely, some of the leaders of Communism are dubbed fanatics, and every step in their policies is related to the blueprint of world conquest emerging from Marxism-Leninism.

The uncertainty about the nature of the challenge is accompanied in Western thought by uncertainty about the nature of policies designed to meet it. If the doctrine of Marx and Engels implants in its devotees an implacable resolve to destroy the capitalist world, then the premise of the ideological motivation of the Soviet system must lead the Western exponents of democracy to concentrate on concrete tasks of defense. If, on the other hand, the doctrine presents danger mainly from the propagandist point of view, isn't the right response to prevent its spread among the underprivileged parts of the globe through technical and economic assistance? To the newspaper reader, the challenge of Communism resolves itself into a blurred composite: a military review in the Red Square; a Communist agitator haranguing an Oriental crowd; Russia's laboratories, with their eager masses of engineers and mathematicians; and somehow behind it all two bearded German thinkers. We no longer are as confident as we once were that this is a rational world. But the Western, especially Anglo-American, tradition still clings to the belief that political and economic problems must have concrete, easily identifiable, and rational solutions. Here we are dealing with a complex of problems that seemingly elude our grasp. Both "reasonableness" and "firmness" fail to arrest the assertiveness of Soviet policies. Emancipation of the colonial peoples and economic help to the underdeveloped areas appear incapable in themselves of endowing the new states with democratic institutions or immunity to Communism. Problems of an international society undergoing an economic and ideological revolution seem to defy the social scientist's expertise, just as they defy the democratic citizen's common-sense analyses and the generosity—granted its qualifications and errors—that has characterized the policy of the leading democratic powers of the West.

It is at least instructive to take a closer look at the origins of the doctrine, which, whatever else it may be, deals with the phenomenon of the economic revolution that has transformed the world during the last century and a half. Knowledge of the origins and structure of Marxism may not help in the solution of an international crisis. But that knowledge is in itself a form of action (the notion Marxism inherited from ancient philosophy) is perhaps the least debatable Marxist tenet. The origins and the structure of the Marxist system explain much about the spread of Marxism and its offshoots like Communism, a spread that has often taken place in societies and circumstances quite different from those that Karl Marx and Friedrich Engels had assumed would welcome their system. If it appears presumptuous to add yet another to the long list of interpretations and explanations of Marxism, then it may be offered as a partial excuse that events since World War II have enabled us to see new dimensions and facets of the problem.

Karl Marx wrote in the midst of and about a revolution that was changing Western society and affecting all parts of the globe—with all its destructive effects on the old orders of Europe. We who have taken the industrial system for granted and assumed that we have seen all its political and social effects, we in the West, have all but lost the conception of the first spontaneous reactions to its arrival: the wonder at the power of technology and science, the bewilderment and resentment at the abrupt destruction of the old social and political institutions and beliefs, and the gropings for a system that would somehow explain it all and put the whole world together again. We have tended to consider reactions to industrialism not found in our own society (or at least assumed not to be found there) as expressions of primitivism, or of the exoticism of a given society, or of a national or economic catastrophe. Even the Bolshevik revolution and its consequences have been usually taken (and this is only to a degree

less true of Western Marxists than of their opponents) as
something quite exceptional, a freak of history, perhaps
attributable to the peculiarities of the Russian national
character.

It is only since World War II that we have realized that we are
in the midst of a yet unfinished revolution. Its character is more
complex than commonplace Communist propaganda would
have it; and it also defies the usual Western editorializing,
which always sees in revolutionary stirrings the result of an
inadequate standard of living, or corruption and oppression by
a particular government. The conditions underlying the
current revolution are in many ways similar to those that
disturbed and transformed Western European society during
the first half of the nineteenth century. Under different
conditions and in a different world situation, we see parts of
Asia, Africa, and Latin America entering the initial or
intermediate stages of the Industrial Revolution. The birth
pains of modern industrial society, which Marx often mistook
for the death throes of capitalism, are being enacted before our
eyes. We can see more clearly what Marxism was *about* than
could the generations for whom it was a movement of protest
against capitalism, an obsolete economic theory, or a
philosophical justification for an international Communist
conspiracy. Also, in another dimension, within the context of a
highly industrialized society, both the insights and the
limitations of Marxism are more clearly perceptible now that a
society based on Marxist ideology is challenging the greatest
nonsocialist state for industrial and political supremacy.

In other words, we can begin to see Marxism not only as a set
of theories and prophecies postulated by its author and his
disciples, but as something that "exists in nature" as well. We
need not agree with Marx's own appraisal of his theories: that
he was discovering the laws of social development. Certainly
his doctrine has been victorious under conditions quite
unforeseen by him, and Marxism got hold of societies which
the very "laws" of Marxism would have precluded from falling
under its influence, while conditions and societies thought by
him most appropriate for the realization of socialism have
developed in a quite different direction. But a thinker may be

supremely important and his thought of world significance not only because he formulates historical laws, but also because his thought reflects the essence of the mood of great historical periods. This has been the great significance of Marx. Philosopher, economist, a would-be politician and revolutionary, his ideas are still alive and important because they are attuned to the two greatest tendencies of the industrial age: the worship of science and mechanization and limitless faith in their power to transform mankind; and the very opposite—protest against the soullessness and destructiveness of the machine age. Every society reaching for industrialization and modernization has its "Marxist" period, when some of the ideas of Marx are relevant to its problems and are reflected in everyday sentiments of the masses of people, even though the name of Marx and his movement may be unknown to them. Hence the attraction for Marxism, and the quasi-Marxist character of social protest in many areas of the world—an attraction which would still exist, though perhaps in a different form, were Marxism not represented by one of the two greatest powers of the world. Hence also the stubborn character of the appeal of Marxism to the intellectual and scientist as well as the masses in a society undergoing industrialization. For Marxism comes to them not entirely as a new argument attempting to convince with facts and figures, but as something which co-ordinates and brings together their own ideas and sentiments.

Marxism, then, is not only the complex of theories bequeathed by Marx and Engels and developed, interpreted, and acted out in countless ways by countless theorists, parties, and movements. To use an analogy from physics: science has learned to produce in the laboratory elements found in nature. Imperfect as such comparisons must be, Marxism to a remarkable degree reproduces the social psychology of the period of transition from a preindustrial to an industrial society. If this is correct, then it is not surprising that Marxian socialism found little response in late nineteenth-century England and a great deal in Russia at the turn of the century. The industrialized United States has experienced Marxism in the last generation only as an intellectual reaction to the

Depression; but large parts of Latin America, drawn increasingly into modern economy and its concomitants, are experiencing social and political turbulence which, while not directed by Marxists and not necessarily inspired by socialism or Communism, is Marxist in its mood if not in its postulates.

It is always dangerous as well as ungracious to condescend to great men's ideas because the passage of time has inevitably shown their incompleteness or partial errors. A college student is not a greater physicist than Newton because he knows the incompleteness or limitations of Newton's theories. The great body of literature that has grown up in the exposition of Marx's errors, the incompatibilities of his theories with historical facts, and his inconsistencies has served—only a little less than the incredible intellectual calisthenics of the defenders of the literal truth of every single postulate of his canon—to obscure the main meaning and importance of his doctrine. It is not proposed here to minimize the importance of critiques of the Marxist system or to consider them merely as emanations of their times.

But it is possible and sensible to look at Marxism not as an infallible canon or as a series of intellectual aberrations. Lenin, for all his dogmatism, used to quote fondly Goethe's saying about the grayness of the dogma and the greenness of the tree of life. In this case the grayness of the dogma often conceals the passion and movement of life. The surplus-labor theory may be "wrong" from the point of view of a non-Marxist economist, yet it implies the supreme value of human labor and individuality in the midst of societies where the worker views himself as an adjunct of the machine. The economic historian may patiently prove that under capitalism the fate of the worker has not grown worse, but this Marxist "error" still communicates to the worker in an *industrializing* society his loss of the stability and security he enjoyed in his previous status of peasant or craftsman.

This does not mean Marx was manufacturing social myths or dealing in symbolism. Again the context of his times enables us to understand how he came to believe with the intensity of a religious fanatic in many, to us, bizarre notions, just as the context of our own times shows how a simplified version of the same ideas can drive people into political action. In many respects, Marx culminates rather than transcends the ideas of his times and society. His economics are in the final flowering of the tradition of classical political economy. His philosophy and dialectic, those sources of exasperation to would-be Marxists in the pragmatic Anglo-Saxon countries, conclude the main Hegelian stream in German philosophy as well as subvert it. In Marx, socialism from sporadic sects and movements and from philosophers became an international movement and a definite body of thought. And even some of the postulates of liberalism, his main intellectual target, are, as we shall see, enshrined in his philosophy more rigorously and dogmatically than in the work of the most typical representatives of liberalism itself.

Marxism, then, as a *system of thought*, cannot be understood except through an understanding of the intellectual traditions that made up nineteenth-century thought. The source of the historical influence of Marxism can be understood only if we realize how *recurrent* the kind of social and intellectual situation of Western Europe in Marx's time has been in other parts of the world up to our own times.

It is not proposed here to establish a new form of determinism. The existence of Marxist situations in large parts of the world does not inevitably portend the victory of Communism there. It was a grouping of fortuitous events and forces that enabled Marxism to triumph in Russia. But it was *not* an accident that in 1917 Marxism in Lenin's version appealed to large segments of Russia's working class and intelligentsia. Similarly today: whether the Marxist situations all over the world become Communist preserves depends mostly on the relative strength and policies of the Western and the Soviet camps. But the outcome must be affected by the naturalness or inappropriateness of the setting for Communism in any given society. The study of the underdeveloped territories, and the attempt at their economic development by Western resources and skills, must take into realistic account the fact that at the crucial point of transition from a pre-industrial society to a modern, at least partly industrialized state, Marxism becomes in a sense the natural ideology of that society and the most alluring solution to its problems.

Another dimension of the contemporary problem of Marxism is equally important to practical politics. What of Marxism in the Soviet Union? If Marxism's alternative roles are the expression of protest against the pains and deprivations of industrialization and modernization and, simultaneously, the ideology under which this modernization and industrialization are accomplished, what are the prospects for Marxism in the largely industrialized Soviet state? Is the ideology still important to an analysis of the Soviet Union, or has it become a mere façade behind which practical people make practical decisions aimed at the maximization of their own power and that of the totalitarian state over which they rule?

To sum up: from a variety of vantage points a study of Marxism is a study not of disembodied ideas, but of crucial social and political ideas; not only of theories but also of human emotions which have shaped and continue to make the modern world.

— 2 —
The Argument

Materialism

It was over the grave of his friend and associate, in 1883, that Friedrich Engels said:

> As Darwin discovered the law of evolution in organic nature, so Marx discovered the law of evolution in human history; the simple fact, previously hidden under ideological growths, that human beings must first of all eat, drink, shelter and clothe themselves, before they can turn their attention to politics, science, art and religion.

Engels was carried away by profound emotion; elsewhere in his address he was to ascribe to Marx important discoveries in mathematics. The father of modern socialism, though modesty was not a prominent trait of his, would not have claimed the discovery of historical materialism. The latter as an explanation of human behavior is as old as recorded thinking about society. Marx in his youth exposed the more naive versions of materialism, culminating in Feuerbach's "Man is what he eats." Admirer of Hobbes, student of the Utilitarians, Marx could not have claimed to have discovered the general principle of materialism which indeed emanated from the intellectual atmosphere of his age.

If Marxism belongs in the great tradition of materialist thought, yet the character of Marx's materialism already displays one of those striking inconsistencies and ambiguities that are interspersed throughout his whole system. We are the products of our material environment, in the sense that our ideas, as well as our mode of existence, are determined by the type of economy within which we live, or more concretely by our status within it. Systems of politics, art, religion, etc., are eventually traced back to their economic roots. Nothing exists in the mind that cannot be traced back to the economic environment. The dominant mode of production determines the character of society; the relationship of an individual or class to the means of production decides his or its social consciousness and mode of behavior. Such is the gist of Marx's materialist argument. Who would quarrel with Marx if he had said that material factors are important—if before each "determined" he had inserted "largely" or even "mostly"? Marx's rigorous dogmatism has set his critics on a gleeful and rather easy hunt for exceptions, qualifications, and inconsistencies in each step of his materialist argument. Yet the fashion for generalizing in dogmatic terms about man's social behavior and history was prevalent in Marx's times. If one accepts Marxism as a historical phenomenon and does not seek to accept or reject it as gospel, there is no reason to get excited over Marx's materialistic dogmatism. It is in the spirit of his era.

The interesting inconsistency lies elsewhere. The first naive question a student is likely to ask about Marxism points up the real problem: If we are determined by our environment, what chance is there for conscious human activity to change society? The passion of Marx and Engels for social justice and revolutionary activity, their propaganda and their literary activity seem to belie their teaching. Whatever unlovely personal characteristics one discovers in Marx himself, one cannot avoid the impression of a Prometheus-like person struggling against the world, attempting to expose the injustices and hypocrisies which, according to his theories, are the unavoidable features of contemporary society.

The above dilemma is that of many a philosopher and scientist who attempts to revolutionize or reform his world. And to the accusation of inconsistency there is the not entirely convincing answer that revolutionary activity, like scientific activity, does not deny the facts of nature, but seeks their understanding and control by men. But the ambiguity in Marx's determinism flows from his search for a *new* type of determinism and a *new* type of materialism. The beginnings of the search are perhaps to be found in an occurrence quite common in young intellectuals: fascination with somebody else's ideas and, at the same time, desire to appropriate them by improving upon them, by seizing them in a new way. Certainly this intent is visible in *Theses on Feuerbach*, the eleven exceedingly epigrammatic statements jotted down by young Marx in 1845. If they were read without bearing in mind Marx's future activity, they would be dismissed as incoherent exercises on the theme, "materialism is not enough," and as a fatuous attempt to grasp for something else. But in the context of Marx's future development they can be seen as not only a projection of ambition, or of the exasperation of a young and sensitive man with an academic approach to human problems and his disgust with both materialism and idealism as then defined. The theses set before him the problem of the search for an understanding of the material world that would contribute to and lead toward a liberation of mankind. The development of his own theories henceforth bore the imprint of an unresolved conflict between, first, submission to the spirit of the age with its materialism and search for laws governing social reality in economics, and second, a romantic's rebellion not only against society but against the current theories of social problems. Materialism is not enough. Idealism is irrelevant, and the contemporary theories of socialism are the works of quacks and moralists. It is a heartfelt cry that is heard at the end of the theses: "The philosophers have only *interpreted* the world in various ways; the point, however, is to *change* it": a direct challenge to Hegelian strictures of philosophy coming too late to teach the world what it should be. Knowledge as formulation of laws by a dispassionate observer versus knowledge as a form of action—these are two clashing concepts before young Marx.

The search for a new type of materialism can be seen in the whole Marxist system. The forces of history work through the changing forces of production and the changing civilizations

that correspond to them. Progress toward freedom is man's
continuing progress in mastering the forces of nature until full
mastery is achieved under socialism. Marx's materialism is an
intricate combination of eighteenth-century mechanistic materialism, common-sense liberal materialism, which saw men
influenced by their "interest," and Hegelian dialectic. In his
own mind and to his own satisfaction, Marx achieved the
creation of a new materialism promised in another thesis on
Feuerbach: "The standpoint of the new [materialism] is
human society or socialized humanity." Thus both a new
interpretation of the world *and* a way of *changing* it are
promised by Marxist philosophy. Man is a slave of his
environment not only in the way he lives but also in his ideas,
until science enables him to break the shackles of his
environment and by liberating his labor liberates his personality. Materialism is thus not only a sober realistic way of
viewing human affairs, an antidote to religions, myths, and
superstitions which have imprisoned the human mind. It is
also the equivalent of the original sin that, until socialism is
reached, keeps mankind imprisoned in the network of selfish
economic interests and makes utopian the postulates of
freedom, equality, and fraternity. It is vain to pray for a change
in men's hearts, for we are all slaves of economic necessity
until . . .

The scaffolding of Marx's argument discloses Marx the
romantic revolutionary assailing his contemporary society for
its preoccupation with money; Marx the materialist rejecting
moralistic and idealistic solutions as fraudulent; and finally
Marx the Hegelian reconciling the two conflicting principles
by a march of history that, through an evolution of material
forces, brings freedom for the first time within the grasp of
mankind. It is a brilliant intellectual exercise, a brilliant
synthesis performed by a mind chafing under the world's
injustices and yet rejecting solutions ignoring the reality of
human relations. But what can be the source of attraction in an
argument so tortuous and involved, with its "negation of
negations" and its "alienation"?

A preliminary answer must acknowledge how universal is
the inner dialectic of Marx's argument. How often we are

struck by the conflict between ideals and "things as they are." How enticing it is to resolve the conflict "realistically" by postulating a material progress, whether of individuals or societies, that will bring about the desired moral results. Behind its complicated structure, Marx's concept of materialism has all the power of a commonplace. And much more than that: within the fully developed system, Marxist economic determinism (which is the form his materialism takes) acts not to weaken but to strengthen the moral component of the revolutionary impulse. Superficially, no moral blame can, strictly speaking, be attached to the capitalist as capitalist: he acts in accordance with economic forces that determine his behavior. Yet in a sense his crime is all the greater. His function lies athwart the historic forces that ordain society to move beyond capitalism into socialism. Economic predetermination, like religious predetermination, does not absolve from but enhances moral judgment. Whatever a logician may think of the various steps in its argument, Marxist economic determinism will always retain its human appeal.

To a society encumbered by class, caste, and bureaucratic distinctions, materialism comes as a philosophy of liberation. This is difficult for us to realize, living as we do in a materialistic age and in a materialistic society. Yet in the middle forties of the last century in Germany, materialism burst forth as an iconoclastic creed, challenging the rationale of dynastic and class distinction. In a country attempting to shake off traditionalism and enter the modern industrial world, materialism, often announced with the naive air of discovery, was the first component of a rationalistic revolution against the force of obsolete customs and distinctions. It "exposed" the immemorial customs, privileges, and philosophies of the status quo. That Marxism made its plea for social justice under the guise of materialism rather than in moral terms has always enhanced its appeal in tradition-bound societies. The "discovery" that Marx made has often been the first discovery made by a young man in a social system that denies him advancement or self-expression. A typical Marxist paradox: the most simplified version of Marxist materialism is often the most effective incentive to revolutionary idealism.

Marx's materialism is of course far from being simple. The tortuous arguments of economic determinism have led some, like Professor Schumpeter, to assert that "Marx's philosophy is no more materialistic than is Hegel's."[1] Yet its first appeal is the appeal of the simplicity of materialism: man is made by his environment and not by forces over which he has no control. One does not often pause to reflect that in taking this first step one may be exchanging a religious or psychological determinism for an economic one. The first step offers liberation from the irrationalities of one's society and culture, and also the challenge to remake them. The second step, the postulate of economic determinism, seemingly negates the first one: human control over the social environment is illusory, because it is subject to the rigid laws of economic phases. Nothing can soften the oppression of the serf under feudalism, or of the worker under capitalism, until each system, having fully developed its potentialities, is ready to pass on and be replaced by its successor—feudalism by capitalism and capitalism by socialism. To Marx himself, the contradiction was encompassed by revolutionary optimism and a historical illusion that the birth pains of capitalism in Western Europe were its death throes. A new way of interpreting the world was to demonstrate how to change it, not in the distant future but immediately. As his revolutionary optimism waned, the simple argument of his youth became an elaborate theoretical structure. Perhaps in their own old age Marx and Engels themselves forgot how convincing and how endowed with immediate revolutionary potentialities their original and primitive materialism had seemed to two young intellectuals in a Europe undergoing the most painful phase of economic transition.

In his general formulation of economic determinism Marx drew close to English liberalism and its materialist viewpoint. We shall attempt to show later how, in his fascination with and bitter critique of the English school of political economy and its ally liberalism, Marx managed to import into his creed some of the most rigorous and dogmatic characteristics of the liberal economic *Weltanschauung*. Here it is necessary to note certain general resemblances and differences between the two brands of materialism.

Like Marxism, early liberalism saw in materialism a doctrine of intellectual and political liberation. Rationalism and materialism became practically synonymous to the early liberals. A sober realization of the healthy earthiness and selfishness of human nature is a prerequisite to the study of society and history and a necessary antidote to the obsolete claims of tradition and supranatural religion to dominate human conduct. The world of liberalism, the world of a middle-class, intellectually inclined Englishman of the nineteenth century who read Hume and Bentham, was a world of concrete and tangible objects. This frame of mind did not tolerate myths, deities, or abstract principles as explanations of human behavior. Bentham ridiculed the Declaration of the Rights of Man as a rationale for political emancipation. Adam Smith looked to enlightened self-interest as the basis for prosperous, hence free, society. The institutions of the West have grown within the liberal tradition of the last century and a half. It is something of a shock, therefore, to realize how "Marxist" this tradition was in its original formulation of materialism. The dispassionate language of the early liberals (in comparison with Marx's) and their happy ignorance of Hegelian terminology may blind us to the rigid economic determinism which their writings exude. Indeed, reading Marx, one sometimes gets the impression that he spells out with excessive emphasis what the early liberals asserted almost nonchalantly, so great was their belief in the obviousness of their conclusions.

It goes without saying that there are considerable differences between the two philosophies. The liberals' materialism is unselfconscious. Unlike Marx's, it is unaccompanied by an inner revulsion at the *merely materialistic* basis of human action and hence by a search for a philosophy which *through materialism* will eventually free man from his complete dependence on his economic environment. There is no sense of original sin and therefore no elaborate theology of how to overcome it. The mood of liberalism and of the English political economy is optimistic. The reservations of Ricardo and the pessimism of Malthus find no general response in a generation impressed by the miraculous power of science and the prodigious growth of the productive powers of the economy. If individuals are allowed to carry out their own lives with a minimum of interference by the state or organized religion, if economic forces are permitted to work out their benevolent effects, mankind will emerge from its unhappy condition. Human progress is visible and concrete, not only as a long-run proposition, but as a day-to-day improvement in the assertion of human rationality over obsolete institutions and customs. One does not need, as one does in Marxism, cataclysmic clashes of historical forces to accomplish the liberation of mankind; this is being accomplished, step by step, by the improvement of material environment through science and education.

Such is the general spirit of early liberalism, concealing under its broad-minded view of progress a rigid materialist bias. The absorption of Marxism into the liberal outlook is accompanied by Marxism's dislike of liberal bourgeois society and its rejection of liberal conclusions. As young Marx, largely under the influence of Engels, turned to reading the English political economists and historians, his materialism, from being a mere philosophical postulate, a counterpoint of Hegel, grew into a vision of science, industrial labor, and industrial achievement civilizing and liberating men through the conditions of their lives and not through moral preachings or abstract ideas. The sense of Marxism is materialism not only as a materialist philosophy and as economic determinism, but also as admiration for the tangible fruit of materialism: the bourgeois industrial civilization.

Economics

The trouble with Marxism lies in its economics. Such at least has been the opinion of many would-be Marxists, especially in the English-speaking countries. The assertion of the class struggle and the postulate of socialism are clear and simple challenges to capitalism. Why spoil them by dragging in an involved economic argument and making it the crucial part of the equally unnecessary Hegelian apparatus of history with its dubious "inevitabilities"? In the view of these critics, Marxism gains from its economic theory neither as a system of thought nor as a movement of social protest. No crowds are likely to be driven to storm the bastions of autocracy or capitalism because of Marxist *economics*. The legacy of the economic argument to the succeeding generations of Marxist leaders and intellectuals has been mainly the diversion of energy from concrete political and revolutionary tasks to the defense of a doctrine "so dull and illogical," as Lord Keynes phrased it. If Marxism could only have preserved the simplicity, immediacy, and revolutionary appeal of the *Communist Manifesto*!

Such criticisms are usually grounded in the opinion that Marx's economic theories can be divorced from his revolutionary message and that the surplus-value theory and what follows is merely an intellectual fabrication of one man's mind and not a theoretical expression of the revolutionary ideas current in Marx's society. In fact, the economic argument is, as we shall attempt to demonstrate later on, a sophisticated arrangement of commonly held notions, both liberal and anti-liberal, characteristic of Marx's period. The surplus-value theory may or may not be beyond the ken of a follower of Marxism, but the type of thinking about the economy that it represents will at times find a ready response in the minds of people quite unversed in economic theory. An economist in 1900 or 1950 may barely contain himself while struggling against the illogicalities of the doctrine, yet his predecessor in 1860 or 1850, even though equally anti-Marxist, would have had to admit how close Marxian economics were, in spirit and structure of argument if not in conclusions, to the then dominant school of political economy.

Marx's economic inquiry is characterized by three assumptions. First, that political economy is the science of the distribution of wealth in society and of its rationale; that the aim of economics is to find out "who gets what and why," a notion proceeding from the Physiocrats through the classical English political economists to Marx. Second, that the introduction of machinery, industrialization, constitutes the decisive fact of modern economy, around which all the forces of the modern economy turn. Industrialization is a decisive break with the previous pattern of economic development and will lead to an entirely different relation of man to material forces.

Third, that the economic development of England, roughly in the first half of the nineteenth century, is a preview of eventual economic development everywhere; that the observable data about the economic behavior of various classes there have a fairly universal validity. England in the middle of the century is Marx's laboratory for economic analysis and for what we would call today the psychology of industrialization. His worker is the English worker of the forties and fifties, his capitalist is the contemporary English capitalist.

In his philosophy Marx always goes back to his German origins. In politics he is always attentive to French developments. A man of universal interests, he comments perceptively on developments throughout the whole world. But in economics the contemporary (or rather the recently past, by the time the first volume of *Capital* appeared in 1867) English economic scene crowds out everything else. When, late in his life, he hesitates and inquires whether Russia may not skip the capitalist stage of development, he departs from his main economic point and is not a "Marxist."

Within the three above assumptions, shared by him with the leading intellectuals of that very unsociologically minded era, Marx's economics fall easily within the dominant tendency of the classical political economy (i.e., Ricardian economics), but with an anticapitalist bias. He asks, "What is value?"—a question to us scholastic in its flavor and unanswerable. But this question was asked and always will be asked in a society in which a dramatic transformation of the economy has prompted an inquiry into the sources of new wealth and the claims of individuals and classes to its apportionment. Marx's answer agrees with Ricardo, asserting human labor to be the sole source and the real denominator of economic value. One step further and human labor becomes the only commodity which, in process of its use, expends more value than it uses up. Thus, not as a figure of speech but as a hard fact, human labor becomes the only maker of value, the only magic of economic transformation. From labor is extracted capital accumulation and the capitalist's profit. Its magic propensity gives the capitalist, after he pays the laborers for their labor, the natural wages of any commodity, i.e., the cost of its production, the *surplus labor*. The worker may satisfy his wants by working, say, four hours, but the capitalist system forces him to work longer and to produce *surplus value*. The whole process is one of exploitation, in terms not of human volition (i.e., the malevolence of the employer on the one hand, the worker's stupidity or weakness on the other), but simply of the necessary mechanics of the system. The cupidity of the employer and the chains of the proletariat are alike ordained by the forces of history prescribing the inevitable stages of capitalism, and only these forces, once the system is fully developed, will decree its collapse. In the meantime there is nothing that charity, parliaments, or unions can do to alter the consequences of the law of surplus value.

The howling of critics, the agonized attempts of defenders, and the simple exasperation of men of common sense have followed the surplus-value theory down to our own day. How can you talk about labor or labor power as if it were a concrete substance? How about a ditch digger versus a man operating an atom smasher? How about the role of management, the value of inventors and innovators? How about factors of scarcity, noneconomic influences, and so on? The answer is that *in the context of its times and circumstances* Marx's surplus-value notion did not depart from the best economic thinking.

More than that. In his admirable rephrasing of Marxist economics, Mr. Paul Sweezy[2] has re-emphasized the importance of Marx's attack on what he called "fetishism," a cunning tendency of the bourgeois economists to picture the whole economic process as consisting of relations between *things*, as concealing the essentially *human* nature of social and economic reality. The surplus-value theory was a concrete application of Marx's "new materialism": there are laws of history and economy, but they operate through human beings. There are heroes and villains, exploiters and exploited, even though they are cast in their roles not by their own volition but by historical forces. The mechanistic aspect of the "dismal science" of economics is supplanted by live actors, and here lies the continuing human appeal of an awkward theory.

From the perspective of a modern non-Marxist, the surplus-value theory is a clear example of an ideology masquerading as a scientific theory. It is necessary to meet this objection by repeating how close the economics of Marx are to the British economic thought of the generation preceding their formulation. The notion of the capitalist's being the inevitable exploiter because of the mechanics of the industrial process is parallel, for instance, to Ricardo's picture of the landlord gathering, through no merit or labor of his own, the fruits of the growth of population and industry. If Marx was intruding an ideology into his system, so were the others. If Marx rejected the common-sense version of exploitation (i.e., the cheating of the worker by the capitalist) in favor of a more subtle one, he did so because he was convinced that the economic system is regulated by laws of its own, having all the rigor of scientific laws—if not so rigorous as those of physics then at least those of biology. As a matter of fact, the more Marx studied political economy and the structure and argument of the contemporary bourgeois society, the more he became engrossed in their spirit. The violent diatribes and vituperations that intersperse the theoretical sections of *Capital* give the impression not only of an indictment of bourgeois society and its apologists, but also of an inner irritation at the way the author feels himself drawn into the spirit and the way of reasoning of his opponents. It is not just the statistics, equations, and theorems that replace the simple Communist appeal of Marx's youth; it is also, perhaps, the realization of how much of the capitalist spirit has entered into the edifice of his socialism.

The moving factor of the capitalist development is industrialization. It is difficult, if we follow the main trend of Marx's doctrine, to conceive of capitalism apart from industrialization, impossible to conceive of the capitalist except through his role in the industrial process. And to anticipate, socialism without industrialization is in Marxist terms simply a contradiction in terms, because it follows and is the logical culmination of capitalism. Marx expressed the connection unmistakably:

> Except as personified capital, the capitalist has no historical value, and no right to that historical existence, which to use an expression of the witty Lichnowsky "hasn't got no date." And

so far only is the necessity for his own transitory existence implied in the transitory necessity for the capitalist mode of production. But, so far as he is personified capital, it is not values in use and the enjoyment of them but exchange value and its augmentation, that spur him into action. Fanatically bent on making value expand itself, he ruthlessly forces the human race to produce for production's sake; he thus forces the development of the productive powers of society, and creates those material conditions, which alone can form the real basis of a higher form of society, a society in which the full and free development of every individual forms the ruling principle. Only as personified capital is the capitalist respectable. As such he shares with the miser the passion for wealth as wealth. But that which in the miser is a mere idiosyncracy is, in the capitalist, the effect of the social mechanism, of which he is but one of the wheels. Moreover, the development of capitalist production makes it constantly necessary to keep increasing the amount of the capital laid out in a given industrial understanding, and competition makes the immanent laws of capitalist production to be felt by each individual capitalist, as external coercive laws. It compels him to keep constantly extending his capital, in order to preserve it, but extend it he cannot, except by means of progressive accumulation.[3]

The capitalist is history's agent of accumulation, without which industrial development cannot go on. Without this development the necessary material basis for socialism will not be achieved.

We already find here more than a hint of the industrial fanaticism and the mania for production that has characterized the Communists of our times. But in the context of the economic argument, the immediate importance of the statement is that it pictures the capitalist as the unconscious agent of industrial progress. The logic of industrialization brings about major changes in the capitalist system. The capitalist's psychology fits in with the inherent logic of industrial dynamism, although the latter will eventually bring about his demise when he is no longer necessary. He cannot help but go on accumulating, extracting surplus value from the worker, indulging in catastrophic competition for the market with his fellow capitalist, and thus speeding the day of his doom. The capitalists as a class may not—though isolated individuals may—cease their feverish pursuit of accumulation and more production; they cannot develop the tastes and ethics of other classes and simply let the economy stagnate. Thus the picture of the dynamics of the capitalist mode of production can be understood in terms of two general assumptions of Marxian economics that we noted in the beginning: that the increasing use of machinery is the central and universal characteristic of the modern economy; and (a much more debatable notion) that capitalists everywhere and always will behave the way the English capitalists of Marx's time in effect did.

The drama of capitalism has as its cast of characters the worker, the capitalist, and the machine. Economically speaking, they have no choice in their actions. The worker *has* to sell his labor for the wages oscillating around what in the given society is the level of subsistence. The capitalist has to extract surplus value and sink it into expanding the means of production. Finally, the machine is both the cause and the nemesis of the capitalist economy. Itself nonproductive of value, it increasingly displaces human labor and forces the capitalist to reduce his investment in value-producing human labor as compared with his investment in machines. The organic composition of capital, the proportion of constant capital (mainly machinery) to variable capital (wages), goes up as capitalism progresses. Thus the mechanics of industrialization, of capitalism, must force employers to use less and less surplus-value producing labor and more and more machines, which do not produce more value than they consume!

The triumph that this theory achieves over obvious, palpable common sense did not escape even Marx. He granted that his law contradicted all experience based on observation. Everybody knows, he wrote in the first volume of *Capital*, that a cotton manufacturer who uses a lot of machinery in proportion to workers does not receive less profit or surplus value than does a baker who uses little machinery and a lot of human labor. The logic of the wretched law would have all capital go into the most primitive forms of production, with the capitalists falling all over themselves in destroying machines! Undaunted, Marx observed haughtily that:

For the solution of this apparent contradiction, many intermediate terms are as yet wanted, as from the standpoint of elementary algebra many intermediate terms are wanted to understand that 0/0 may represent an actual magnitude. (p. 335)

He eventually undertook the solution of the dilemma, in the third volume, while reproaching the bourgeois economists of the labor-value theory (i.e., Ricardo and his school) for simply capitulating before this crushing paradox.

By the time the third volume of *Capital* appeared in 1894 with its "solution" of the dilemma of price versus value, the type of economic thinking embodied in the labor theory of value was almost incomprehensible to economists. It has become difficult to appreciate that Marxist economics were not only a logical conclusion of the tradition of classical economy, but embodied ideas about the production and distribution of wealth in which many "practical" people quite innocent of economics believed. Not only many a worker or radical agitator, but quite a few manufacturers in England from about 1820 to 1860 instinctively talked and acted as if they were demonstrating the Marxist "laws." By the nineties, the economic situation and intellectual atmosphere that had produced Ricardian as well as Marxist economics had largely become things of the past for Western Europe. The imperfections of Ricardo's theory, the cul-de-sac to which his theory of value led, were treated tolerantly by the then dominant school of economics. Great men, after the passage of time, have the privilege of being proved partly wrong. But Ricardo did not place economics as a basis of an elaborate political philosophy, or so it seemed, and the full fury of the marginal-utility-theory economists fell upon Marx.

The "solution" that Marx offered to his own riddle provides at the same time his exposition of the dynamic development of capitalist economy leading to its self-destruction. Although the capitalist cannot derive any profit from the machine, he is increasingly forced to use it, because he is in competition with other capitalists and because a technological advantage translated even temporarily into a cheapening of the given commodity is to him a matter of life and death. A technical innovation, a more extensive use of machines, enables him to grab a bigger share of the market and to force his more backward competitor from the rank of capitalists. Hence, even at the price of reducing the proportion of human labor employed and, therefore, at the price of reducing his profit, he is drawn toward greater and greater mechanization. It is this process of competition, this toll exacted by the mechanizing propensity of modern industrial civilization, that distributes among the surviving capitalists at a fairly equal rate the total sum of surplus value exacted from all the workers. Commodities exchange not according to the amount of labor embodied in them, but according to that amount as modified by the constant competition among the producers. The machine, which is the blessing of modern civilization, is at the same time the curse of capitalism. It undermines profit; it threatens the producer, unless he is constantly in the forefront of mechanical progress, with removal from the rank of manufacturers. Since the capitalists as an order have to pay an ever-increasing ransom to the machine, their profit is bound to decline and their number is bound to decrease. Industrial progress is forever devouring its children—the capitalists.

It is immaterial, from the point of view of the analysis of Marxism expounded here, to concern ourselves with the extent to which Volume III of *Capital* contradicts Volume I, or with the question of whether the organic composition of capital creates the tendency for the rate of profit to fall continually. The important thing to note is that Marx's exposition reflects a peculiarity of his period: human perplexity at the effects of scientific and mechanical progress. We may sympathize with thinkers of the first half of the nineteenth century, for, after having become quite used to and blasé about mechanization, we have been confronted most recently by the implications of automation and atomic energy. It is perhaps easier for us than for someone in 1900 to visualize resentment at forces of our own making that yet control our lives, independently, as it were, of our will. The century and the class that prided themselves on shedding the shackles of superstition and custom were confronted with progress itself as seemingly defying human volition. In more prosaic terms, the English economists and philosophers were confronted with the necessity of formulating a theory—"laws"—for a constantly changing situation, the necessity of prescribing a stable and unalterable pattern of relations for an economy in a state of revolution. The most profound of them, even while sharing in the enthusiasm for progress and technology, could not but reflect in their theories the very human if unscientific worry: "Where will it all end?" Full accommodation to the Moloch of industrialization was beyond their vision, just as it is difficult for us to visualize how the world will come to terms with atomic energy. Marx shared their fascination and perplexity, but because of his premises, his new materialism, *he* knew how it would all end. Advanced industrialism is incompatible with capitalism. Mechanization by reducing the share of labor in a finished product impinges on profit-capitalism. Yet mechanization is both necessary and unavoidable because of competition among the capitalists. The final result can only be the replacement of capitalism by a system that does not need the profit motive and hence can live and thrive on technological progress—socialism.

It is with an almost voluptuous delight that Marx sketches several aspects of capitalism's race toward self-destruction. Periodic crises of overproduction destroy the weaker strata of capitalists, but also plunge whole societies in misery. Whether Marx was an "underconsumptionist" or not is a question of primary interest to the economists. Certainly within the body of his writings there are several suggestions about how the pleasing prospect of capitalism's self-strangulation is to become reality. Concentration of capital to an absurd degree and on a world scale is one such possibility. The world reduced to a few capitalists and hordes of paupers is a vision sufficient in itself. The most frequent economic argument for collapse is more varied. The perpetuation of capitalism under conditions of technological progress means a continuous effort by the capitalist to squeeze more surplus value out of his diminishing labor force. He will attempt to cut his workers' wages closer to the minimum subsistence level or to prolong their hours of work or to work them more intensely or God knows what else. The worker has no option but to take work on the capitalist's terms, because the mechanics of industrialization, progressively decimating the number of business firms, increase the number of unemployed, the "reserve industrial army of the proletariat." Periodic crises of increasing severity shake up the capitalist economy until the final one spells its destruction. Capitalism is doomed because it cannot accommodate technological progress to the profit motive. It is doomed because it *creates* socialism in the sense of concentrating the means of production in huge units, thus making the notion of private property an absurdity as well as a fetter on the productive system. It is finally doomed because in its fight for survival it has to bring increasing misery, exploitation, and unemployment to the mass of the population.

Such is the culmination of Marxist economics, the elaboration of which took the great revolutionary a major part of his life. Economists have written voluminously about its obvious weak points: the inconsistencies concerning the relationship of value and price and the belief that industrialism under capitalism is bound to make the working class more and more miserable. The latter point, Marx's "immiseration" theory as Schumpeter called it, is a tenet of Marxism most decisively refuted by history. Nobody would claim that the worker in England or France today is worse off than was his grandfather a hundred years ago. One may attempt, as the neo-Marxians have done, to plead that Marx meant a "relative" as opposed to absolute worsening of the standard of life. Such an interpretation is not borne out by a study of all that Marx had to say on the subject, and its content has not come true anyway. By contrast, Marx has been praised even by his adversaries for predicting the trend toward the centralization of industry and, eventually, monopolies.

Both the defenders and opponents of Marxism have thus distributed pluses and minuses to various points of its economic analyses. To the defenders of the over-all system as a correct analysis of and prediction about capitalism and its development everywhere was left the unenviable task of stretching every conceivable line of argument: Marx was interested in discovering the "laws of motion" of capitalist society rather than in describing its operations precisely; Marxist laws still describe correctly the natural tendency of capitalism, although at times this tendency is held in check by countertendencies; the downfall of capitalism is postponed by such extraneous factors as the imperialism of the great industrial countries. It was claimed that the Great Depression of the 1930's was a vindication of Marx's analysis—comparable to the vindication of a doctor who predicted that his patient would die of cancer within one year, only to have the man die twenty years later of a heart attack! The devotion of the believers, and the attacks or condescension of the opponents as well, overlook, ironically enough, the clear moral of Marxism itself: the rather commonplace idea that no social doctrine or system of economics can transcend its historical and social circumstances. The main point about Marxist economics is not the correctness or error of this or that item of his analysis, even though such a question in itself is of great intellectual interest. More important to the historian as well as the student of contemporary society is to ascertain the social and intellectual forces that gave rise to the Marxist structure, and to see where in the modern world the same or similar forces endow Marxist economics with relevance and persuasiveness.

The Class Struggle

The eternal battle array of history always ranges the oppressor against the oppressed, most commonly the owner of the means of production against the man who works with them. Only in the very beginning of human society was there no class struggle, just as there will be none in its culmination. Between the most primitive tribal community and the socialist-Communist era, "the history of all hitherto existing society is the history of class struggles."[4] Capitalism witnesses this struggle in the most simplified form: the proletariat against the capitalists. The victory of the proletariat will bring with it the abolition of the class struggle. The discovery of private property disrupted the social innocence of mankind. The full utilization of mankind's productive powers under socialism will restore it. With the disappearance of private property and of the class struggle, most of the social evils will disappear and with them the rationale for oppressive institutions, including the state.

This is the most clear-cut and internally consistent of all

Marxist arguments. From its ringing formulation in the *Communist Manifesto* to the end of their lives, Marx and Engels never doubted that they had found the operating pattern of history, that the reality of social and political life is expressed, not in the struggle of ideas, dynasties, or nations, but in the class struggle grounded in economic motivation. To their followers, the principle was a satisfactory explanation and a reliable guide to action, with none of the puzzling qualities of Marxist economics or overall philosophy. Class struggle became, in effect, the major portion of the revolutionary appeal of Marxism. Workers do not strike or storm the barricades in order to abolish surplus value. They strike and revolt against oppressive conditions, against the capitalists. From the point of view of political action, the slogan of class struggle is the simplest guide. It is also the simplest, most convincing revolutionary explanation of politics and history.

A deceptive simplicity! It has misled both the critics and the followers of Marxism. It has led Marxist movements too often to identify Marxist politics with a simple posture of opposition to the exploiting classes. The dominant faction of the German Social Democrats before World War I defined their Marxism as hostility to the imperial institutions and middle-class parties of their country. It led the Bolsheviks, in the first flush of their victory in 1917, to believe that by destroying the capitalists they were destroying capitalism. It has led people versed in Marxism to express surprise that many secondary features of capitalism "suddenly" made their appearance in Soviet Russia in the 1930's. Marxism became identified with insurrectionary action or with hostility, open and uncompromising, to capitalism and to everything and everyone connected with it.

It is necessary to repeat (as it will be again) what is perhaps the most pregnant sentence in Marx's view of social revolution, describing the role of the capitalist: "He thus forces the development of the productive powers of society, and creates *those material conditions, which alone can form the real basis of a higher form of society*, a society in which the full and free development of every individual forms the ruling principle."[5] Nothing in the *main body* of Marx and Engels' writing suggests that any political development, even a seizure of power by the proletariat, can abrogate the laws governing the material development of mankind. From the earliest days of their association, the days filled with the most immediate revolutionary hope, Marx and Engels believed in the primacy of material factors over political action. It is always possible to find an incident or a statement by one or the other that would range them in the camp of believers in revolution pure and simple and hang the stage of economic development. (Thus the brief "Blanquist" period of Marx's early revolutionary activity, and, late in his life, his opinion that Russia might skip the full capitalist phase and pass into socialism from pre-capitalism.) But it is impossible to claim that such incidents or utterances represent the main tendency of Marxism or, as M. Rubel claims in his excellent biography, that Marx ultimately abandoned economic determinism in favor of unconditional faith in the ideal of human liberation.[6]

What bridges the gap between economic determinism on the one hand and class struggle and the call to the proletariat to seize power on the other is Marx's revolutionary optimism. In the 1840's and early '50's, he believed that capitalism was on its last legs, that the economic as well as the political conditions for its downfall were at hand. It is true, as M. Rubel reminds us, that Marx was a socialist long before he discovered his economic system. It is true that the fascination of political economy engrossed and captured him, pushing his thought in directions he had perhaps not envisaged as a young man. But his socialism and his "discovery" of the class struggle did not precede his distaste for the existing moralistic brands of socialism and the determination to place *his* socialism on a firm, materialistic, scientific basis.

Again, what is difficult for us to understand from the perspective of a hundred years becomes easier if we immerse ourselves in the feeling of the period. How could a man believe both that capitalism was a necessary phase of the development of mankind and that Western European capitalism circa 1850 had played its role and was ready to leave the stage? The simple answer is that Marx and Engels shared not only the expectations of many radicals and socialists of the day, but also the apprehensions of many capitalists and liberal economists.

Social and economic unrest had risen in ascending proportion from the introduction of what are *to us* the rudimentary institutions of capitalism to the middle of the nineteenth century. Was it entirely unreasonable to expect a fairly early economic collapse as well as a political revolution? Or to see a democratic revolution as a far-reaching step toward socialism? Many revolutionaries live expecting their revolution to take place any day. In Marx the faith of a revolutionary was complemented by the analysis of a social scientist. It is easy for us to say that Marx was wrong: capitalism did not collapse in Europe in 1850 or in 1860. But he was also right, though on wrong premises: what he assumed were relatively late stages of industrialization and modernization in France and England were in effect the early stages of industrialization and modernization in those countries, and in those stages capitalism is most vulnerable to class struggle.

Without revolutionary optimism, the doctrine of the class struggle, when joined with economic determinism, is a somber and tragic lesson. Except at the turning points in history, there is nothing the oppressed can do against the oppressor. The slave cannot prevail against his master, the serf against the landowner; and one type of oppression disappears only to be reborn in a different form of exploitation of man by man. Class struggle is compounded in the character of law and civilization imposed by each dominant class. Systems of religion and ethics serve to reinforce and to conceal at the same time the interest of the dominant class. Ever since he had seen, as a young man, the diet of his province discuss draconic laws against the removal of timber from state and private forests by the poor, all of Marx's instincts rebelled at the myth of the impartial state, impartial law. The system of private property under capitalism embodies best the double deception by which each exploiting class masks its exploiting role. It protects the capitalist against any tampering with his property, and it seeks to create the illusion of equality and impartiality for all. The plea for democratic franchise that the bourgeoisie makes is likewise a weapon of its class struggle. It seeks to strip the landlords of the remnants of their power and to delude the proletariat into believing that the essential issues are political in nature. The principle of class struggle illuminates world history by stripping it of its theatrical aspects of national struggles or contests about principles, and by demonstrating its material nature. Marx's is the "inside story" of world history, with economic interest its moving principle.

The "exposure" of history and politics was not unique to Marx. The dominant role of "interest" in politics and recent history was a cardinal tenet of the liberalism of his time. The sense of politics consisted in the struggle of classes seeking the advancement of their material interests. Thus the political struggle in the England of the thirties and forties between the Whigs and the Tories was interpreted as centering around the contest between the agricultural and the manufacturing interests. Liberal economists saw in their doctrine a guide to public policies that would secure a "harmony of interests," but they were far from assuming that the correctness of their theories would of itself secure their adoption, or that a collusion of vested interests could not—as well as ignorance— hamper public welfare. The liberal version was already a "suspicious" theory of history, with the material interests of classes lurking behind the struggle for politics and principles.

Marx elevates this suspicion into certainty. Thus, for example, the Glorious Revolution of 1688 is not primarily a victory of parliamentarianism over royal despotism, but a harbinger of bourgeois domination, with the Stock Exchange and other rudimentary institutions of capitalism soon to be established. In a sense, the Marxist class-struggle interpretation of history is more "historical" than the liberal one. In the liberal outlook, history had been a period of darkness and superstition until the sixteenth and seventeenth centuries, and only then had scientific principle begun to assert itself in thinking about human affairs. To Marx, on the other hand, the class struggle provided the rationale of social systems and philosophies from earliest times; the pattern of history is always meaningful if we follow the class-struggle principle and its economic underpinning. The Middle Ages are thus not merely a period of darkness and obscurantism: their social and religious ideas are perfectly understandable in terms of the then dominant mode of production and system of property. Marxist historical analysis and methods of investigation have had an influence on many historians, some of whom would repudiate indignantly the charge of having anything to do with Marxism.

The class struggle under capitalism ranges the proprietors of the means of production against the proletariat. To a man like Marx with an acute sense of contemporary social reality, it was obvious that the picture was much more complicated than that. The class struggles in France, Germany, and England in the forties and fifties demonstrated the presence of other classes, as well as the differentiation of the two principal ones. The aristocracy, a remnant of the feudal age, was still fighting a retreating battle. The peasants had some characteristics of a separate class; from another point of view, they constituted a part of the petty bourgeoisie. The bourgeoisie itself had elements of the financial class as well as of the industrial one.

Marx cannot be reproached with having overlooked the differentiation and proliferation of social classes in his society. Indeed, ostensible political activity consists in various classes and subclasses playing for, or being played for, power in the state. But the essence of the class struggle and its eventual determination is much simpler. Only two classes really count —the capitalists and the proletariat. Other classes and subclasses play increasingly minor roles in the drama of capitalism. Sooner or later they retire into the wings, leaving the stage to the two great antagonists. Insofar as it is the logic of history, i.e., the development of productive forces, and not the temporary whims or affiliations of groups of population that ordain social stratifications, only two classes will remain, and they are "really" the only classes in the true sense of the word. Capitalism is already destroying the landowning nobility, and it will destroy the peasants.

Marx's conclusions about the class struggle, its character, and its participants make sense only if one keeps in mind his economic presuppositions. Like many philosophers of history of his period, he worked on the assumption that history operated neatly and always solved the problems it had posed. It did not occur to him that an advanced capitalism might still shelter a peasant problem or that a concentrated system of retailing might not completely replace the local grocer. Indeed, what "spoils" his analysis of society and his remarkable social acumen, so much more penetrating than that of his contemporary liberals, is precisely his analytical gift, his conviction that the observable tendencies in his society *must* work themselves out fully! History likes to chastise those who presume to understand it fully—a remark Marx would have classified as sheer obscurantism!

The two classes that are to square off in the last phase of the class struggle are quite dissimilar in many characteristics. The capitalist class is forever growing smaller in numbers; the proletariat, the exploited, ever larger. The rationale of the capitalist process, while it makes the capitalists aware of certain interests they have in common, still obliges them to engage in suicidal competition. The capitalist-industrial process makes the workers more and more unified in the realization of their common interest and in their class solidarity. The peasants, for instance, because of their dispersion, because of the peculiarity of their way of living, can never achieve real solidarity and a real community of interest and feeling; and thus, apart from their marginal economic significance, they can never constitute a true class. The workers, on the contrary, are disciplined by the circumstances of their work, brought together in great aggregations where they can feel the community of their privations and realize the logic of capitalism as leading to socialism. The *spontaneous growth* of class consciousness accompanies the growth of the capitalist-industrial system.

We shall see later how this concept of the spontaneous growth of class feelings and of its character was rooted in the experience of the early days of industrialization, and what trouble it brought to those followers of Marx who had to expound it under conditions of mature capitalism. Here we may observe certain interesting connotations of the concept. It is *rationalistic* in the extreme. The working class will not be distracted from the obligation and the realization of the inevitability of the class struggle by nationalistic or religious slogans and considerations. Only a degenerate, rootless portion of it, the *Lumpenproletariat*, may capitulate to the schemes of reactionaries and adventurers. The vast majority of the workers will understand their historical position and historical mission. The vision of the working class is Hegelian in its underpinnings. The proletariat is the universal class, carrying in its future the destiny of mankind, thus parallel in its function to Rousseau's General Will and Hegel's State. The loss of individuality caused and made inevitable by factory labor, the worker's *alienation*, carries in it the seeds of the fullest assertion of individuality under socialism, which comes as a Hegelian "negation of a negation." In more prosaic terms, the factory system is inevitably oppressive and inevitably felt by the worker as such. This oppression *inherent* in the system produces the class feeling. Capitalism = factory system = class consciousness is the line of argument, and a closer examination of each term of the triad will illuminate the nature and conditions of the appeal of Marxism.

The doctrines of the classes and the class struggle have, within the context of the Marxist system, some further rather unexpected connotations. Take the class struggle between the bourgeoisie and the proletariat. The latter, through strikes and political action, resists the inevitable tendency of the capitalists to increase the exploitation of the workers. Yet nothing is clearer according to the logic of the doctrine than that the class struggle cannot paralyze capitalism until the system is fully developed and ready to pass on, or until the proletariat is fully capable of wresting power from the bourgeoisie. What might be called guerrilla class warfare, endemic industrial strife, which would paralyze the system, is clearly against the logic of Marxist thought, even if paradoxically within its spirit: the worker has to get used to the hated factory system, has to undergo exploitation, before the material conditions of the society will allow the transition to socialism. From the perspective of a hundred years, we may appreciate how the Russian and Chinese Communists have taken to heart the logic of the last proposition.

There is no *mystique* of the working class in early Marxism, no extolling of humble material circumstances as being conducive to virtue. Workers are not asserted or called upon to be heroic. They are asserted and called upon to be rational, to develop class consciousness. To Marx, nothing would have been more distasteful than the emotional undertones of later syndicalism. The ideal (in Weber's sense of the term) Marxist worker is a curiously unemotional creature. He has no country, no real family life; and his main objective in life is not an amelioration of his condition, but the overthrow of the whole capitalist system. His sense of suffering injustice, of being exploited, does not deceive him into immediate action against the immediate agents of oppression—the factory and the employer—but into a *planned* struggle against capitalism and the capitalist state. In his political writings and speeches, Marx makes eloquent and emotion-tinged appeals, but the fact is that the main tenet of his theory about the worker and the class struggle is coldly rational in its logic. Human passion and generosity cannot in the last analysis prevail against the facts of history. The drama of the class struggle and the heroic exploits of the working-class revolutionaries are secondary to the working out of material forces. One cannot divorce economic evolution from the human drama that underlies it, but one must not ignore the laws of economics in revolutionary action. It is only a superficial reader of Marxism who would read into it the assumption that the proletariat may by political or insurrectionary action void the laws of history and avoid, say, by seizing power before capitalism is fully established, the hardships and privation of the factory system.

The idea of the class struggle serves to disprove the facile optimism of the liberals for whom, in all the clashes of interests, an "invisible hand" assured in a rationally organized society the harmony of individual and class self-interest with the general welfare. Marx's "invisible hand" is the very visible forces of production, which by their evolution confront each succeeding civilization with a different type of class warfare until, finally developed, they bring about classless society.

The centering of the social problem around the individual is, according to Marx, another pious hypocrisy of liberalism. Individual liberty and due process of law are, within a capitalist society, simply contradictions in terms. They are at most scraps of concessions thrown by the bourgeois state to deceive the proletariat, and in the circumstances of the workers' life under capitalism, they are of no value to them. This contemptuous attitude toward civil liberties, of such great historical significance to Marxism, is attuned to the circumstances of the worst period of the Industrial Revolution: with the proletarian working twelve and fourteen hours a day, and his wife and underage children also in unregulated industrial labor, the Bill of Rights did not, in fact, appear of overwhelming importance to the working class. The class struggle becomes the doctrine of total distrust of the capitalist state, with its laws, bureaucracy, and ideology. The violence of this distrust and opposition, the difficulty Marx and Engels experienced in acknowledging even the slightest social-welfare aspect of the bourgeois state, have often led to the optical illusion that Marxism was opposed to the state as such. It has enabled the revolutionary Marxists to denounce *the state*, with all the accents and conviction of anarchists, forgetting, for the moment, that the centralized state, like the capitalism of which it is a necessary ingredient, is an inevitable part of the historical process.

An alteration in the character of the capitalist state—such as the development of the workers' class consciousness into something other than the class struggle—is a possibility early Marxism cannot admit. "The civilization and justice of bourgeois order comes out in its lurid light whenever the slaves and drudges of that order rise against their masters. Then this civilization and justice stand forth as undisguised savagery and lawless revenge,"[7] wrote Marx about the supression of the Paris Commune. The lures of legalism, of parliamentarianism, of social reform by the state are illusions and deceptions. When Marx or Engels admit the possibility of a peaceful transition to socialism under exceptional conditions, they do so grudgingly. Theirs is a theory grounded in the period when self-confident factory masters confronted the helpless workers, and the state backed up the masters with its police powers and philosophy of self-reliance. Like Marxist economics, the Marxist postulate of the class struggle ill fits the reality of full-grown capitalism— the reality of strong trade unions, social welfare legislation, and parliamentary socialism.

Here, then, is a theory attuned even more closely than other parts of Marxism to the facts and feelings of an early period of industrialization. The class struggle is the salt of Marxism, its most operative revolutionary part. As a historical and psychological concept, it expresses a gross oversimplification, but it is the oversimplification of a genius. The formula of the class struggle seizes the essence of the mood of a great historical moment—a revolution in basic economy—and generalizes it into a historical law. It extracts the grievances of groups of politically conscious workers in Western Europe, then a very small part of the whole proletariat, and sees in it the portent and meaning of the awakening of the whole working class everywhere. The *first* reaction of the worker to industrialization, his feelings of grievance and impotence before the machine, his employer, and the state which stands behind the employer, are assumed by Marx to be typical of the general reactions of the worker to industrialization. What does change in the process of the development of industry is that the worker's feeling of impotence gives way to class consciousness, which in turn leads him to class struggle and socialism. Marx's worker is the historical worker, but he is the historical worker of a specific period of industrial and political development.

Even in interpreting the psychology of the worker of the transitional period, Marx exhibited a rationalistic bias. The worker's opposition to the capitalist order is a total opposition to its laws, its factories, and its government. But this revolutionary consciousness of the worker is to take him next to Marxist socialism, where he will accept the factory system and the state, the *only* difference being the abolition of capitalism. Why shouldn't the revolutionary protest of the worker flow into other channels: into rejection of industrialism as well as capitalism, into rejection of the socialist as well as the capitalist state? It is here that Marx is most definitely the child of his age, the child of rationalistic optimism: the workers will undoubtedly translate their anarchistic protests and grievances into a sophisticated philosophy of history. They will undoubtedly realize that the forces of industrialism and modern life, which strip them of property, status, and economic security, are in themselves benevolent in their ultimate effects and that it is only capitalism and the capitalists which make them into instruments of oppression. The chains felt by the proletariat are the chains of the industrial system. The chains Marx urges them to throw off are those of capitalism. Will the workers understand the difference? And if they do, will they still feel that in destroying capitalism they have a "world to win"?

Socialism

How different will the better world of socialism be from the old one of capitalism? Marx and Engels have notoriously little to say about the wonderful new world their criticism and theories imply. The wealth of observations and historical data illustrating the nature of capitalism is paralleled by a skimpiness of reference concerning socialism: a few epigrammatic statements about the general nature of socialist society, a few items of the political program for the socialist parties, incidental references to the contemporary socialist movements and such revolutions as the Paris Commune, and that is all. The task of expounding the Marxist canon in the very un-Marxist world of Western Europe of the 1880's fell mainly to Engels. He wrote chattily and attractively, a fact that makes him, rather than his great companion, the favorite of the popularizers of Marxism. His thought on the main issues had, of course, for a long time merged with that of Marx. There is in Engels, at the same time, a certain dilettantism and a tendency to write around rather than to address himself directly to the most important theoretical issues. At his death in 1895, the canon of Marxism was frozen, and the vital questions of the socialist role in parliamentarianism, of the nature of transition from capitalism, and of socialism itself, remained to be fought over by the Revisionists and the orthodox Marxists. The fight, although accompanied by continuous invocation of the scriptures, points up the really enigmatic and ambiguous nature of the Marxist argument as it touches the actual problem of socialism.

The apparent enigma disappears if one refuses to be distracted by the revolutionary phraseology of Marxism into believing that *from the economic point of view* the stage of socialism represents a drastic break with capitalism. Quite the contrary: socialism, once it assumes power, has as its mission the fullest development of the productive resources of society. Though private ownership of the means of production and the profit motive are abolished, the state takes on the mission, formerly performed by individual capitalists, of creating "those material conditions which alone can form the real basis of a higher form of society." The logic of the doctrine implies that in so doing the state will in no wise proceed differently from the capitalist: i.e., it will take the worker's surplus labor in the form of surplus value and will sink it in further investment. From the earliest, most revolutionary writings of Marx and Engels until the very end of their activity, there is no indication that society, until full material abundance is achieved (whatever that may be), can dispense with the organization of labor and production typical of capitalism. What, then, is socialism? *It is simply capitalism without the capitalists.* There is no need for elaborate descriptions of socialism. Except for the abolition of private property in the means of production (its rationalization), socialism continues and intensifies all the main characteristics of capitalism. The Bolsheviks and especially Stalin have been accused of perverting Marxism into state capitalism. Yet we need not burden Marx and Engels with the responsibility for Stalinism to perceive that the notion of socialism as state capitalism is found in the canon of Marxism under all the revolutionary and anarchistic phraseology.

When they wrote the *Communist Manifesto*, Marx and Engels were very young men. They could not deny themselves a certain youthful bravado ("Communism is already acknowledged by all European powers to be itself a power." (p. 320)—a ridiculous statement in the Europe of 1848) and a most literal attempt to *épater les bourgeois* ("The Communists have no need to introduce community of women; it has existed almost from time immemorial."—p. 340). Yet even in the midst of all this pathos, so typical of revolutionary manifestoes mushrooming all over Europe in 1848, there is a chilling reminder:

The proletariat will use its political supremacy to wrest, by

degrees, all capital from the bourgeoisie, to centralize all
instruments of production in the hands of the State, i.e., of the
proletariat organized as a ruling class; and to increase the total
of productive forces as rapidly as possible. (p. 342)

Even at the most revolutionary moment in their career, Marx
and Engels do not envisage the worker getting away from the
treadmill of the factory system, do not allow the industrial
system other functions than the ceaseless race for more and
more production, more and more accumulation. Nothing in
the logic of Marxism should enable the worker to expect his
standard of life to rise *immediately* following the revolution.
Nothing in the doctrine extends to the worker the prospect of
greater control over conditions of his work once socialism is
established. The state runs the factories; and the socialist state,
as much if not more than the capitalist, is interested in
increasing production and productivity. The devices of
workers' control, industrial democracy, and profit sharing by
the workers receive in Marxism all the sympathy they would
receive from an early nineteenth-century capitalist. To be sure,
the worker will have the pleasure of seeing "the expropriators
expropriated," and crises and unemployment will disappear
once the profit motive is eliminated. Yet the worker remains
subject to factory discipline. Socialism demands that everybody
work, but it repudiates the idea that everybody should be paid
equally. The emphasis on technology and productivity
promises, as a matter of fact, that there will be a very
considerable inequality in wages and salaries under Marxist
socialism. How many proletarians would be likely to stir into
revolutionary action if the logic of Marxism were thus
expounded to them?
  If there is a clear line leading from the logic of Marxism to
certain central features of the development of the Soviet Union,
we must still be on our guard against the gross and unhistorical
tendency of reading into original Marxism a blueprint for
Stalinism. Just as Marx's economic determinism and revolutionary activity are bridged by his revolutionary optimism,
which makes him see *both* the economic forces and political
action of the proletariat leading simultaneously to a revolution

in the near future—so his rationalistic and democratic faith enable him to envisage a workers' state that continues some of the principal features of capitalism. The workers under capitalism hate the factory system with its discipline and monotony. Somehow, once the capitalists are gone, they will understand and approve the necessity of the very same system under socialism. They hate the centralized bourgeois state with its bureaucracy and police, yet under socialism they will accept and increase the powers of the state. Marx, in effect, promulgates an "abstinence" theory of the worker's socialism: once in power the workers are willing to forego the immediate fruits of their victory in order to build the material base for the next step, Communism.

It was inherent in Marx's rationalist faith, a product of the century, to believe that the centralized state of socialism would somehow be drastically different from the bourgeois state just by virtue of being a workers' state. In commenting upon the Paris Commune of 1871, both Marx and Engels approved its democratic character, its "smashing" of the bureaucracy and the police, its making all offices, including the judicial ones, elective and revocable. *The Civil War in France* seemingly gives the lie to the accusation that Marxism under socialism means state capitalism and the old capitalist state. It praises the egalitarian character of the Commune's short-lived institutions and democratic instincts. Yet what is essentially a political pamphlet addressed to the political needs of the hour does not change the clear logic of the Marxist system. Marx approved the spontaneous democracy of the Paris workers after its suppression by the French government. Yet, had it survived, this democracy would have been expected to centralize the industrial system, to abandon its anarchistic undertones, and to recreate a society devoted to production. Marx could afford to be both a democrat and a Marxist because of his untested belief that the workers, having seized power under democratic and anarchist slogans, would willingly accept the Marxist, i.e., centralized, state and the industrial system and discipline of capitalism.

What would Marx have said of the Commune had it continued and expanded in power, but under the leadership and in the ideology of the Proudhonists and Blanquists who had led it in its failure? He was happy in his conviction that the absolute priority of building the economic prerequisites of the new order would be as evident to the workers once socialism won as it was to him now. He did not face the possibility that the worker who won power under anarchistic slogans might require an elaborate bureaucracy, secret police, and suppression of real democracy—in brief, totalitarianism—to make him submit to measures necessary for the creation of "those material conditions which alone can form the real basis for a higher form of society."

To approximate Marx's vision of the socialist state and socialist society, let us use a tangible example. Let us take the official theory and the constitution of the USSR, forgetting for the moment the *reality* of the political picture there. We see universal democracy, public officials freely elected and subject to recall. We see national self-determination and the fullest regional autonomy. Yet through the free working agreement of all parties concerned, Soviet Russia has a highly centralized planned economy. The citizens of their own free will, unanimously, forsake immediate improvement in their standard of living to build at a rapid rate the productive powers of the economy. This society has no desire for morbid introspection or highly personalized subjects in the arts and literature. There is no need, except in marginal cases, for the police or for oppression. Crime, when found, is a distant reflection of the pre-socialist past. The sense of creative partnership in socialist labor pervades everyone, and no one feels the presence of undue privilege or of a barrier to the full development of one's personality. This fairyland of Soviet propaganda probably comes close to what Marx imagined would be the reality of socialist life. He would not have approved some elements of even the official picture. No egalitarian, still he would almost certainly have been shocked at the extent and scope of the officially and cheerfully acknowledged disparities in pay and ranks, at the uniforms and official pomp. No model of intellectual tolerance, he was still a man of the nineteenth century for whom an officially approved theory did not put an end to a scientific discussion. But in general we shall not err by taking the romanticized self-portrait painted over the reality of Soviet life as coming close to the vision of Marxism. The logic of the doctrine found its fulfillment in Soviet Russia, but the accompanying dream of a democratic and humanitarian society found its place as window dressing.

That this should have happened is a peculiar irony of history. Marxism boasts of being scientific socialism, and the assertion is made with all the implications of being hardboiled, realistic, and done with all the moralistic nonsense that pervades other brands of socialism. Marx's revolution against the contemporary schools of socialism is in fact more fundamental than his revolution against capitalism. Capitalism is a definite part of the historical process. Important elements of capitalism entered the blood stream of Marxism. The leading contemporary schools of socialism—those of Fourier, Proudhon, and Saint-Simon—are, on the contrary, but secondary symptoms of the disturbance and misery produced by capitalism and of no major historical significance or revolutionary value in themselves. There is a very human reflection of ideological rivalry in this appraisal of Marx's. The story of his personal relations with other socialist leaders is a partly humorous and partly pathetic tale of exacerbated vanity, charges of plagiarism, and the confrontation of the rigid and sensitive German academician with the easygoing Gallic nature of a Proudhon or the Slavic disorderliness of a Bakunin. These stories and the related one of Marx's anti-Semitic vulgarity about Lassalle have provided excellent material for those writers who feel Marx's chief failing to be his own and his theory's lack of humor and other redeeming, if not dialectical, human characteristics.

The major reasons for Marx's criticisms of other socialist sects and their apostles are, however, more fundamental. In the first place, there is the obvious criticism of the "utopian" and other socialists for their belief that an amelioration of the condition of the working class can come by good will, or by propaganda, and without the realization by the proletariat that only the full development of the productive forces of society as well as the class struggle can bring about real socialism. For instance, in his *Critique of the Gotha Program* (1875), Marx assailed the newly born German Social Democratic Party for the Lassallean phraseology of its program. Much of the criticism is petty, a testimony to Marx's vindictiveness toward his colorful contemporary. But there is also a sincere effort to teach the German socialists that socialism is not merely vague talk about equality and vague promises of social reforms, and that the Socialist Party should teach its own followers a definite economic and political creed grounded in the laws of historical development. Even in a political program, one should not try to delude the workers into believing that under socialism the total social product will be distributed among them, with no deductions for the communal needs, administration, and further investments. Nor should one equate socialism with complete equality. The first stages of socialist society will require considerable inequality, teaches Marx. "Right can never be higher than the economic structure of society and the cultural development thereby determined."[8] Even equality of pay according to the individuals' needs (an ambiguous formula) is left for that rather distant, "higher" stage of socialism—Communism, in which the full abundance of material goods and the full development of the individual will permit the disappearance of the state and divisions of labor and allow the establishment of the principle, "From each according to his ability, to each according to his needs."[9] Only the remotest reach of the historical process is given over to the anarchistic dream of equality and no state.

What *loose reading* of Marxist politics would lead one to believe is that the immediate objectives of socialism are its distant by-products, according to the *Critique*. It is no wonder that the pamphlet, despite its brevity and compactness, has never been favored reading for the purpose of Communist agitation.

The other reason for Marx's revulsion against other brands of socialism is actually a variant of the preceding one: the revolutionary appeal of Marxism, despite its quite different logic, is essentially the same, addressed to the same instincts, as that of many contemporary socialist and anarchist movements. If "Property is theft" is the most effective Marxist appeal, it was also a slogan thrown by Proudhon; but in reality, of course, the

Marxist theory teaches that property is something else. Had Marx been more cynical he might have urged his followers not to be carried away by their own propaganda. As it is, the revolutionary fervor of a Marxist is quite likely to carry him into anarchism, just as his sober realization of the material prerequisites of socialism may induce him to be patient with capitalism. The secret of the proper blending of the two elements was something that the master tried to infuse in his followers. Thus, to apply the frightful semantics of the Communists, Marxism as a child revealed its parentage by being susceptible both to "right" and "left" deviationism. To Marx, the greatest danger came from the possibility of confusing Marxism with mere revolutionary socialism, with simple opposition to capitalism, and with the desire only for the destruction of the old order. Hence his intense irritation with his closest ideological relatives.

The vocabulary describing socialism and Communism is as vague as it is rapturous. Following the destruction or collapse of capitalism, we are to get "the revolutionary dictatorship of the proletariat." The meaning of this celebrated phrase is quite obscure. Is it to be like the Paris Commune? Not likely, because, despite Marx's eulogy over the grave of the Commune, it had been dominated by the essentially anarchistic followers of Proudhon and Blanqui. We have said that Marx probably had in mind something on the order of what the Soviets pretend they have in fact. But the formula is certainly vague enough to accommodate a multitude of interpretations. All that Marx insists upon is that the essential features of the industrial system be preserved under socialism. Granted that it is difficult to see how "the revolutionary dictatorship of the proletariat"—which is helpfully defined as in fact being a democracy, because, unlike bourgeois democracy, it represents the domination of a vast majority over a small minority of ex-capitalists—could be very democratic. Would the dictatorship of the proletariat look kindly upon the formulation of political parties demanding *immediate* equality of wages, workers' control of the individual industrial enterprises, or the abolition of factory discipline?

The next and final stage of historical development,

Communism, was painted by Marx and Engels in terms so
nebulous as to suggest their relative lack of interest. We are told
that Communism will come after the productive powers of the
society have been developed to their fullest and after human
personality, freed of the fetters of capitalism, has reached its
highest growth. Instead of the detailed constitutions of heaven
offered by Owen, Fourier, and Saint-Simon, the Marxists have
to be content with epigrammatic phrases about the passage
from the realm of necessity to freedom and about the fullest
development of everything. The practical sense in Marx
scorned the easy task of building utopias. The important thing
is to get rid of capitalism without disturbing its industrial
machine. The distant phase of Communism is simply
everything that capitalism is not, a consolation, perhaps, for
the fact that socialism will have to be so much like capitalism.
It is a concession, an empty one, to the anarchist in every
revolutionary: the wondrous future where there is no state and
no division of labor.

Engels, in the famous passage in *Anti-Dühring*, was eager to
fill in some details. The abundance of goods under socialism
brings with it progressive attenuations of the repressive and
planning functions of the society. Labor becomes lighter and
less regulated, and various functions of the state superfluous.
Finally the state withers away. Human nature has been
basically transformed. It is only in this anarchistic and
individualistic paradise, which to a skeptic does not seem to
afford much scope for human activity, that Marx and Engels
meet with Proudhon, Bakunin, and Fourier, and the subject of
their quarrels, the state, is finally laid aside.

Volumes have been devoted to the questions of whether
socialism abolishes classes or class antagonism, what degree of
material influence must precede the passage from socialism to
Communism, etc. Such disquisitions might best be left to the
Communist leaders and their philosophical attendants, who
indulge in them in the line of duty and as a relaxation from
more practical matters. In Marx's theory, the importance of
Communism, in the technical sense of the term, is negligible.
On the other hand, in the Marxist movement, the propaganda
value of the fact that Communism is often mistakenly read into

the Marxist definition of socialism has been enormous.

The relationship of revolution—i.e., seizure of power by the socialists—to the stage of economic development of the given society has justly been considered the most perplexing problem of practical, as well as theoretical, Marxism. To young Marx, the problem was relatively simple: capitalism in the most advanced capitalist countries (particularly England) was drawing to the end of its course; thus, there was no contradiction between the political and the economic aspects of the problem. A democratic, i.e., Chartist, revolution in England would soon be followed by a socialist one: witness the strong socialist undertones of Chartism. This fantastic optical illusion, a product of Marx's revolutionary optimism, that Western European capitalism circa 1850 had nearly reached its full economic as well as political development, could not withstand the experience of the three remaining decades of his life. What Marx subsequently meant on the subject but never quite brought himself to say was that a socialist revolution (i.e., the seizure of power by revolutionary socialists) and the end of capitalism *as an economic system* need not coincide. The socialists may—should—seize power if an opportunity warrants, even if capitalism has not reached its full development. This is indeed clearly forecast in his *Address to the Communist League* in 1850, which the Bolsheviks rightly considered almost a blueprint for their tactics in 1917 in Russia.

According to the *Address*, a democratic revolution in Germany is to be turned by the Communists to their own use and made the starting point of a socialist one. Germany, no matter what her stage of economic development, is to be seized by the socialists. If capitalism has not fully completed its preparatory task for socialism, then the socialist state should, first, finish the work of capitalism. Thus, if small peasant holdings have not been converted into huge capitalist estates, then it will have to be socialism rather than capitalism that delivers the *coup de grâce* to the independent peasant. If full state centralization has not been achieved, the socialists will have to press for it or accomplish it, and "they need not be misled by democratic platitudes about freedom of the communes, self-determination, etc."[10] Marx does not say, and the omission is understandable in a political address, that there are other tasks which socialism, in a country unripe for socialism, might have to perform in lieu of capitalism— breaking in the worker to factory discipline, discouraging the notions of the workers' control of industry, etc. Though the *Address* is principally tactical advice to the "workers" about what they should do after having overthrown, in alliance with the bourgeois democrats, the old regime, it is also a prescription for the socialists' measures after the death of "unripe capitalism." The revolutionary in Marx cannot quite wait for capitalism to die of old age, but the economic determinist in him knows that the necessary historical tasks of capitalism must be performed even under socialism.

The dazzling profusion of terms—capitalism, socialism, Communism—each having a political as well as an economic meaning, and one shading into the other, may well induce the exasperation of the follower or critic. A witty British critic suggested that the title of a future book on the subject might be *What Marx Really Meant, Actually*. The confusion is reduced if we remember that there are two consistent lines in Marx: one, of a revolutionary always against the status quo, feudal, capitalist, or whatever; the other, of a believer in the immutable laws of material development, which no *political* revolutionary could affect. At first, in Western Europe of the 1840's, it was easy to be both; later on it became increasingly difficult. It fell to his successors to try to reconcile the logic of the theory with its revolutionary emotion, in a world quite different from the one in which Marx and Engels had spent their formative years.

The circumstances of the times also dictated some secondary characteristics of the theory of revolution and socialism. To an age that was beginning to witness the stirring of subject nationalities, nationalism still appeared a passing phenomenon. The small politically minded element among the English, French, and German workers was internationally oriented, as were the middle-class democrats of these countries. If the fight against autocratic oppression by the Poles or Hungarians was felt by the enlightened men in the West to be a part of their own struggle, was the future fight against capitalism to be confined within narrow national bounds? And the national question was just a reflection of the economic and political oppression. With this oppression gone, nationalism itself was to find its fulfillment in internationalism, dictated by the ever-spreading network of industrialization. The logic of industrialization, which makes the workers into socialists, forbids them to become chauvinists. Hence the tasks and the natural inclinations of the proletariat are international in their character, and the bonds of the common chains infinitely stronger than the accidental ones of nationality or religion. This optimism, though it too did not remain unscathed by the developments after 1870 following the Franco-Prussian War, is never repudiated. And, sadly distorted as it has become in the main Marxist movement, it remains in Marxism an attractive reminder of the rationalist faith of the era when enlightened men believed that the conquest of the forces of nature would automatically banish injustice and intolerance.

An account of the original Marxist argument must close with a repetition of its major intellectual premise: history works out tidily, creating no problems it cannot solve. The observable economic forces of Marx's times must work themselves out fully to their logical conclusion, leaving no nooks and crannies of the social system where anachronistic economic phenomena lurk. Likewise, in individual consciousness no reflexes or instincts characteristic of pre-industrial society will be allowed to remain. Such is the Marxist world, into which generations of Marxists have had to fit their contemporary reality.

— 3 —
The Sources and Dynamics of Marxism

If it seems illogical to follow a discussion of theory by detailing its sources, one must plead special justification in the case of Marxism. To see the main sources of Marxism is to explain its appeal. If the Marxist system as a whole strikes us as something too vast, overpowering, and complicated to exercise an immediate attraction on the minds and emotions of men, then the answer must be found in the character of some of its components. From Pareto to Schumpeter, unfriendly critics have sought the explanation of the appeal of a doctrine "so illogical and so dull" by consigning it to the realm of religion. An involved theology to amuse the intellectual and an appeal to the most primitive emotions to stir up the masses—such is the essence of Marxism under the veneer of its philosophical and economic system. If this were so, we would still be begging the question. Why Marxism rather than some competing religious system, also masquerading as ideology? To ascribe the cause of major historical events to human irrationality and the propensity to be duped does not explain anything except the underlying premises of the authors of such an explanation.

The source of the abiding influence of Marxism must be ascribed to the lasting character of human reactions to social change. These reactions may be rational or irrational, depending on one's definition of the term. But under certain conditions and at certain times, they will always characterize the human response to industrialization. The childhood and even the prenatal conditions of Marxism explain its fortunes as a mature doctrine and a fully grown political movement. The history of its sources is an explanation of its appeal.

Industrialization

In the midst of revolutionary fulminations and economic theories, one postulate of Marx's may strike the reader with its unexpectedness: "Combination of agriculture with manufacturing industries; gradual abolition of the distinction between town and country by a more equable distribution of the population over the country."[1] This is a postulate of socialism, and the year is 1848. The modern reader will be puzzled. This is not the apprehension of an atomic war, or the answer to the spectacle of huge urban conglomerations creating insufferable traffic and supply problems. Even the "most advanced countries," to which the plan was addressed, presented in 1848, from our point of view, a picture of bucolic simplicity: overwhelmingly rural Germany, prevailingly rural France, and even England, where industrialization had not as yet destroyed the largely agricultural character of the economy. Why should a socialist basing his revolutionary expectations on the urban proletariat have reservations about the growth of the cities? And the apprehensions about urban civilization are balanced by a frank dislike of the countryside, of what Marx in the *Manifesto* engagingly calls "the idiocy of rural life." The misery and degradations of the cities and the primitiveness and lethargic condition of the country are constant themes of Marx and Engels. Socialism cannot be fully established nor Communism begin to grow until the distinction between the city and the countryside is obliterated. Why?

The answer will go a long way to explain the assembly of interests and emotions that are the sources and the moving forces of the Marxist appeal. Marxism is *about* industrialism. It is not about equality. Even the anticapitalist argument is secondary to the concentration on the phenomenon of industrialization, with its destructiveness and its promises. The city is the symbol and the reality of modern industrial civilization. It concentrates people joined by nothing other than the accidents of employment and the necessity of earning a livelihood in industry or service. It is a visible demonstration of the soullessness and alienation of the machine age. Yet it is necessary, for without it there is no progress in industry, no progress in culture. Its crowded conditions, the friendless intimacy into which it forces the proletariat, the contrasts, visible to hundreds of thousands, between wealth and poverty, between crime and the protection afforded by authority to the rich and privileged, are in themselves lessons in the class struggle.

The countryside, on the other hand, presents the illusion of orderliness and social placidity. To the city proletarian, who has not yet lost his roots in the country, it is the place where he had status and stable livelihood, where the system of authority, being traditional, appeared less oppressive. Even the economic and political forces that destroyed the quiet of the village and made him come to Manchester or Lyons were somehow of city making, divorced from the natural mechanism of agrarian existence. For the actuality of agrarian pre-industrial existence, Marxism has nothing but contempt. Villages in the industrial age are locations of social torpor and superstition; and the peasant, unless stirred up by unusual exactions or distress, is a patient beast of burden, a potential tool in the hands of reaction. But for the ideal of human existence as embodied in the proletarian's dream of a "natural," stable, and egalitarian agrarian community, Marxism has the highest respect. That ideal, according to Marxism, embodies not only a temporary grievance and consequently an overidealized version of the immediate past, but a constant element of the proletarian's psychology. It is not merely a reflection of a period of adjustment and economic distress, of sentiments that will pass or change once the economic situation improves and a new set of values takes hold. The longing for the simple community and the nonindustrial life is a constant source of revolutionary feeling and of the worker's unalterable opposition to the agent of the change, the capitalist. Socialism, then, must mean extracting from the proletarian's dream its justifiable human aspiration to a more dignified, leisurely, and stable existence than that provided by the city—the modern industry. But it must also mean the rejection of the reactionary, utopian part of the dream, the idealization of the coarse and unenlightened past of the peasant and the artisan, and the illusion that that past may be recreated by rejecting the machine civilization and its consequences, the city and the state. Only the highest development of modern industrial forces can bring about the ideal of human dignity and equality inherent in the dream of the small agrarian community free from the tension of modern industrial life.

The city and the countryside: two ways of life clashing—neither of them in itself complete and adequate to the requirements of modern life—both of them having to undergo changes and amalgamation before socialism can be established. Such is the message of Marxism. Unlike some of his contemporaries, Marx is not given to rhapsodies over the picture of model factories amidst green fields or to dreams of erecting little self-sufficient communities free from the taint of industrialism. Behind the Hegelian phraseology of two opposites merging in a synthesis, there is evoked an acute intuition of the incompatibility of two ways of thinking, two ways of life put in sharp contrast by the rise of industry: first, the older agrarian order, based on ancient traditions, providing if not material progress then a modicum of economic and social security; second, the new industrial order, whose only constant characteristic is change, continual revolution in the productive forces, and consequent instability of employment and economic insecurity for the mass of the population. One appears "natural," sanctioned by long usage and habituation; the other "unnatural," bewildering in the variety of new habits, concepts, and skills it requires and constantly changes. This is the clash that makes Marxism and fills its formulas with life. The uprooted peasants and craftsmen recruited into the proletariat seek a personalization of the forces of change and disturbance. Marxism intuitively, though not without help, hits on a formula that explains and apportions blame for the destruction of a world which, as it recedes into the past, looks all the more—and unrealistically—stable and uncomplicated. Hence the proposal to combine the stability and simplicity of the past with unavoidable technological improvement. Hence the real meaning of "combination of agriculture with manufacturing industries" and "gradual abolition of distinction between town and country," which Marxism inscribes on its banners.

Across a century, a noted practitioner of Marxism restated the problem in more concrete if oversimplified terms. Wrote Stalin:

> The problem of eliminating the antithesis between town and country, between industry and agriculture, is a familiar problem which Marx and Engels posed a long time ago. The economic basis of this opposition is the exploitation of the countryside by the city, the expropriation of the peasantry and the ruin of the bulk of the rural population by the entire process of development of industry, trade and the credit system, under capitalism. Therefore, the opposition between city and country under capitalism must be regarded as an opposition of interests. On this foundation a hostile attitude arose on the part of the countryside toward the city and "city folk" generally.[2]

We may amend the statement in some respects to get at the meaning of the conflict. The ruin of the countryside by the development "of industry, trade and the credit system"—in short, by industrialism—is the basis of the resentment, whether the development is done by capitalism or by any other system, as Stalin, of all people, had occasion to observe. Then the "hostile attitude toward the city and 'city folk' " is not a peculiarity of the peasants under industrialization; it is felt even more acutely by the mass of the "city folk," the proletariat. It is the basic, the instinctive form of Marxism among the dispossessed peasants, craftsmen, and unemployed workers who constitute the first waves of the industrial army.

Anti-industrial feeling is the basis of Marxist emotion, just as its opposite, worship of science and technology and faith in their limitless possibilities, is the basis of Marxist logic. Without the first, Marxism would not be a revolutionary movement, always relevent when industrialization hits a hitherto mainly agrarian and traditionalist society. Without the second, it would, like many of its contemporaries among socialist movements, spend its energies battling the unavoidable forces of modern life, unable to construct a working social system, even if it were to succeed as a revolution.

The anti-industrial feeling on which the Marxist movement subsists is not infrequently also the breeding ground of its

elaborate theories. Human grievances do not indefinitely
persist in abstract expression, as resentment against impersonal "forces." The anguish of industrialization finds a more
advanced complaint in the proletarian's exaltation of the role
of labor and in his hostility toward the visible agent and
beneficiary of the economic revolution, the capitalist.

> This was the plain sound, raw material of average working class
> opinion or instinct out of which, with the tools of Ricardian
> economics and the measuring rod of Patric Calquhoun's
> estimate that the wage earners received a bare quarter of the
> national income, scattered thinkers of that generation had
> constructed those theories of value, doctrines of the right to the
> whole produce of labour, which Karl Marx was subsequently to
> put into crabbed dialectical shape.[3]

The relationship is not that simple, and the genius of Marx
consisted not only in distilling out of the proletarians'
grievances their unconscious theoretical substratum, but in
bending it into a system that harnessed the social protest to a
philosophy and objective quite opposite to the worker's
immediate aims. But anti-industrialism does find its practical
meaning in anti-capitalism. In an industrializing society the
appeal of Marxism rests on the fact that its *intermediate* aim,
the overthrow of capitalism, coincides with the proletariat's
instinctive reaction against industrialism.

Anti-industrialism and the most absolute faith in industrialization are the two interwoven themes of Marxism. They are so
closely knit together that it is difficult to discern either in its
full complexity or intensity. The anti-industrialism of the
doctrine matches or surpasses in intensity the most violent
anarchist sentiments. Its underlying faith in progress through
science and industry sometimes leaves behind as pale and
unsubstantial the most uninhibited liberal optimism about the
benevolent effects of industry and free market.

It is necessary to explain more fully the phenomenon around
which the two most actively operative parts of Marxism turn—
industrialization. The setting is the first half of the nineteenth
century in Western Europe. In our thinking about the

phenomenon of industrialization, we visualize factories, railways, canals, etc. Or we think in more abstract terms about capital accumulation and the rate of growth. It is difficult for us—for we live in a highly industrialized society with more than a century of habits and techniques appropriate to it behind us—to realize the full complexity and meaning of the process. To be sure, even in the West, as we have entered since World War II the second industrial revolution, we have also witnessed a certain rebirth of anti-industrialism. It lurks beneath the surface of the more extreme varieties of environmentalism, it is evident in "no-growth" philosophies, it is implicit in the writings of many, both on the left and on the right, on the political spectrum who condemn our civilization as being overly materialistic. Still, all these phenomena are not comparable in their intensity to the outburst of anti-industrialism that accompanied the first industrial revolution. Thus, for a citizen of today's more advanced country, it is still difficult to grasp the problem of human adjustment to the economic change at that time and the revolution in values and habits that had to precede and accompany the functioning of the new society.

In Western Europe of that time, the process, although prepared for by the Enlightenment and by long commercial development, still manifested some elements of the shock that primitive societies, the "underdeveloped countries" of today's jargon, undergo when submitted to "Westernization." "Detribalization" may be too strong a term to apply to the situation of an English or Irish peasant whom combined economic and legal forces eject from his holding and force into a cotton factory, but it may not be too inapproprate a description of his situation and of his reactions to it. The bewilderment at the change, the confusion about its economic and political causes, and the shattering impact upon previously held beliefs are present in both cases. In the twentieth century, industrialization comes seemingly prepared by planning and buttressed by various devices (like social security) to ward off its most immediate anarchic and disruptive effects. But in the first half of the nineteenth century, Western Europe was at a disadvantage. Nobody, least of all the bulk of the industrial workers, was quite sure what was happening to the economy. Voices were heard quite late in the period questioning the veracity of official statistics that the population of England was growing under the Industrial Revolution, and maintaining that in fact the population was declining—this at the period of its greatest increase in history! A more serious debate divided those who saw further industrialization and depreciation of the agricultural interest as the surest road to economic ruin from others who urged manufacturing and trade as the only roads to salvation. The curious propensity of philosophers for seeing premonitions of disaster in the growth of material wealth was not escaped even by some of the most ardent advocates of the new age. The fear of mechanization as leading to widespread unemployment and the exhaustion of natural resources already exerted its gloomy fascination on some of the acutest minds of the era. How then could the common uneducated worker see the unmistakable proofs of progress in what was happening around him and to him?

Industrialization in the most immediate sense means an adjustment to the machine. This adjustment takes the form of the factory system, which in addition to the specific skills it requires of the workers, even at its most primitive, has the basic requirements of division of labor and industrial discipline. We need go no further to find the social basis and sentiment of Marx's "alienation of labor." Whether the worker feels that he produces the whole value or not, he will always feel oppressed by the discipline and monotony of factory labor. If the conditioning in industrialism, the immeasurably better terms of labor, and the immeasurably higher standards of living have not entirely erased these feelings among the workers in the most advanced industrial countries, how do the conditions of factory life strike those who are unused to it and who have to experience it under the most primitive and degrading conditions? Marx drew upon the reports of the Factory Inspectors to picture some of the worst cases of the worker's misery in the beginning phases of industrial capitalism. But any discussion of the excesses dulls the perception of the general shock that the shift to industrial life produces even *without* unreasonably hard conditions.

About labor migration and its connection with industrialism, a British historian wrote:

> It is hard for one born in a mature industrial region, inhabited by a *race of patient and disciplined factory workers,* to realize the difficulties involved in the deliberate formation of a factory community, even where industrial habits and traditions are already well established among the local population. *In the course of a generation or two* it becomes quite "natural" for people to work together by hundreds in hot, humid, barrack-like buildings for a fixed number of hours each day, regulating their exertions constantly by the movements of tremendously powerful machinery. After a great war, or any other prolonged dislocation of industry, there may be some temporary restlessness among the "hands," but the routine soon reestablishes itself as part of the ordinary discipline of life.[4]

Before the *race of patient and disciplined workers* is created, it is not unlikely that these people experience their own version of what Marx tried to express by "alienation"; and it may take more than one or two generations before general anti-industrial feeling ceases to provide fertile soil for revolutionary protest.

The adjustment to the machine not only means the habituation of the worker to the factory existence. It means learning and accepting a whole network of ideas and customs. A commonplace feature of attempts at Westernization of backward areas has been the opposition often encountered among the population to the most ordinary and beneficial scientific or public health measures if they somehow clash with local customs and beliefs. The difficulties attendant upon the acceptance of science and rational criteria are compounded in the replacement of men by machines: this causes additional confusion and bewilderment, and, ultimately, in an agrarian society urged into industrialism, often results in revolutionary protest. Here again the recent experience of the more primitive communities in the process of seizure by modernization is helpful. Revolutionary movements are not infrequent when ancient superstitions, nascent nationalism, and distorted echoes of Western political ideas blend into a hopeless revolt against the new.

It is a far cry from an African territory of today, or the China of the Taiping rebellion, to even the most primitive area of England or France at the beginning of the nineteenth century. But some of the elements of protest are similar. The Luddite movement, when, to the accompaniment of fantastic rumors, the displaced workers destroyed machines; similar developments of the first two decades of the century in France and elsewhere; the opposition to smallpox vaccination—these are but the most primitive symptoms of the incipient revolt of the simple people against the mysteriously changing circumstances of their lives. Progress and education may ride roughshod over uncivilized protests, but the shock of industrialization, instead of disappearing, will become greater even though the reaction to it becomes more indirect and subtle.

Beyond the machine and its consequences, the most important, though subtle, element of transition from pre-industrial to industrial mode of existence hinges on the notion of *property*. An agrarian society is built around the concept of property. Land is property, however much the concept may be attenuated by tenantship, serfdom, or membership in a commune. So is the artisan's shop and his tools of trade. The status that a peasant or craftsman acquires from the mode and quantity of his property is much more important than any other aspect of his social personality. What happens to the connection of status and personality under the industrial process is dramatically if exaggeratedly described by Marx in the *Manifesto*:

> Hard won, self-acquired, self-earned property! Do you mean the property of the petty artisan and of the small peasant, a form of property that preceded the bourgeois form? There is no need to abolish that; the development of industry has to a great extent already destroyed it, and is still destroying it daily. . . . In your existing society, private property is already done away with for nine-tenths of the population; its existence for the few is solely due to its non-existence in the hands of those nine-tenths. (p. 335-337)

The process has not been that drastic or automatic, as Marxism has to its sorrow discovered. But the fact remains that one of the basic features of industrialization, transmuted into one of the most potent spurs to revolutionary feeling, is exactly the loss of "property"—hence, status—which the peasant or small craftsman experiences in becoming a proletarian. His previous existence or that of his father may have been, probably was, economically marginal, and his fresh status may mean a material advance. But as likely as not he will feel degraded, he will have the illusion of being impoverished, by the loss of his property. In a mature industrial society, where a man's status is measured mainly by the quantity of goods and services he commands, by his income, the social grievance caused by the exchange of a petty property inadequate to eke out a livelihood for the more varied and materially satisfying life will appear incomprehensible. But it will take more than one or two generations for the workers to lose the feeling of having been declassed just by the fact of being workers and of being cut off from their previous mode of existence and status.

The problem of the small producer, most commonly the peasant, so brusquely disposed of in the *Manifesto,* so readily assumed by Marxism to be solved by the very dynamics of industrialization and capitalism, has been both the crux of and the main impediment to the revolutionary appeal of socialism. Here it is sufficient to observe how varied are the revolutionary ramifications of the pressure exercised by the "city" upon the "countryside" during the initial, intense period of industrialization. Economic forces that make small-scale agriculture and crafts unfeasible or less and less profitable are at the same time the instruments for creating the labor force for the factories, the preconditions for science and sanitation, which lead, at first, to a prodigious growth of population. Economic crises and revolutionary stirrings reach not only the proletarian, but also the peasant or craftsman who is fighting, with the odds against him, against becoming a proletarian. Such is the initial impact of intense industrialization, and it is against this background that Marxism drew its conclusions about capitalism and the class struggle.

Politically, industrialization means acceptance of the state. That the centralized and strong state is a necessary feature of industrialization may seem a paradox in view of the fact that the industrialization of Western Europe was carried through under the auspices of liberalism, which proclaimed as its political philosophy governmental noninterference with business and the fullest autonomy of the individual. Here the insight of Marxism shows more than historical appearances. A moment's reflection will show how much the laissez-faire state had to legislate in order to establish laissez faire; how the mass of regional peculiarities, of paternalistic laws, of pre-industrial customs had to be legislated away before the establishment of the legal and political prerequisites for the industrial order. When Rousseau wrote about the General Will and Hegel about the State's being the march of God in history, they were, in a way, giving expression to the longing for an authority strong enough to establish mores and an outlook for the whole society, something the most autocratic *pre*-industrial state could not do. There was no need for an English liberal to be lyrical or to engage in high-flown oratory about the state. The liberal state was legislating, almost unconsciously, a social and economic revolution, engaging, especially in the England of the thirties and forties, in what we would call today social engineering. The liberal ethos was finding its legislative expression, as in the New Poor Law of 1834. Not only the exclusive privileges of the land-owning aristocracy, but the whole network of legal and customary impediments to the business civilization, were being swept away by the action of the state. Politics was obediently doing the bidding of economic forces, of the ascending economic interests.

Even in the most mechanical sense of the term, industrialization means the age of regulation and a tendency to uniformity. Authority in a pre-industrial age may appear oppressive at the same time that it appears a part of the natural order of things. *Ideally* it does not interfere with the personal world of the lower orders: religion, family, "property," and daily life. Since nothing remains ideal there are moments of stress and rebellion, occasioned by unduly harsh exactions on the part of the authority, economic distress, or national and religious grievances. But in general a pre-industrial society will give a deceptive picture of placidity and harmony, for the natural radicalism of its typical member—the peasant—the product of his economic and legal helplessness, is held in check by his natural conservatism, by his attachment to and the belief in the permanence of his way of life. Once the "idiocy of rural life" gives way to the hustle and exactions of industrial existence, political authority appears in a different light. It is the state that somehow stands behind the forces disrupting the previous routine of life. It is the state that stands behind the factory owner and overseer. It is the rulers of the state who can decide whether food will be dear or cheap, who could, if they would, mitigate poverty and unemployment. To the disfranchised proletarian, there are no laws of economics superior to human volition; and if political authority has sanctioned the disruption of economic life, then it has the clear obligation to set it right, and its refusal to do so can mean only its unwillingness.

In the context of natural radicalism bred in the workers by the circumstances of industrialization, it is almost superfluous for Marx to teach the proletariat that the bourgeois state is the executive committee of the exploiting class. The state, in both its activity and its inactivity, as the policeman and the legislator, appears as the enemy. Perhaps the diagnosis is extended further. Authority of any kind, religious or political, is essentially a screen for economic oppression. Instinctive anarchism of the large part of the proletariat is the legacy of the pre-industrial age to the period of industrialization, of the "countryside" to the "city."

Anti-Industrialism

"I have great pleasure in conversing with the lower part of mankind, who have very curious ideas," wrote James Boswell.[5] Boswell's pleasure might have been lessened had he foreseen how within two generations the curious ideas of the lower orders would come to affect the destiny of the more elegant part of society. No sociological surveys enable us to ascertain exactly the ideas of the French and English proletariat during the period of the great economic transformation. The wealth of memoirs, political reports, and even rudimentary economic surveys helps, but the picture of the impact of industrialism is still like that of the proverbial iceberg: a small part of it is visible in the form of theories, statistics, and political and social movements; the greater part of it, the feelings and thoughts of the people affected by industrialization, is submerged. We are forced to speculate about the latter from an analysis of the former. But such deductions must be made with the caution that our assumptions about the feelings of the proletariat are based on the opinions of a small but very active minority. The historical and economic literature of industrialization in the West supplements the raw emotions of the political tracts.

To the affluent contemporary reader, the social historian pictures the unspeakable horrors of the era which employed children as mine workers and chimney sweeps. The economic historian adds his reservations: for all the wealth of the data illustrating the horrors, we must not conclude that the standard of living, say in England between 1820 and 1850, was lower than before, that the most intense period of industrialization was, as the agitator and Karl Marx proclaimed, a period of unremitting suffering for the worker.[6] Both the economic and the social historian may be right, each from his own point of view. Real wages may be on the increase and yet the confusing newness and lack of security of industrial life may create the illusion of a lowered standard of living and give the worker the feeling that the industrial process leads to his increasing misery.

The content of the "curious ideas" of the lower orders in the face of industrialization does not come readily out of the statistics or the contemporary parliamentary debates. It does not come with full freshness and directness from the plans of the reformers and system makers. The latter may infuse too much theory and logic into what is initially a spontaneous and bewildered reaction to a new world. It is best to approach the character of innate radicalism of the working masses by looking at earlier movements that embodied some of the angry bewilderment and opposition to industrialism. Their appeal to the masses may have been ephemeral because they have no well-thought-out reforms or even utopias to offer, or because what they demanded was clearly ruled out of order by the political and economic forces of the moment. But the very incoherence and temporary popularity of the protest help explain the abiding appeal of the more "artificially" constructed theories of reform and revolution.

A tangible example is the career of William Cobbett. Tory, then Radical, pamphleteer, and propagandist, he remains in history mainly as a colorful figure of English politics in the first third of the nineteenth century rather than as a major reformer or thinker. No primary, practical reform can be associated with Cobbett's name, at it can with Francis Place's. No specific socialist philosophy was developed by him, as it was by Robert Owen. And among those who struggled against and tempered the worst effects of the Industrial Revolution, he cannot be ranged at the side of Lord Ashley or John Fielden. Yet on the contemporary scene Cobbett was a man of considerable influence and of great appeal to the lower classes. His *Political Register* at times reached a circulation of sixty thousand—enormous, by the period's standards. The reasons for Cobbett's popularity must be sought, with all the due allowance for his genius as propagandist and libeler, in his faithful portrayal of the common man's prejudices and grievances. No aspect of anti-industrial radicalism fails to appear in Cobbett's writings, which are a vast compilation of the emotions and prejudices on which radicalism, both left and right, feeds.

Cobbett's writings, from the beginning, when he was a Tory, to the end, when as a Radical he espoused the principle of universal suffrage, have the character of a criminal inquest on the subject, "Who is destroying the old England?" More specifically, what is destroying the most useful social class, the small farmers, "a set of men industrious and careful by habit; cool, thoughtful and sensitive from the instructions of nature"?[7] At the foundation of the *Political Register* in 1802, the criminals were identified as domestic and foreign enemies of the Tory establishment: the political reformers and Napoleon. But the list soon lengthened to include the Tories, the system of government with its sinecures and corruption, and the royal family itself. Behind the outward agents of the change, Cobbett soon perceived the world of finance and industry which was taking over early nineteenth-century England: bankers, stock jobbers, rich Jews, and manufacturers. The oscillation from extreme conservatism and chauvinism, to radicalism is quite typical of the unreflecting radicalism aroused by the destruction of the allegedly simple, virtuous, and prosperous agrarian society. This radicalism was probably the secret of Cobbett's popularity among his countrymen. So was the idealization of the old: the love for the countryside, the harmonious life of the small cultivator, the virtues of family life on the land; and the defense of the traditional sports of bull baiting and fisticuffs. Farming, gardening, and animal husbandry receive from Cobbett almost as much attention as do the opprobrious inroads of the new civilization relentlessly defacing and destroying rural England.

At the later and more advanced stage of his activity, the simple picture of the clash of the two worlds was elaborated into an indictment of industrialism and of its social and political appurtenances. The enemy is now the machine, challenging the natural order of the world, which demands that "nine-tenths of the people should be employed on, and in the affairs of the land."[8] For the machine, as for such corresponding phenomena of modernity as smallpox vaccination, Cobbett had no use. The encroachments of science provoke a defiant reassertion of a number of popular superstitions (for example, horse hairs may occasionally turn into living things!).

In the same spirit, Cobbett, now a Radical, opposed any schemes for a national system of education. In brief, his radicalism became basically a passionate thrashing around in an anti-industrial fury. Compassion for the poor and exploited, and hatred of the exploiters and the privileged are not absent from his writings, but the driving force is uncomprehending hostility toward the new order.

The radical stage of Cobbett's activity coincided with the enhanced pace of industrialization and the intensification of social problems that followed the end of the Napoleonic wars. How simple radicalism and nostalgia for the idealized past may shade into political radicalism and a sort of home-made theory of class struggle becomes readily visible: "The march of circumstances is precisely what it was in France, just previous to the French Revolution. . . . The middle class are fast sinking down to the state of the lower class. A community of feeling between these classes . . . is what the aristocracy has to dread."[9] The formerly idealized landowner has now become an oppressor, only a shade better than the manufacturer or the banker, and the chauvinism of the earlier days gives way to the perception that the French wars were begun by the English ruling class to prevent reforms at home. Along with many other Radicals, Cobbett, who once objected to the King's dropping the "King of France" from his titles, now considered the victory at Waterloo as a sad defeat for the liberties of England.

Social indignation often turns into a generalized suspicion of the motives of the rulers, then into mistrust of the whole social and political system, and finally into the certainty that the system exists merely as a cloak over exploitation and oppression. It became necessary for Cobbett to illustrate how the last three centuries of English history had been, in effect, the history of the class struggle, how the Reformation had predestined the birth of the Stock Exchange and of the Bank of England, and how the Glorious Revolution had accelerated the race toward industrial towns and hypocritical political economists. The latter, headed by Malthus and Ricardo, were in Cobbett's view but the lackeys of the plutocracy, as were the greater part of the Liberal reformers headed by "Jerry Bentham, an egotist and coxcomb."

The indiscriminate attack upon men and institutions had one unifying theme—hostility toward anything and anybody connected with turning England into an industrial society. A Protestant, Cobbett was driven into a eulogy of the Catholic Church, because that church was identified with the allegedly happy agrarian past and with the nonindustrial virtues of charity and toleration toward the poor. The full virulence of an extremely virulent pen is turned against those ethnic and religious groups that seem to thrive on industrialization and commercialism and that embody the virtues demanded by the new order of society. It is embarrassing for those who would claim Cobbett for a progenitor of English socialism to face his inflammatory language about the Jews and the Quakers. A relatively mild sample is his observation about the two groups:

> Till excises and loan mongering began, these vermin were never heard of in England. They seem to have been hatched by that fraudulent system, as maggots are bred by putrid meat, or as the flounders come to live in the livers of rotten sheep. The base vermin do not pretend to work; all they talk about is dealing, and the government, in place of making laws that would put them in the stocks, or cause them to be whipped at the cart's tail, really seem anxious to encourage them and to increase their number.[10]

And the Methodist ministers are hardly better; they preach to the poor to be content with their miserable lot.

Writing at a much later date, Alfred Marshall employed the language of early liberalism in discussing the mental traits required of the pioneer capitalist entrepreneur. He had to have the ability to concentrate on the practical, an openness and alertness to new ideas, and a sense of proportion. Concludes Marshall, and the sentiment he expresses was a favorite motif of the great economist as it had been of the early liberals: "These are faculties which have been conspicuous in the Jewish race longer than in any other: but they were also such as could be, and were, quickly and strongly developed in that sturdy English character, of which the foundation had been laid by the sea rovers."[11]

Industrialism and anti-industrialism are at opposite poles on the subject of the groups that seem to embody values destructive of the older order. In *On the Jewish Question*, young Marx gave proof of his affinity to anti-industrialism. The Jew expresses the essence of the bourgeois society; he is the carrier of the capitalist values. It is too much to read into Marx, or to explain his theories, by a species of masochistic anti-Semitism. The original, undifferentiated, anti-industrial radicalism is prone to anti-Semitism, for the same reason that the liberal and business circles of early nineteenth-century England and France were filo-Semitic and pioneered in the social and political emancipation of the Jews. Over and above abstract principles and religious considerations, the dividing line was the acceptance or rejection of the civilization and its values, which the Jew (and, in England, some of the dissenting communities) appeared to symbolize. Cobbett's is the inflammatory language of anti-industrial radicalism. The element of ethnic hostility in it may become subdued or muted if that radicalism is assimilated into socialism. Or it may become expanded if the radicalism is absorbed into a revolutionary movement with nationalistic or fascist characteristics.

The stubborn refusal to recognize the facts of social and economic improvements is frequently a common characteristic of the conservative and the radical. The Marxist diagnosis of capitalism as leading to the worsening of the workers' standard of living is matched and surpassed by Cobbett's triumph over the facts in his assertion that population under industrialism tends to decrease. England's population during the Middle Ages must have exceeded her population of the 1820's.

> Populousness is a thing not to be proved by positive facts, because there are not records of the people in former times; and because those which we have in our days are notoriously false, if they be not, the English nation has added a *third* to its population during the last twenty years. In short, our modern records I have over and over again *proved* false.[12]

The demographic revelations of Cobbett find a parallel in his historical discoveries. James II was a conscientious and freedom-loving king, his opponents scoundrels. History and economics of the past are frankly seen through the prism of the author's acknowledged biases. The rough and ready philosophy of history pictures it as a continuous story of trickery and exploitation of the ruled, engendered by the ascendancy of the materialist tendency ever since the Reformation. There is no well-conceived scheme of reform. The only solution is a return to the solid virtues of the past, the restoration of the yeomen class as the backbone of the nation, and a halt to industrialization and urbanization. Political reform, i.e., universal manhood suffrage and annual parliaments, is advocated by Cobbett in a spirit of pique at the upper and middle classes, rather than in a democratic spirit, of which he had very little.

The great agitator remains amidst the gallery of English politicians and reformers of his day as a uniquely naughty and biased, but thereby human, figure. His terrible prejudices are somewhat softened by a sense of humor, which made him ask of himself, in the midst of spouting historical nonsense, "Is this what you call writing a history?" The fact that he has appealed to people as diverse in their political philosophies as G. K. Chesterton and G. D. H. Cole shows the enigmatic character of the instincts and emotions of which he has been a spokesman. More than anybody else of the period, Cobbett with his likes and dislikes demonstrates the content of the "curious ideas" of the common man. "Cobbett and the people *felt alike*; that was the secret of his ascendancy."[13]

The stock of prejudices and superstitions and the blind opposition to the forces of modern life that Cobbett represents are merely the breeding ground of indiscriminate radicalism. There is not enough of systematic theory in his fulminations to classify Cobbett as anything but an anti-industrialist, but we shall not be far wrong if we borrow a term for the kind of response that Cobbett, the common man of the 1820's, evidenced toward industrialism and call it basically anarchist. Unyielding conservatism in the face of economic change, rejection of the most basic means of accommodation to the organizational and scientific requirements of modern life, what else is the basis of anarchist sentiment? This sentiment often masquerades under pretended reverence for the older and now impractical forms of authority and social organization, but it does not offer solutions for fitting the older values into the changed social and economic structure. Where can universal suffrage lead without a system of universal education? How can a class of prosperous small farmers be preserved, if there is to be no paper money, no centralized banking system, but on the contrary a positive discouragement of industry and technology? Insofar as it expresses anything, Cobbett's philosophy is simply the anarchistic radicalism of the displaced countryman, with its inconsistent but very human mixture of individualism and authoritarianism, of xenophobic nationalism and humanitarianism, a radicalism that can flow into a more practical political movement of the left or the right, but of itself can accomplish nothing because it negates the simple facts of life, because it is an emotion and not an ideology.

The idea of the "good old times" is in fact the springboard of as much revolutionary as reactionary feeling. Young Engels could write of the disappearing craftsman-peasant, whom he and Marx were soon to classify as part of the passing "idiocy of rural life," in the following terms:

> True, he was a bad farmer and managed his land inefficiently, often obtaining but poor crops; nevertheless, he was no proletarian; he had a stake in the country, he was permanently settled and stood one step higher in society than the English workman of today.... They did not need to overwork.... They were, for the most part strong, well-built people.[14]

The recovery of the lost virtues of the past through the most intense development of the new—such is the scheme of Marxism. And it is in the rejection and condemnation of the present that it strikes a sympathetic chord in the proletarian. In this sense, it is superfluous to seek elaborate proofs of the paternity of this or that theory of Marxism in Cobbett, the Chartists, or the contemporary French socialists. Marxism simply breathes the same air of half-nostalgic and half-revolutionary rejection of the bourgeois world and incorporates it in its revolutionary appeal.

By the time the *Manifesto* was published, the "Marxist" period of English politics was, in fact, drawing to its end. Cobbett had been its precursor, and Chartism its political expression. If Cobbett is sheer, unorganized, anti-industrial sentiment appealing to instincts only one step more advanced than those expressed in Luddite riots and smashing of factory equipment, then Chartism means a further advance: the grappling for political power. The Chartist movement was not, despite Marx's dictum, a working-class *party*. It was a movement, mass action, groping to become a party. Its antecedents were not unconnected with the feelings that gave rise to the kind of historical nonsense Cobbett propagated: a

Chartist like Doubleday could say that universal suffrage had been the custom of the country until Henry VI, and since then the common people had been despoiled by the aristocracy and the middle class. The movement could still find its "practical" proposals in schemes like Feargus O'Connor's proposed mass resettlement of the proletariat on land. But its unhistoricity and nostalgia are secondary to the two great prerequisites of the Marxist feeling: the identification of anti-industrialism with capitalism, and the idea that only political action by the proletariat can secure its economic emancipation.

Neither of these premises of Chartism is unblurred or true of the whole movement. Real Marxism obviously required a Marx, whom the Chartists did not have, while they did count a number of middle-class reformers and moderates in their ranks. But Disraeli expresses the opinion of a large part of the movement when he makes the worker in his *Sybil* say:

> The Capitalist has found a slave that has supplanted the labor and ingenuity of man. Once he was an artisan; at best he now only watches machines; and even that occupation slips from his grasp to the woman and child. The capitalist flourishes, he amasses immense wealth; we sink lower and lower. . . . And yet they tell us that the interests of Capital and Labor are identical.[15]

We are closer to the formula with which Marxism transmutes anti-industrialism into anticapitalism. In the speeches and writings of the radical Chartists, we repeatedly get the claim for the worker of the "whole product" of labor. The primitive statement of the labor theory of value (and the obvious deduction from it) had been something of a commonplace among radical pamphleteers and socialists before Chartism, but in the latter it became elevated into a political principle and a part of political propaganda rather than of theoretical disquisitions.

From the point of view of political action, abortive concepts of insurrections and general strikes, Chartism also impresses us as a harbinger of Marxism. Radical revolutionary movements up to that time were either conspiracies or demonstrations which, often to the surprise of the participants, turned out to be revolutions. The latter had been the traditional pattern of French politics since the Revolution. In Chartism we get for the first time attempts at this "controlled spontaneity," which later on became so characteristic of the Marxist movement— attempts at the synchronization of revolutionary activity and awaiting the appropriate moment to bring out the "masses." The proponents of physical force in the movement (like James Bronterre O'Brien, who argued that usurping governments never abdicate of their own free will but only because of force or fear) had their counterpart in the advocates of "moral force," remote ancestors of the revisionists and gradualists of the Marxian movement.

The official platform of Chartism was, of course, the People's Charter, published in 1838 with its Six Points demanding universal manhood suffrage, equal representation, annual parliaments, no property qualifications for Members of Parliament, ballot, and payment of the Members of Parliament. The ostensible program was political and constitutional: a demand by the working class, or its politically conscious segment, for the extension to them of political power, which the middle class had secured in the Reform Act of 1832. As such, the movement was viewed sympathetically by some Tories, out of spite, no doubt, at the middle class, and even by some democrats within the business community. Essentially, Chartism soon took on the undertones of social radicalism and became a reflection of the workingmen's grievances at the new order established by the partial victory of liberalism in 1832. Chartism's high points of agitation—1839, 1842, and the final spurt of 1848—coincided with periods of economic distress for the working class and amounted to a near-revolutionary situation which certainly alarmed the possessing classes.

The triumph of liberal ideology and of the business interests, which in the mid-forties set England on the road to free trade, separated Chartism from many of its middle-class supporters. About the same time, the beginnings of protective legislation on labor put rudimentary curbs on the greatest abuses of laissez faire and thus set the stamp on the character of liberal society in England during the next fifty years. It was to be a society dominated by commercial and industrial values, buttressed by the liberal ideology. The gradual extension of the democratic principle to politics, and the very gradual and primitive adoption of rudiments of social legislation and recognition of unionism, were to temper the radical protest. And the development of industry and the rise in the general standard of living stripped this protest of its mainly anti-industrial character. The forces of social and economic development were going to thwart decisively the challenge to industrialism and liberalism that Chartism had represented at its most intense. They were to make sure that when socialism as a political force again came to England it was to come under different auspices and in a different spirit from that of anti-industrialism. "The Marxist situation" was gone forever from the English scene after 1850. With it went the possibility of developing a political movement of the Marxist type, toward which some Chartists like Harney and Ernest Jones had groped before 1850, but which when enunciated after that date was simply to be an eccentric political cult bypassed by the main social and intellectual currents.

The wrath of the working class as embodied in Chartism appeared to Engels in 1845 certain to "break out into a revolution in comparison with which the French Revolution and the year 1794 will prove to have been a child's play."[16] This wrath spilled over from behind the political petitions for the Six Points of reform into what appears in retrospect to have been the last desperate stand against industrialism and the modern state. The Poor Law Amendment Act of 1834 embodied the central points of the new liberal philosophy, with its mixture of philosophical radicalism of the Benthamite school, belief in the benevolence of free market and the virtues of self-reliance, and echoes of Malthus.

The Act abolished the old Poor Law, one of the remnants of the patriarchal notions of society dating from Elizabethan and preceding times, and substituted a "scientific" and "modern" principle of relief. Outdoor relief was, in effect, eliminated, and public support was to be extended only to those undoubtedly indigent, under conditions as strict as life in the poorhouses was to be unpleasant. The administration of the new law was centralized and nationalized. The premise seemed to be that unemployment and poverty were a sin if not a crime, and the liberal state took as its motto what was to become an echo of fundamentalist liberalism in Marxism: "Those who do not work, neither shall they eat."

For Cobbett, just before his death, the new law was the dissolution of the unwritten social compact by which the possessing classes held their wealth on the condition of help extended to the poor. For the radical Chartists, it was a device by which freshly triumphant capitalism was to create an industrial reserve army to do its bidding. "Yes, my friends, the New Poor Law is the last blood-stained prop by which the money monster hopes to sustain the tottering fabric of his cannibal system—of that merciless system, which first makes you poor in the midst of wealth of your own producing, and would then bastile and starve you for the fruits of its own barbarity," cried Chartist James O'Brien.[17] From the liberal point of view the law abolished an inefficient and antiquated system, promoted mobility of workmen and removed inducements to their idleness and reliance on public charity. This point of view was incomprehensible to the Tory anti-industrialists and proponents of the protection of the workingman, like the famous Richard Oastler, who openly incited to violence and defiance of the law. To the class-conscious Chartist leaders like O'Brien, the intent was all too clear, and only complete political democracy, whether arrived at peacefully or not, could prevent the fastening of the relentless yoke of capitalism on the British worker.

The richness and multi-varied character of radicalism as exhibited in Chartism still requires systematic treatment. What is important here, in this brief notice of its importance for Marxism, is exactly its partly contrived and partly spontaneous character. It is no longer merely a nostalgic look at the unreal past, nor is it yet an organized political movement with a theology and schemes of its own. Some Chartists persisted in die-hard opposition to the symptoms of the new—paper money and the factory—others wanted a managed currency and a central banking system to spur industrial production. There was the voice of the worker, too, still confused by what was happening around him but now asking questions. Thus, when the London Workingman's Association, led by the pioneer Chartist William Lovett, drafted an address to the American workers in the late 1830's, it congratulated them on having what the British did not, namely, a republic and virtual universal suffrage. But then it proceeded to ask:

> Why have lawyers a prepondering influence in your country?— men whose interests lie in your corruptions and dissensions, and in making intricate the plainest questions affecting your welfare. Why has so much of your fertile country been parcelled out between swindling bankers and grinding capitalists. . . . Why have so many of your cities, towns, railroads, canals and manufactures become the monopolized property of those who toil not, neither do they spin![18]

Why indeed? The stage is all set for Dr. Karl Marx to enter and provide the English workers with a precise answer why suffrage in itself is unavailing and what can be done about it. When in effect he does enter on the British scene with his answers, the London workers will no longer be terribly interested. It is too much to proclaim Marxism a child of Chartism. But it is not too much to affirm Marxism as being shaped by the *impression* of English politics and economics of the 1840's. In the course of a generation, the English working class appears to have progressed from uncomprehending protests against industrialism, through premature efforts at unionization, to the point of revolutionary action, to the point at which it asked questions about the relationship of politics and economics. It was not too much to expect that the next step must be a fuller understanding both of industrialism and of the necessity for socialism, and then a spontaneous revolutionary movement of the whole class. It is also not too much to read into the picture the universal and unavoidable characteristics of modern capitalism and of the effect it produces on the working class. Crude formulations of what later on become Marxist dogmas are commonplace in the mouth of the Chartist leaders: history as a panorama of the class struggle, progressive impoverishment of the worker under capitalism, the labor theory of value and its moral, the industrial reserve army of the unemployed and the monopolistic tendency of capitalism— they all find repeated expression, not as something the speaker announces as a discovery, but as something he assumes the workers know from their own experience. It is hardly important to trace these ideas to the French Revolution, to Ricardo or Robert Owen; the fact is that they appear to comprise what Marx was to call the class consciousness of the advanced worker of the Chartist period.

In observing the English scene in the forties and even the fifties, it was a pardonable illusion for the author of the *Manifesto* to believe that the industrial process under capitalism enables the worker, with barely any help from an agitator or economist, to approach his own *Weltanschauung* and to reach the Marxist conclusion. From this point of view, the English development between 1830 and 1850 was much more Marxist than the French one. In France during this period, one can observe a variety of revolutionary movements and stirrings, often of working-class origin, and a variety of socialist schemes and utopias propagated by individuals and sects. But there is little connection yet between the two, little evidence that *the industrial process in itself* educates the worker about capitalism in the way Marx and Engels believed it did in England. The revolt of the Lyons workers in 1831 was a reflection of misery pure and simple, and its only motto was "Work or death." Even the uprising of the Paris proletariat in June 1848 was caused mainly by indignation over the fact that the Second Republic had not ameliorated the worker's misery. In France, contrived socialist ideas floated on the surface of the revolutionary wave stirred by the misery and dislocation of industrialism and the general instability of the state. In England, socialism appeared to be generated by the revolution- ary wave itself, but this wave beat impotently against the strength of the liberal establishment.

Marx and Engels did not become convinced of the strength of the latter until long after the demise of Chartism. For them the next step was to be a clearly socialist, clearly Marxist phase of

the English revolutionary movement. The best commentary on
such hopes is provided by the story of the individual Chartist
leaders after 1848. Many of them who had fancied themselves
before as the Marats and Robespierres of the coming English
revolution spent their last days in pathetic Victorian middle-
class respectability. Their revolutionary and reforming drive
was channeled into petty and socially approved paths of
reform, temperance, "elevating" the working class through
education, and so on. The most typical worker among them,
William Lovett, sought unsuccessfully to become a small
businessman and toward the end of his life looked with horror
upon socialism. He retained his belief that the British Museum
should be open on Sunday, so that the workers could go there
and "their vicious habits would yield to more rational
pursuits."[19] The upper-class recruit to Chartism, Ernest Jones,
whom Marx considered after 1848 as the most likely leader of
the English Marxist movement and who was the most dashing
and revolutionary of the left Chartists, ended as a candidate for
a liberal nomination for Parliament. Jones, who for years after
1848 preached near-Marxist socialism and theorized about the
monopolistic tendency for self-destruction of capitalism,
finished his life almost as a Gladstonian liberal. Another left
Chartist, George Julian Harney, lived as an inconsequential
radical long enough to have his eightieth birthday fund
subscribed to by, among others, the embodiment of big
business and radicalism turned to imperialism, Mr. Joseph
Chamberlain.

The stories are symptomatic not so much of men naturally
abandoning the radicalism of their youth, as of the triumphant
ascendance of the Victorian social and political spirit, which
made the earlier radicalism simply unthinkable for later
generations. Biographers of the Chartist leaders are often
moved to ascribe to the movement the historical merit of
initiating the democratic reform which eventually swept
England and of setting up the foundations for the rebirth of
English socialism in the eighties and nineties. This homage to
men who, whatever they were "responding" to, were often
courageous fighters against injustice confuses the nature of
two socialisms. Modern English socialism, the product of

Fabianism and the trade unions, is the result of mature industrialism, with few if any ties to the anti-industrial, anti-state feeling so important in Chartism. Of the older type, traces can certainly be found in the socialism of William Morris, in the early Independent Labor Party, and in the guild tradition. But the main current, as we shall see, is quite different.

As to democratic reform, it is interesting to speculate what would have happened had the Chartists' Six Points been in fact adopted, instead of the gradual approach to universal suffrage, achieved in practice in the middle eighties. One thing is fairly certain: the dynamic of England's industrialization and the formation of the "cake of custom" appropriate to it would have certainly been disrupted had a Chartist Parliament been installed. One can imagine reforms on the order of the National Workshops of France of 1848 being tried alongside state-supported schemes of land settlement. If acceptance of industrialization, in the social sense of the term, is a prerequisite to stable democratic institutions, then the victory of Chartism might not have benefited the long-term prospects of democracy and might have made the English development similar to that of France, or led to a situation in which Karl Marx's hopes would not have been entirely disappointed.

Liberalism

The term *liberalism* has faded to the extent that everybody in the West who is not a self-declared fascist lays claim to being a liberal of sorts and programs ranging from extreme conservatism to Communism are advocated in the name of "liberalism." Something of the *original* flavor of English liberalism comes out in Francis Place's prophecy about the socialists in the Chartist movement:

As the best men in the working class proceed in their attainment of knowledge, they will cease to enforce their mistaken notions, and this will be called abandoning their caste by those who remain unenlightened; and these men, and such other men as have power over multitudes of other men, and have sinister objects to accomplish, will misinterpret to the many the actions

and opinions of those who have become more enlightened. . . .
In the meantime many of the incorrigible leaders and large
numbers of their followers who are unteachable will be wearied
out with continued and rapidly recurring disappointments,
will draw off to be replaced by better men; and notwithstanding
the times of inactivity and despair which will occasionally
occur, the progress of actual improvement in right thinking
will go on with increased velocity.[20]

Thus Francis Place, not a middle-class manufacturer or
economist, but a radical political reformer sprung from the
proletariat. What is "right thinking" is determined by the
principles of Utilitarianism and of political economy. The
"mistaken notions" are those of socialism, or of the power of
the trade unions to affect the workers' wages in defiance of
economic "laws."

The quotation is typical of the deterministic rigidity of the
liberalism that ruled the intellectual climate of England from
the 1820's until the end of the century, its greatest and most
extensive reign over morals, legislation, and the economy
occupying the first forty years of the period. The power and
self-assurance of English liberalism dwarfed movements and
opinions opposing it. Though there were no public-opinion
polls at the time, it is not unreasonable to assume that the
conglomeration of opinions and movements known as
Chartism enjoyed at times in the forties some measure of
sympathy from the majority of the nation. Yet the waves of
Chartism beat ineffectually against the rising liberal establishment. The ideology or parts of it made the round of the world.
At home all the animadversions of the Carlyles, Ruskins, and
Newmans could not keep it from becoming the ascendant
intellectual doctrine, any more than the Cobbetts, the Tories,
and the Chartists could keep it from becoming the basis of
English laws and institutions for nearly a century.

The content of early liberalism is not easy to decipher. We do
not begin to describe it by seeing it, as did Mr. Laski, mainly as
the philosophy of business civilization or as a cloak thrown
over vested interests. Nor is it sufficient to center it around the
belief in the self-regulating market, the belief which, according

to Karl Polanyi, was the major historical error of liberalism and the source of all our troubles since.[21] We gain little in comprehension by reading our contemporary ideas and alternatives into the past. Complete determinism and its relative in historiography—"What happened had to happen the way it did"—are no worse than their opposites, which, for instance, would tax Cobden and Gladstone with not anticipating the ideas of Keynes and Beveridge. There is no denying that liberalism became, par excellence, the philosophy of the bourgeoisie and a rationale of the laissez-faire system, and that the connection influenced the philosophy itself. But it was not invented for this purpose, nor was it merely a reflection of business interests.

In dealing with liberalism, it is again wise to recognize the distinction between the great body of theories and philosophies that comprise its basis and what might be called the liberal outlook characteristic of a class and a generation. The philosophers from Adam Smith to John Stuart Mill largely shape this outlook and express some of its most salient characteristics. But liberalism as a whole is not simply the sum of its parts. The liberal spirit is at once broader and perhaps less sophisticated than the theory or theories of liberalism. The distinction, though it may seem fanciful, is always an important one to bear in mind in the case of a social or political philosophy that is not only a body of theories but also the basis of a popular movement. In the theoreticians of liberalism we find not infrequently a note of pessimism about material progress, questioning of whether the ever-expanding productive capacity of society may not be arrested sometime or whether it indeed leads to human happiness. The father of liberal economics, David Ricardo, expresses this (heretical from the liberal point of view) doubt:

> Happiness is the object to be desired, and we cannot be quite sure that, provided he is equally well fed, a man may not be happier in the enjoyment of the luxury of idleness than in the enjoyment of the luxuries of a neat cottage and good clothes. And after all we do not know if these would fall to his share. His labour might only increase the enjoyment of his employer.[22]

This line of pessimism runs through Malthus to the man who expresses the transition from earlier to latter-day liberalism, John Stuart Mill. Yet how unrepresentative this is of the general spirit of liberalism and of what the followers of Ricardo and Mill took to be the main tendency of their teachers. Their tendency was one of triumphant materialism, of continued and indefinite improvement of mankind through material progress. This unsophisticated confidence, which permeated the middle class and spread to the rest of the nation in a manner unmatched in any other European country, was necessary to beat down and then practically extinguish the almost equally massive surge of anti-industrialism, as exhibited in Chartism. The workman William Lovett, coming to abhor the anti-industrial socialism of his youth, is matched by the Tory statesman writing, "If you had to constitute new societies, you might on moral grounds prefer corn fields to cotton factories; an agricultural to a manufacturing population. But our lot is cast, we cannot change it and we cannot recede."[23] The nostalgic retreat of other viewpoints, the helpless acquiescence of other classes, would not have been possible without the solid and unbroken confidence of middle-class liberalism.

Liberal materialism, then, came to be identical with belief in industrialism. To the middle-class reader who cared but little about the constitutional schemes and devices of Jeremy Bentham, the practicality and iconoclasm of Utilitarianism became a social gospel. Distrust of sentimentality on social questions, of too abstract principles in politics, the questioning of every institution by the standard of usefulness—these were the basic instincts of practical men, who now found a philosophy telling them what they felt. Materialism, which to young Marx meant emancipation from the miasma of Hegelianism and endless philosophical discussions, and a road to finding out how people, classes, and nations really behaved, was to the middle-class liberal the concrete reality of his social and professional life. Progress in science and technology was an unqualified good, and the task of society was to sweep away all impediments to it.

It is no wonder that this massive self-confidence in industrialism was to lead to England's industrial supremacy in the world, just as it was to lead to the squalor and ugliness of the English industrial cities. The liberal spirit considered mechanical works and other trophies of industrialism more aesthetically pleasing than castles and green fields. The humanitarian objection was swept aside as unreal. Place no impediments on material progress and other social goods will eventually be added: education and a higher standard of living for all. Tamper with industry in the name of the most elevated idea and everything will be jeopardized. Had he felt the need to justify his function, the liberal businessman would have subscribed to one part of Marx's portrait of the capitalist: "he thus forces the development of the productive forces of society, and creates those material conditions, which alone can form the real basis of a higher form of society, a society in which the full development of every individual forms the ruling principle."[24] Compared with this function, what is that of a carping critic or a social reformer? How ridiculous it is to glorify the pre-industrial past with its long history of barbarity, superstition, and wars, or agrarian existence with its "idiocy of rural life"! And how mischievous it is to propose to turn political power to the as yet uninstructed masses, who would use it to destroy the only means of bringing them out of their present misery and ignorance, industrialization!

The liberal spirit made the same selective use of the economic theories of Smith and Ricardo as it did of the politics and social psychology of Bentham. From the latter it took its utilitarianism and iconoclasm and largely ignored its extreme democratic conclusions and bureaucratic hints. The economics of Smith and Ricardo were not unqualified endorsements of free trade and industrialism. They were born in the still prevailing agrarian country, where manufacturing was of the small-unit variety and the most fundamental economic questions turned around fiscal and trade policy. The liberal spirit lost many of its earlier economic inhibitions in the worship of industrialization pure and simple. Here again, Marx is a reliable guide as to liberalism's appraisal of the task it was performing:

> The bourgeoisie cannot exist without constantly revolutioniz-
> ing the instruments of production, and thereby the relations of
> production, and with them the whole relations of society. . . .
> The bourgeoisie has through its exploitation of the world
> market given a cosmopolitan character to production and
> consumption in every country. To the great chagrin of
> reactionaries, it has drawn from under the feet of industry the
> national ground on which it stood. . . . It has created enormous
> cities, has greatly increased the urban population as compared
> with the rural, and has thus rescued a considerable part of the
> population from the idiocy of rural life. . . . Independent, or but
> loosely connected provinces, with separate interests, laws,
> governments and systems of taxation, became lumped together
> into one nation, with one government, one code of laws, one
> national class interest, one frontier, and one customs tariff. (p.
> 324-326)

And the famous tribute:

> The bourgeoisie, during its rule of scarce one hundred years, has
> created more massive and more colossal productive forces than
> have all preceding generations together. Subjection of nature's
> forces to man, machinery, application of chemistry to industry
> and agriculture, steam navigation, railways, electric telegraphs,
> clearing of whole continents for cultivation, canalization of
> rivers, whole populations conjured out of the ground—what
> earlier century had even a presentiment that such productive
> forces slumbered in the lap of social labor? (p. 326)

The sober businessman could not have approached the
lyricism of Marx in the *Manifesto*, but would have granted that
the passionate German did justice to the historical task of
liberalism. The meaning of Marx's words becomes more clear
cut if for the "bourgeoisie" we substitute "industrialism." The
belief in the all-encompassing, benevolent powers of industrialization is the central point of the liberal spirit, the belief
which in its most fanatical and unconditional form is the
legacy of liberalism to Marxian socialism.

The industrial orientation of liberalism combines with its
class-interest component in the plea for state noninterference.
In the fathers of liberal economics, there was never a clear-cut

argument of *absolute* laissez faire. Bentham's political philosophy bears a bureaucratic tinge. Voices for factory legislation in the 1840's were raised not infrequently by liberal manufacturers, though more typical was the liberal member of the Commons who argued that his profit was made in the last two hours of his workmen's labor and that to cut off those hours would make him bankrupt and his men unemployed. Class selfishness, in other words, though prevalent, was not as strong as the industrial mania. The two coalesced easily in the belief that social reform and economic regulation were the devices by which the aristocracy was fighting a retreating action and would thwart the benefits of industrialization and free trade. The typical liberal, as in Morley's portrait of Bright,

> was carried along by vehement political anger and deeper than that, there glowed a wrath as stern as that of an ancient prophet. To cling to a mischievous error seemed to him to savour of moral depravity and corruption of heart. What he saw was the selfishness of the aristocracy and the landlords and he was too deeply moved by the hatred of this, to care to deal very patiently with the bad reasoning which their own self-interest inclined his adversaries to mistake for good. His invective was not the expression of mere irritation, but a profound and menacing passion.[25]

If we supplant, as the object of hatred, the aristocracy by the bourgeoisie, the description could be Marx's.

Moral anger aroused at the irrational privilege, at the fostering of what it considered economic superstitions, made the liberal spirit suspicious of state action. Yet it is not entirely inconceivable to imagine, in different historical circumstances, the same men working to build industrial society, with the same passions and uncompromising vigor, as state-installed managers and bureaucrats, rather than individual entrepreneurs. But not in a society in which the British "are a servile aristocracy-loving, lord ridden people, who regard the land with as much reverence as we still do the peerage and baronetage."[26] Social antagonism can be a powerful spur in economic activity. The liberal industrialist, in his furious activity, was not without the grim comfort that his exertions were showing up the social uselessness and parasitism of the aristocracy. A century later, the same masochistic self-sacrifice on the altar of industrialization was to be urged upon the Soviet worker and manager.

If Marxism inherited much of the industrial mania of the early liberal spirit, then this spirit itself was not without a certain one-sidedness and intolerance for different standards of value. The source of this intolerance, again a paradox and an analogy to Communism, was not so much class selfishness but precisely the sense of social mission, of performing the necessary and inevitable task of industrialization and modernization, of rescuing England and then the whole world from superstition and backwardness. One cannot blame a contemporary observer like Marx for incorporating in his theory the conviction that industrial fanaticism and self-righteousness were indelible traits of the capitalist. That the capitalist would grow more humane, that he would slacken in his ceaseless pursuit of accumulation and expansion, were not impressions readily warranted by the English social scene of the 1840's and '50's. It appeared then equally unlikely that the capitalist would modify his values or submit without the use of force to the full panoply of the welfare state: state regulation, unionism, and high taxes. The continuously and increasingly dissatisfied worker facing the inflexible capitalist—this fairly realistic picture of early industrialization is taken by Marx to express the eternal law of capitalism.

Sources of the ethos of industrialism have been sought in religion, more specifically in the Puritan tradition and Calvinism. Theories of this kind, whether presented with the scholarship of Max Weber or with the vulgar exaggeration of Cobbett, are elusive of proof. It is equally difficult to establish related notions of religious influence: for example, the often stated assertion that Methodism had a quieting effect on the revolutionary turbulence of the masses. Industrialization and unbridled laissez faire were both attacked and defended from the religious point of view. There is no question that the spirit of liberalism was a secularizing one, temperamentally antipathetic to excessively doctrinal and ritualistic creeds; and yet no strict lines of religious divergence can be established paralleling the defenders and attackers of the new order.

What is more important here is attention to what might be called the general assimilationist bent of liberalism and its premises. It would not have occurred to the average liberal to demand conformity, strongly addicted as the movement was to individual freedom. Yet rationalism and industrial and political progress were equated in his mind. The spread of industrialization undermines the irrational institutions of the past, in themselves reflections of obsolete economic forms. Industrialization and education will eventually impose the same rationalistic, materialistic, middle-class stamp on men everywhere. The average liberal would have thought it inconceivable that a fully industrialized and rational society would shelter such phenomena as Catholicism, nonobjective art, Christian Science, militarism, and socialism. Tolerance, which is justly associated with the liberal spirit, was initially due to its invincible conviction that it was the "wave of the future."

We might digress here and anticipate the discussion of Soviet society. The startlingly Victorian code of morals (if we omit the religious element) and arts that the Stalinist period fastened on Soviet society flows rather logically from this fundamentalist liberalism ensconced in Marxism. What the liberals—and Marx—assumed would result automatically from the development of economic forces and the adjustment of social values to them was in the Soviet Union created by decree. Both early liberalism and Marxism carry in them the premise of conformity, even if this premise is coupled with the promise of the fullest flowering of individualism once the social environment (largely through this conformity) provides the appropriate material basis.

The passion for freedom in liberalism is not unconnected with this rather oversimplified—from our point of view—estimate of human nature. No doubt about man being formed by his environment, no doubt about material progress beneficently transforming human nature. The outlook of Dr. Marx stares at us from many of the preconceptions of liberalism, but it is in vain that one looks for Dr. Freud. It is difficult to find a society so self-congratulatory for its virtues, for dissipating the darkness of the past, and for discovering the true principles of moral and social improvement, as English liberalism of the mid-nineteenth century.

> Give me a sober Englishman possessing the truthfulness common to his country, and the energy so peculiarly his own, and I will match him for being capable of equalling any other man in the everyday struggles of life. He has a self depending and self governing instinct which carries him triumphantly through all difficulties and dangers,

writes Cobden.[27] The drunkenness of the lower classes and the perversity of the upper ones were blemishes that the progress of education and of democracy would remove, thus eventually uniting the whole nation in the industrious and sober virtues appropriate to modern civilization. The note of nationalism was seldom chauvinistic. Industry and commerce would inculcate in other nations the virtues suitable to self-government and individual freedom. If liberalism did not aspire to build internationals, it was for the same reason that it disdained to legislate conformity. The forces of history would chase away militarism and despotism. Noninterference abroad was the concomitant of individualism at home. Revolutions abroad, if directed against the type of forces that had opposed the Reform Act of 1832, were justified. With a great deal of reason, liberalism considered itself a revolutionary force on a world scale; and, had it known the frightful semantics of the twentieth century, it would have classified upstart socialism as "counterrevolutionary."

The preceding statement is of necessity an oversimplification. Just as social historians have in this century poked holes in "capitalist realism," with its picture of steady material and national improvement, so novelists and biographers have penetrated behind the façade of monotonous virtue and optimism of liberal society. Contemporary critiques, both conservative and pre-Marxian socialist, take as their point of departure a simple dislike of the new order. More recent criticisms illustrate the inner doubts, psychic suffering, and pessimism behind the Victorian facade of self-assurance. But the oversimplified view brings us perhaps closer to the viewpoint of a revolutionary like Marx, to whom liberal society did not even pay the compliment of political persecution, and who spent the greater part of his life in England, unnoticed and ignored. In his absorption with drawing up a list of indictments against liberal society, Marx was carried a long way toward acceptance of its values and ethos.

The main accusation against liberalism is not the unreality of its values—industrialization, rationalism, and individualism—but the hypocrisy inherent in their being combined with the bourgeois system of property. The unreal Marxist worker does not reject the gospel of hard industrial labor, the aim of comfortable existence, the plea for democracy and education. His quarrel with bourgeois society is that through its institution of property it denies to him the realization of his essentially bourgeois and liberal values. Marx's technological and scientific enthusiasm and his acceptance of industrialism have often been compared or traced to Saint-Simon. The great French philosopher had a mania for science and technology and some interesting ideas as to how the world might be arranged to further their development. But the technological obsession of liberalism was expressed not in extravagant theories but in the actual development and transformation of French and especially British societies. Just as Marx's conclusions about the revolutionary propensity of the proletariat are affected more by the reality of contemporary *movements* like Chartism than by revolutionary socialist *theories*, so the technological and industrial component of his socialism owes more to the absorption in and the reaction to the reality of industrial life under liberalism than to any theoretical cult of industrialism.

The reluctance of Marx to draw up any detailed socialist utopias may be another reflection of the air of practicality that characterized political life of the prototype of industrialism, England. Chartism, for all its land schemes, concentrated on the struggle for political rights. English liberalism progressed from the day of Bentham, with his constitutional models ready down to the last detail, to practical matters of political and economic reform. This air of practicality, of ready and immediate application of broader principles to political action, which was to give Marxism its unsurpassed advantage in competition with other socialist movements, is a direct inheritance of a society and a period which, whether in reform or revolution, was given less to brooding about right, wrong, and the ideal than to action. The great moral of contemporary liberalism is that an ideology which cannot be translated into political action is pointless. Revolutionary movements in Europe of that day often had one strategy, *coup d'état*, and one aim, the realization of a particular political or social utopia. By observing English liberalism between 1830 and 1850, we can draw closer to the conception of the political party inherent in later Marxism: *a political movement in being*, having its ultimate aim (even a utopia) but going after its objectives step by step, if need be forming temporary alliances, compromising, but never abandoning its objectives. What in contemporary British society was the result of fortuitous circumstances becomes, in mature Marxism, elaborated into a conscious system: a political party with a rigid program and ideology, but capable of basing its political tactics on an analysis of shifting social and economic forces in the given country.

The earliest political Marxism of the *Manifesto* still has the revolutionary impatience and immediacy of the utopian socialists. Later Marxism, although Marx and Engels never lose their revolutionary optimism, is mellowed into conceding the possiblity of gradualism. One may at least conjecture that this fact, which gives Marxian socialism staying power not possessed by its rival revolutionary doctrines, penetrates the doctrine from an impression of the triumphant ascent of English liberalism.

"And notwithstanding the times of inactivity and despair which will occasionally occur, the progress of actual improvement in right thinking will go on with increased velocity."[28] This is a sentiment that Marxism, in effect, enrolls among its own. Place's condescension toward those who do not see the world the way he does is repeated by Marx's, even though the latter expresses it with greater violence and bitterness. The "other side" of Marxism is in effect a kind of integral liberalism of the early variety, liberalism unmellowed by absorption in democratic politics and untempered by conversion to social legislation. The *intellectual* atmosphere of Marxism has that excessive rationalism, historical iconoclasm, and defiant refusal to go below the material surface to probe human motives which have often made early liberalism unmarketable to the masses while endearing it to the scientist, engineer, and social planner, all struggling against inherited irrationalities of every social system and all seeing in science and technology the only roads to human emancipation. Marx and Engels, by setting their industrial and scientific creed within the frame of a revolutionary movement, shifted the emphasis of the early liberals. To the latter, democracy and individualism were the end products of free development of social and economic forces. Even a reasonable degree of economic equality was not beyond the ken of the earlier liberals, but they envisaged this development as the end result of a free growth of capitalism. "Time is a great equalizer," Bentham said, while rejecting progressive taxation as a logical corollary of his "felicific calculus." The liberal's realm of freedom was, like Marx's, to follow the realm of capitalism, but there was no intervening period of socialism. Furthermore, liberalism soon underwent "secularization," i.e., adjustment to actual politics: political and social reforms soon became tangible measures of freedom and ends in themselves, and these ends had a suspicious correspondence to the aims of the middle classes. Just as the revolutionary side of Marxism is couched in the violent and bitter language of contemporary, essentially anarchist, socialism, its "positive" side is couched in the liberal idiom of the century, and its better world to come is described in the humanitarian, cosmopolitan, and democratic terms of the liberal paradise.

To repeat, unlike the conservative or anarchist critics of bourgeois civilization, Marx and Engels are not really shocked by the appearence of bourgeois industrialism, by its money grubbing, or by its bad taste. Bourgeois civilization is bad because its values can be realized only by a small minority of the population and because it is predicated upon the growing misery of the masses. Once the revolution is effected, the logic of Marxism parts company with such aesthetic protests against capitalism as those voiced by Ruskin, Herzen, or William Morris and finds a more congenial association in the values and the spirit of the early liberal entrepreneur.

Liberalism as an enthusiastic response to industrialization and modernization and then as a rationale of their most intense development is a direct ancestor of Marxism. We shall not be surprised to see Marxist revolutions, carried out under anarchist, anti-industrial slogans, turn around after victory and sacrifice on the altar of industrialization and its logical corollary, the centralized state, the slogans that brought them to power. Suppose we make the absurd assumption that the real objective of Marx and Engels was to wean the masses of the freshly created proletariat from their unconstructive anti-industrial feelings and to convert them to the necessity of an industrialized society and a strong state. What better ideology could have been devised than one that asserted the inevitability of thorough industrialization and centralization and that placed the blame for the miseries of the transition, not on industrialism as such, but on the anachronistic and hence vicious role of the capitalist and "his" state. This legend is helpful in making us realize how much of raw liberalism there is in the Marxist system, and how the industrial mania of his Communist followers was not unanticipated by the father of the movement.

Apart from inculcating on Marxism the industrial mania, English liberalism was instrumental in the formulation of other related points of the dogma. Economic determinism, although it had been proclaimed before by Marx and was implicit in contemporary socialist and liberal thinkers, could take on flesh and bones from the observation of English society and the ascendance and character of its liberalism. From a historical perspective, we can now say that Britain was not the norm, but one of the rare examples of a society where, for a time, economic forces, the prevailing social ideology, and political power supplemented each other and made possible a feat of economic transformation which in its completeness and relative speed was approached in the twentieth century only by a totalitarian state employing totalitarian means. The naive complacency of a Francis Place over the dying out of the anti-industrial spirit and its "wrong" ideas was not disturbed by the reflection that this was due not only to the inevitable assimilation of the liberal values by the nation, but also to England's advantage of being first in the industrial race, dominating international trade and finance, and not having, after 1815, major wars. The permanent ascendance of liberal values based on their healthy materialism and their eventual spread to all parts of the world were taken for granted by the early liberals. As young Marx, in this respect a faithful interpreter of the liberal spirit, asserted in the *Manifesto*, the growth of industry and rationalism everywhere would do away with wars, despotisms, and protection. At home the full flowering of industrialism would put an end alike to the pretensions of the aristocracy and to the illusions of the proletariat about trade unions. The road to domestic as well as international utopia lay through the forces of production, which (again Marx) "alone can form the real basis of a higher form of society, a society in which the full development of every individual forms the ruling principle."[29] The universal enthronement of individualism, enlightened democracy, and perhaps a world order were to liberalism the inevitable result of economic forces, just as to Marx the same forces were creating universal socialism. No national differences, no social or economic lags, could, in the long run, interfere with this process.

How close to our own feelings this aspect of early liberalism is; how evident it is, for example, in the whole program and plan for economic assistance to underdeveloped nations; and yet how unreal to us is the easy optimism that underlies it. Today a variant of this materialistic utopianism is found only in the official speeches of Communist leaders. But even they, in fact, are no more confident that material forces, unaided, can bring victory to their side than is a Western statesman when he declares that an improvement in the standard of living will bring democracy in Africa or Asia. Contemporary expressions of both liberal and revolutionary optimism sound hollow when compared with their original prototypes. We know now that no other society in the nineteenth century became so thoroughly industrialized, in fact as well as in spirit, as England. Furthermore, even a considerable degree of industrialization has not brought to many other societies the benefit of stable democracy. Rigid determinism of the Francis Place type showed itself to be an illusion based on the observation of one society during one period of its development, just as the related Marxist determinism misinterpreted even more fundamentally the social meaning of England's industrialization.

Professor Dicey traced to about 1870 the decline of the original individualistic liberalism and the shift to its collectivistic stage in England. The shift in the intellectual atmosphere is best epitomized by J. S. Mill's words in his *Autobiography* when he forsakes his earlier belief in the automatism of economic forces and qualifies his democratic belief by the need for state action to provide the framework for meaningful citizenship. There is a straight line from his avowal to Fabian socialism. With this later liberalism, so prone to turn into welfare-state socialism, Marxism has nothing in common. Neither its social analysis nor the chosen path of reform, through the democratic process, is understandable in Marxist terms. Nor did Marx and Engels foresee that at the close of the nineteenth century working-class socialism in England would arise from satiation with industrial values rather than as a reaction to industrialism and liberalism as had been true of earlier working-class radicalism. The industrial mania of earlier liberalism was mellowed and qualified by the achievement of industrialization and the subsequent realization that in itself industrialization did not provide all the answers to the social problems of mankind. The dogmatism and spiritual aridity of the earlier liberal spirit gave way to a variety of, actually, more tolerant, if also less self-assured and certain, liberal opinions. But Marxism persisted in seeing in the capitalist of 1900 his ancestor of 1850; in the democratic state the limited-suffrage institution dominated by the bourgeoisie; and in the social welfare philosophies the rationale of the class interest of the exploiters. With its anachronistic picture (insofar as the West was concerned) of its old enemy—liberal society—Marxism also preserved unimpaired its original characteristics—uncomplicated materialism, belief in economic "laws," and passion for industrialization.

Socialism and Anarchism

In considering the relationship of Marx to earlier and contemporaneous socialist thinkers and movements, it is well to keep several points in mind. Marx was a great synthesizer and a voracious assimilator of ideas and social facts. At the same time, his receptivity to new ideas and movements definitely slackened after about 1850, when the main outlines of his system were laid and he entered on the task of elaboration. Thus his thought, it is hardly worth repeating, bears the imprint of many minds and many movements. But beyond identifying the great intellectual traditions in which Marx and Engels were nurtured—Hegelianism, English political economy, and socialism—it is difficult as well as almost superfluous to trace this or that idea of his to this or that socialist thinker. Many of his most startling concepts to us were virtual commonplaces of the English and Continental radicalism and socialism of his formative years. Were the radical implications of the labor theory of value taken by Marx from John Francis Bray, William Thompson, or John Gray? It is fairly unimportant to decide, for not only they but a host of others, economists, agitators, and politicians, voiced rough and ready versions of the same theory. Modern economists, while assailing Marx's economics, praise him for forseeing at that early date the future tendency of capitalism toward economic concentration and monopolies. To be sure, the classical economists of the period thought in terms of perfect competition and lived in the era of a multitude of small producing units. But predictions of the future bigness and concentration of business were not unique among the radical reformers and socialists. That most impractical of men, Charles Fourier, feared the coming of the era of "industrial feudalism." So did Sismondi, Blanc, and a host of others. The old academic game of "tracing the influence" of this or that thinker or theory does not go far enough in explaining the sources of Marxism or of its influence. To ascertain the doctrine's affinities to and differences from other socialisms, we must look at the principle of selection that Marx employed in taking and rejecting items from the common fund of contemporary radicalism.

It is also worth keeping in mind that Marxism is interested in "ideas in action," ideas that are not only the product of an individual's mind, but that are, or appear to be, postulates or practical demands of a class. Hence it has been asserted here that Marx was more influenced, both consciously and unconsciously, by Chartism on one hand and liberalism on the other than by all the productions of the plethora of individual socialists. The splendidly arrogant words of the *Manifesto* claim for Marxism this double advantage of being a part of actual life—of the thought and feeling of the working class—and of transcending that thought and feeling by understanding history and, hence, the future:

> The Communists, therefore, are on the one hand practically the most advanced and resolute section of the working-class parties of every country, that section which pushes forward all others; on the other hand, theoretically, they have over the great mass of the proletariat the advantage of clearly understanding the line of march, the conditions, and the ultimate general results of the proletarian movement. (p. 334)

Other socialist theories, according to Marx, fall to the ground on either of these two counts: they are unthinking reflections of the *immediate* feelings of the proletariat and pay no attention to the historical causes of the given situation; or they are intellectual creations divorced from the life and aspirations of the worker. This self-proclaimed function of Marxist socialism as the vanguard of the working class has, of course, been established as the organizational principle of the Communist Party of the Soviet Union. It enabled Marx to view other socialist thinkers either as stragglers wandering off the road of the historical march of the working class, or as persons in the ranks, their view obstructed by the multitude around them, and thus unable to see clearly what the head of the column, i.e., Dr. Karl Marx and Friedrich Engels, saw. This vision persisted through the days when, inexplicably, the masses became separated from the vanguard, and the latter, instead of leading a victorious march, found itself doing scholarly work in the British Museum. History seemed to have punished Marx for the presumption of his youth; and when he was on his deathbed in 1883, his theory must have appeared to many just as "utopian" as those he and Engels had scorned.

From a longer perspective it must be admitted that Marxism's self-appraisal and judgment on the competing socialist cults contain a great deal of truth. No other brand of socialism was so insistently a blend of actual workingmen's grievances and acceptance of the logic of the system that had led to those grievances. Many of the contemporary socialists say, in effect: "Give me but a chance to put into effect my own scheme, and human grievances and dissatisfactions will disappear." Others are just as ready to lead a revolution without inquiring where it will eventually lead them. Fourier on one hand and Blanqui on the other, stand as examples respectively of the fanciful deviser of utopias and the unreflecting exponent of revolutionary action. Petitioning the great of this world to put their fancies into effect or storming the barricades, are the recipes of these early socialists for realizing their ideas.

A modern socialist may well conclude that Marx was right in his slighting condescension toward his rivals. Yet a more balanced judgment must acknowledge the tremendous importance of the early socialist thinkers. A closer look at them will explain not only certain points of original Marxism, but even more clearly the factors that influenced the acceptance or rejection of Marxism by sections of society in various countries.

To return to the simile: the claim to be both a part and the vanguard of the working class illustrates not only the strength but also a certain weakness of Marxism. One cannot have one's cake and eat it too, even if one specifies that the two actions are to be separate parts of the historical process. Marxism *has* to sacrifice a certain part of its sensitivity and appeal to the working-class grievances when it accepts the logic of industrialization, just as this acceptance *has* to be modified toward revolutionary appeal. To that extent, Marxism is a much less faithful reproduction of the actual worker's revolutionary feelings than that found in some Chartists (for the British worker) or in Blanqui or Proudhon (for the French). The absoluteness of the belief in the environment's shaping of man comes out more strongly in Robert Owen and the technocratic cult appears more forcefully in Saint-Simon than even in Marx. A brief consideration of some of the early socialists may bring out which elements in Marxism will appeal to which social force or intellectual tradition in a given country.

The dates of some of the great precursors of socialism give a clue to the characters of their doctrines: Saint-Simon, 1760-1825—Robert Owen, 1771-1859—Fourier, 1772-1837. Their roots are very definitely in the spirit of the Enlightenment. Theirs is the temperament of the reforming *philosophe*, with his neat schemes and model settlements, and the unthinkability of achieving reform aims through popular or political action. It is the Englishman Owen who comes closest to the notion of political action among the working class and political agitation. But even Owen was ready to memorialize William IV, the monarchs of Europe, and Metternich on behalf of his scheme, and to preach conversion to his ideas through the example of model communities.

And then there are the stories about Saint-Simon writing to Napoleon and Fourier pathetically awaiting a rich philanthropist to finance his phalansteries. Alas, our heroes lived before the age of the Carnegie, Ford, and other American foundations! But their delusions about the eventual appearance of an "angel" who would finance the one certain way to salvation are not just tragicomic incidents of their biographies. Nothing is more alien to their spirit than the Marxist dictum that the emancipation of the working class can be only achieved by the working class itself. Their mechanistic approach to the social problem and their expectation of patronage in the construction of a new political and social system separate them from the spirit of modern politics.

Equally outdated in terms of nineteenth- and twentieth-century politics, though in a different way, is the type of socialism represented by Auguste Blanqui (1805-1881). This is insurrectionism pure and simple, with but little thought of devising elaborate schemes for the day after the revolution. Blanqui's socialism lives entirely in the conspiratorial world. It is akin to the conspiratorial groups of revolutionaries, whether quasi-socialist or nationalist in character, that flourished on the Continent between 1815 and 1848 and constituted the backwash of the revolutionary and nationalist excitement stirred up by the French Revolution and the Napoleonic wars. The dazzling possibilities of a *coup d'état* on behalf of an oppressed class or nationality stirred up men's minds from Paris to St. Petersburg. The immature revolutionism that would persuade a group of students, young officers, or radical workers that political power in the modern state could be seized and consolidated by a demonstration or conspiracy is another, if more advanced, variant of the model-community-building mania of the earlier socialists. In neither case is there any idea of converting a large part of the nation to one's revolutionary program or of fitting the program in with the postulates and interests of a class. The realities of politics, especially of Continental politics, make utopian expectations of conversion by the example of a model community or romantic revolutionism the only ways for those who would change the world. We are still in the days of mass illiteracy, of no or limited suffrage and parliamentary institutions. By the same token, the Leviathan, the modern state, is still in the process of growing. It appears not unthinkable that the course of a society may be changed by the actions of an enlightened autocrat, the good will of the great, or a determined action by a relative handful of men.

In the *Communist Manifesto* and in the activities of the Communist League, we find numerous traces of romantic insurrectionism; in another decade after 1848 it is almost gone from the European scene, and the last traces, barring distant echoes in Russia, will be found in the Paris Commune. In pouring abuse and ridicule on most of the contemporary socialists, Marx and Engels were blind to the element of utopianism and insurrectionism in their own manifesto. The specter that haunted the Guizots and the Metternichs of the day was not one of the little group headed by Marx and Engels but of the general revolutionary excitement unleashed by the forces of modern life upon the old or slowly changing order: nationalism, schemes of social reform, and democratic and liberal stirrings. The heritage of earlier utopia-building, sheer revolutionary excitability, and conspiracy thus becomes a part of early Marxism, but already because of the British example it is subordinated to the study of the organic growth of society and of its "laws." Thus in the edifice of Marxism, in addition to its exposition of the logic of industrialism and its summation of anti-industrial grievances, are present unreflecting revolutionary enthusiasm and utopianism.

What lies behind them is the vivid recollection of the French Revolution and the Napoleonic period. Continental socialism in its beginnings was not a response to the social question. The poverty of the most numerous class and the attempt to alleviate its lot were almost an afterthought, even with Saint-Simon. Socialism, even before it became harnessed to the task of revolution or reform or concentrated around the phenomenon of modern industry and the modern state, was born out of one central intellectual current and one great historical experience. The intellectual current was the scientific curiosity of the Enlightenment, which made men think of applying social engineering to society. Yet it would not have occurred to Rousseau, Mably, or Condorcet, any more than it would have to Sir Thomas More, to found a movement to push toward the realization of their ideas. The French Revolution and Napoleon provided the examples both of popular passion stirred up on behalf of political ideas and of attempts at social engineering on a vast scale, and a tangible refutation of the conservative thesis that social change is the work of generations and cannot be accomplished by a man or a movement. Socialism, which had always existed as an intellectual or religious fad or literary exercise, thus emerged in the form of schools of thought after the great historical experience. It was another and even more pervasive experience—industrialization—that turned socialism from utopian projects and schemes of *coup d'état* into political movements.

The France of Marx's youth and mature age provides the classical example of the evolution of socialism from intellectual fancies into a political movement. In England, the tempo of industrial advance catapulted the quasi-socialism of the Chartists into the political spotlight, only to grind it equally quickly under its wheels. In Germany, the national problem subordinated the social one. It was in France that socialism preserved longest its "academic" character: an individual's search for a solution to the puzzle of a changing world and the first attempts to anchor this solution to the feelings and interests of the people.

This really primitive phase of socialism has some interesting characteristics, which appear in unequal proportions in its leading exponents. One is the obsession with the religious problem. The religious mania, in the form either of defiant atheism or attack on religion as identified with and comprising the established order, is no more pronounced than the religious or quasi-religious character given by the critics to their own systems. With the liberals or with Marx, the whole matter of religion is definitely pushed to the secondary plane. For them religious values either fit the values of the rising industrial society or they are an anachronism, in the process of being removed by material progress and education. The preoccupation with the religious problem of a socialist or a radical thinker is an indication in itself that a basic prerequisite of industrialization, a certain secularization of thought and life, has not been achieved, and that *the problem of reform or revolution in itself appears as a religious one.* That a religious dogma might dominate a society practicing *his* system would be as inconceivable to Robert Owen as to Saint-Simon, Fourier, or Proudhon, for their systems are essentially religious cults.

This characteristic intolerance was partly inherited by Marxism but with much less intensity, for Marx also partook of the liberal assumption that the problem would solve itself, and, this being the case, why attack the obsolete remnants of a dying order while a more potent enemy was at hand? Thoroughgoing materialism in a materialistically minded society cannot be intensely violent or intolerant on the religious issue. The passion and energy expounded by some early socialists in their love-hatred complex about Christianity were devoted by Marx to the assault upon capitalism, and by a liberal to a concrete political, economic, or religious reform. But enough of the older socialist tradition rubbed off on Marxism so that, in some future "underdeveloped" society, Marxism will appeal to a young intellectual as a liberating religious cult. Actually, the main interest of the doctrine lies elsewhere.

The preoccupations of the fathers of socialism tell us a great deal about their underlying premises. Politics was still viewed from the religious standpoint; the way of putting their theories into life, apart from the immediate instrument of a benevolent patron, lay essentially in indoctrination in the given cult. The mantle of a prophet was needed, for it covered the authoritarian conviction that the masses would never achieve or learn anything through the actual circumstances of their lives, but would have to be taught like children through example, authority, and indoctrination. The essential goodness of man and his perfect malleability by the environment were the common sentiments in the profuse socialist literature. But what could be done to lift from the masses the dead weight of superstition and traditionalism, abetted and exploited by kings, aristocrats, and priests? Only the moral passion of a new religion or doctrine could accomplish the task, not ballots or the forces of production.

It might seem that this irrationalist view of human nature and the consequent authoritarian premise would be absent in Saint-Simon. Admirer of science and technology, praiser of British parliamentary institutions who wanted a parliamentary confederation of Europe, lover of liberty, Saint-Simon seemingly stands as an exception to what has been said here about pre-Marxian socialism. Yet, what this apparent rationalist recommends in the end, is a religion of science and social welfare—and the word *religion* is employed not as a figure of speech but in the literal sense. "Princes, listen to the voice and God, who speaks through my mouth" proclaims the author of New Christianity. In his new Christian society, the preachers will "make their audience tremble by painting the horrible situation which is the fate in this life of a man who has incurred public disesteem; [they] will even show the arm of God raised against a man, all of whose feelings are not dominated by those of philanthropy."[30] The poets will be required to help the "preachers" by writing their poetry in what might be called "new Christian realism," and so will the musicians with their music. The Catholics and the Protestants are heretics for reasons that are spelled out by Saint-Simon with more eloquence than coherence. How rationalist and scientific is the spirit of this cult of rationalism and science?

The same question might be addressed to Robert Owen, with his inflexible conviction that "each individual is so organized that he *must believe* according to the strongest conviction that is made upon his mind; which conviction cannot be given to him by his will, nor be withheld by him." Hence the positive evil of all religions.

> It is necessary, therefore, that all doubt respecting the fact stated in this law of our nature should be forever removed from the human mind and until this shall be effectually done, it will be impracticable to train man to become rational in their thoughts, feelings, and actions, and equally impossible to form arrange-ments to train them to become intelligent, sincere and permanently happy.[31]

The same note appears in Fourier and others and culminates in Proudhon's interminable tirades about religion and his own exposition of the essence of Christianity. Though none of the great precursors of socialism advocated the use of force—which appears in nineteenth-century anarchism à la Blanqui—their authoritarianism is unmistakable. Mankind will see the light and somehow extinguish the old superstitions and adopt the right principles of behavior. Yet, their disciples will ask, what if the superstitions cannot be removed simply by demonstrat-ing their error because they are abetted by powerful vested interests? Isn't the moral fervor of early socialism eventually bound to flow into these socialist movements, which takes a less optimistic but a more activist view about the propagation of their doctrine?

The reverse side of the religious obsession of the early socialists is their scientific mania. Here again, the actual meaning of their use of the term *science*, like that of "religion," has to be carefully considered. When we spoke before of the cult or religion of science and technology inherent in early liberalism and taken over from it by Marxism, we used a figure of speech describing the intensity of the feeling and wonder about the freshly demonstrated powers of science and industry. But the wonder at all those things (which today we can appreciate only by recalling our reaction to the harnessing of nuclear power) in liberalism or even Marxism never takes the form of an *actual* religion, with the appurtenances of worship, saints like Newton and Descartes, or confusions of one's own dogma with the law of gravitation—in brief, the form of obscurantism. A doctine that worships science against the background of industrial development is unlikely to get unhinged and enthusiastically incoherent on the subject, just as a materialistic doctrine does not get violent on the subject of religion if it is posed against the background of a materialistic society. Industrialization makes a society absorb its original wonder at science. If it proceeds rapidly, science becomes an accepted and unsensational part of daily life. The anti-industrial obscurantism of a Cobbett is no more characteristic of the period of transition than the scientific obscurantism of the early socialists and their attempt to base their theories, whether pro- or anti-industrial, on "science." The pitiful complaint of Fourier expresses this spirit:

> Philosophy maintains that God has not made the code for our industrial and social relations, that his providence has not provided for them; but he made this code for creations infinitely greater and smaller than we are; the stars and the insects. Is it not possible that the Revelator of these laws of attraction should be destined to fulfill this role for mankind? Opinion of the world extols Newton who began the calculus of attraction and has luminously treated the material world: would it not be advisable to accord a test to the continuator of Newton, the man who has explored other branches of attraction and whose theory follows on all points that of Newton?[32]

—that is, to Fourier himself! Science is something wonderful and magical. It is not integrated with any specific economic or social force. In the name of science, Saint-Simon demands centralization and economic planning; and in the same name, Fourier and Robert Owen demand small autonomous communities of essentially agrarian character. This reception of science is really quite "unscientific"; and the strange ideological concoctions which in a backward society are often the products of the impact of a technologically more advanced civilization, the mixtures of scientific, traditionalist, and religious ideas, are somewhat of the same order.

It may be that this view of the use of science in earlier socialism does injustice to Saint-Simon. In his sensitivity to scientific progress, his plea for government by a scientific and managerial elite and for international organization, some have found a remarkable preview of the main tendencies of modern life. His appreciation of the development of history has been favorably compared with that of Marx. Engels' laudatory comment in *Anti-Dühring* sets Saint-Simon alongside Hegel as a great thinker. It is impossible at the same time to dissociate Saint-Simon from the general characteristics of which we spoke before. On many counts he shows a remarkable intuition and insight; but the total effect is a bewildering profusion of schemes, plans, and associations, most of them bearing but little relationship to the actual or the possible. If he is a pioneer and prophet of modern industrialism or of modern science, then he is so only in the sense that one could consider Jules Verne the pioneer of the idea of space travel, or H. G. Wells of the use of atomic energy. The story of his followers, the Saint-Simonians, is instructive in this respect: after participating in a sect which in religious eccentricity and obscurantism far surpassed their master's ideas, many of them turned to amazingly successful careers in finance, business, and engineering. The original dogma could attract men of the speculative and enterprising spirit and could intensify as well as channel those abilities. But it was entirely incapable of creating a movement that would affect in the slightest the destiny of a modern society. The parallel to, as well as the difference from, Marxism is striking.

What is the general significance of the precursors of socialism, and what is their importance in explaining the future course of the development and appeal of socialist movements? The nexus *religion-science* demonstrates amply the fertile soil provided socialist theories by a society in the process of modernization, in which the traditionalist religious ideas are being upset and science and scientific thinking have not yet been integrated into modern life. We are still one step away from the full impact of modernization and industrialization, but their prerequisites, science and secularism, already create confusion and the consequent attempts at a synthesis— explanation of the old and new, some of them being socialist in character.

If we feel too condescending toward the fantasies of the early socialists, if we feel like scoffing at Robert Owen's theories because of his spiritualism, or at Fourier's because of his undoubted madness, it is well to keep in mind the variety of similar phenomena that have quite recently accompanied or ushered in the nationalist movements of the formerly colonial nations. Or it is unnecessary to go that far: one can think of the profusion of new religious cults in America in the nineteenth century, many of them bearing the imprint of the same reaction to the bewildering onrush of modernity: the cult of withdrawal into small communities separated from the whirlpool of industrial life, a combination of science and religion, evangelism, or communal living as a protective device against the too rapidly changing, too oppressive forces of modern civilization. There is no thought here of attributing all these to one main cause or of studying why in this country religious or quasi-religious activity has often been the response to industrialism. But it is well to keep them in mind as a corrective to the idea that the usual response to the onrush of industrialism consists in the reading of John Stuart Mill, or, at the present time, in the study of plans of economic development.

Why should socialism, and eventually Marxist socialism, be the main legatee of the strivings for reform produced by the chaos of the intellectual and industrial revolutions? The answer can be suggested by a look at some of the proposals of the precursors. Owen and Fourier are essentially advocates of cooperation. Science, they assume, has enabled mankind to live comfortably and, by their lights, virtuously, without the misery and oppression of the former ages. Societies should and will be transformed into vast networks of self-sustaining communities, living according to the right principles, tolerating no exploitation or superstition. It is unimportant, from our point of view, to go into details, to consider how egalitarian or authoritarian those societies are to be, or who is to direct them. The important thing is to note how, despite all the worship of science and industry, despite even an exaggerated view (for the first quarter of the nineteenth century) of their potentialities, the basic appeal is to the anti-industrial and pro-agrarian instincts. Owen's actual cooperative colonies and Fourier's projected phalansteries are to be islands of harmony and natural life, away from the turbulence of commercialism and competition. Their members achieve status and function as partners in an organic community, not as single individuals tossed to and fro by the mechanism of the market, requirements of the industry, or command of the state. Despite his madness, Fourier expresses, for instance, the very basic and universal objection to industrialism: the abhorrence of division of labor. His fantastic community will fit jobs according to each man's aptitude and tastes. Furthermore, no man or woman will be tied down to one job any more than to one spouse: there will be pleasing alternation and variety in both respects.

In the name of science and industry, Fourier and Owen dispense with those central or accompanying factors of industrialization: the centralized state, the market mechanism, and "bourgeois" morality. The strictly regulated "freedom" of a small community liberates man from the nauseating influences of society at large. It gives him the full life denied by the hurried pace of modern economy. It frees him from the shackles of church and state and restores him to the vocation of human being. Let it be added that, as behooves a Frenchman, Fourier is much more explicit on the sensual joys of communal living. The man who made the undeniable discovery that the "English influence," i.e., industrialization, was injuring the French cuisine devoted an inordinate part of his writings to the gastronomical question. Who, living in the day of business lunches and ready processed food, can deny Fourier the credit of foreseeing and denouncing one of the most devastating effects of industrialization?

That the visions of Owen and Fourier attracted devotees and

even practitioners not only in the countries of their origin but in places as far away as America and Russia, and that, for all their impracticality and often absurdity, many practical men throughout the nineteenth century were drawn to these doctrines, is proof of the strength of their underlying appeal, of the vision of a world freed from competitive individualism, commercialism, and political compulsion. Yet in time Owen's and Fourier's ideas lost their meaning as a *practical* protest against the organization of the modern world. What movement and what party was to embody the same elements of protest while linking them to a more realistic appraisal of social and economic forces and a concrete program of action?

And a somewhat similar process affected the propagation of the ideas of Saint-Simon. The mere cult of technology did not change the social reality. Passion for science, the conviction that through technology one can solve the problems of poverty and backwardness were united with the desire to accomplish actual improvement in the life "of the most numerous and poorest class." But the road of petitioning of princes and bankers appears ridiculous and unavailing against the reality of nineteenth-century Europe. The Saint-Simonians in France, after disbanding their cult, entered upon individual careers of active technological and industrial endeavor, but in another society less industrially developed, less subject to the liberal spirit, the doctrine appeals not as a plea for a scientific and managerial elite but as a rationale for political and social revolution. Even if the early socialist ideas are propagated in the spirit of nonviolence, even if those socialists admit the most scrupulous regard for private property, their effect in the turbulent Europe of 1830-1850 is most often revolutionary. Their critique of the existing society and their common reverence for labor make them the basis of the actual socialism of the radical movements.

The net effect of the socialist theories of Owen and Fourier, and to a much lesser extent those of Saint-Simon, is to appeal to the inherent anarchism of popular response to industrialization. Taken out of the context of model communities, the feeling underlying the cooperative idea is one of protest and revolution. Even the implication of the technological cult of

Saint-Simon is twisted in this direction. Science, he said, has now enabled mankind to put into practice the only true principle of Christianity: "love each other as brothers." Why don't governments and princes put into effect schemes of social betterment? Why do industry and the state ruin or displace the peasant, crush the craftsman, rather than enable him to lead a freer, more dignified and stable existence than that of the proletarian? The practical significance of the early socialist ideas lies not in the experiments—New Harmony, Brook Farm, or the Saint-Simonian church—but first in their symptomatic importance as some individuals' response to the social malaise of the transition, and then in their reception in wider circles as surrogates of a revolutionary response to the actual political and economic environment. People grasp at fantasies because they do not quite understand, but they do dislike, what is happening. The moorings of the old system, with its agrarian economy and its traditional Christian belief, were slipping, and the new industrial and secular psychology was far from having penetrated the mass of people, who refused to accept it on the word of a middle-class economist or capitalist.

The next step in socialist thought is focused, not in the schemes of philosophers and inventors, not in isolated cults and discussion groups of intellectuals, but in the more immediate sentiments of certain segments of the laboring classes. As observed before, the connection between socialist theories or feelings and the actual sentiments of the working class is never as straightforward in France as it is in England during the period under discussion. In England between 1830 and 1850, the advanced section of the workers reached *almost* the level of the Marxist revolutionary analysis of capitalism, and Chartism behaved *almost* like a Marxist movement. In France during the parallel period, which lasted until the Commune of 1871, the revolutionary protest remained at the lower form of socialism (from the viewpoint of the Marxist measuring scale). The protest against industrialization, unlike that of Chartism, did not begin to be transmuted into a straightforward revolution against capitalism. French socialism fought not only the capitalists but even more the Industrial Revolution, and it never quite stopped refighting some old battles of the Revolution of 1789. Because French capitalism was weaker, because the industrial ethos of liberalism never acquired the absoluteness of domination that it acquired over English society, socialism in France was, from the Marxist perspective, less socialist and more primitive than the socialism that seemed on the point of emergence from Chartism.

By the same token, French socialism, whether it is the unreflective philosophy of the *coup d'etat* of Blanqui or the free-ranging, universal social critique of Proudhon, is a "purer" form of socialism. It represents a more instinctive form of the reaction of the radical part of the working class to industrialization. It is less affected by the arguments borrowed from the armory of its enemy, liberalism, and its proponents are less likely to end up in submission to the spirit of liberalism.

The main tendency of French socialism is perhaps best found in Proudhon (1809-1865). He is a generation or two removed from the utopia builders, in some respects a continuer of their thought, but, in accordance with the new age, not so much an individual philosopher in search of patrons and disciples as a spokesman for popular radicalism. It will not be unfair to Proudhon to assert that the most striking impression produced by his writings is one of incoherence. This is produced not by the derangement of the author, for in contrast to Fourier or even Saint-Simon, Proudhon was eminently sane, nor by the inevitable inconsistencies of a writer who deals with everything under the sun. Proudhon's inconsistencies were produced exactly by a sense of reality and practicality and intelligence, combined with a vivid dislike of whatever was practical in terms of nineteenth-century politics and economics. (This, to digress, has not been atypical of French politics down to our own day.) The man who is best known for his (perhaps borrowed) aphorism, "Property is theft," was a great believer in private property. A proponent of equality and democracy, he adjudged the people a quiet beast interested only in eating, sleeping, and love-making. What could a sober liberal or Marxist socialist do with the social reformer and moralist who at one point dismissed all "long-run" theories and wrote, "On the contrary, profound moralists have held that life consists exactly in those brief moments when the soul and senses are engrossed in desire and voluptuousness, and he who has known this intoxication with life for a single moment, has lived!"[33]

Born a peasant, becoming a craftsman and a self-taught philosopher whom Marx never forgave for the presumption of claiming to understand Hegel, Proudhon stands as the personification of the attachment to peasant values which are under the impact of industrialism being transformed into socialism. The family and small property are the anchors of human existence. But something has happened to property in the modern world. It now appears as an antisocial force. On the family, Proudhon has, as an Anglo-Saxon writer would put it, very Continental views. The father of anarchism has the peasant's ideal of a harmonious household ruled by the father. Proudhon's opinions on women, which scandalized many of his foreign admirers, were very definite. Woman's place is either in the kitchen or on the streets. The housewife and the prostitute are the two vocations granted to women by nature. To demonstrate woman's inherent inferiority, Proudhon goes into some very weird mathematical exercises. The same *petit-bourgeois* spirit pervades his views of morality. The main source of his abhorrence of the Fourierists and Saint-Simonians, one feels, is their views about the equality of women and their dissolution of the family. The man who believed that woman is inferior to man in proportion 28 to 7 and that the institution of marriage is the model of justice could yet hold love to be an unnecessary element in marriage and extol the father's absoute authority over children. Enemy of authority of all kinds, Proudhon shows a similar inconsistency in opposing the softening of laws against sexual deviants and the legalization of divorce. In brief, one feels that Proudhon does not need a phalanstery or any other model of ideal community. His utopia is the small household with its plot of ground, and his enemy everything that intrudes upon this idyllic unit: the state, industrial economy, the religious power of the Church, and the socialist who would centralize and dissolve the family.

The religion-science obsession of the earlier socialists is still at its full strength in Proudhon. In addition to the family and land, religion is the third natural element of the order from which he arose. But Christianity has become perverted from its original ethical precepts and the Church has become an ally of the vested interests. The language of a secularist alternates with that of a passionate atheist, the Hegelian phrasing of the religious problem with the almost pagan accusations against God for leaving man in uncertainty and enduring human misery and suffering. Nothing can be done in France except through religion, he says in one place, only to return to his leitmotif elsewhere: "And I say that the first duty of an intelligent and free man is to chase unceasingly the idea of God from his mind and conscience."[34] This is something that Proudhon, no more than many another revolutionary of his type, never completely succeeded in doing. God appears almost as the unjust father of mankind, the prototype of all tyrannical authority. The Church is the originator of one of the main evils of civilization: centralization. It has no place for science, for democracy, for the true feeling of brotherhood. The catalogue of reproaches links Proudhon's feelings to the religious obsession of early socialists. But there is a marked difference in tone. To Saint-Simon or even Owen, religion was an ethical problem, and the aberration of churches denoted the betrayal of their social mission toward the masses. The intensely religious feeling which underlies Proudhon's atheism has in addition something else: the primitive man's intimate personal dialogue with God. Education and radicalism may transmute that feeling into atheism—never into secularism or liberalism.

Hence the other divinity of the early socialists—science—never appears with the same intensity as the religious problem. Yet it is "science" that the workers need more than democracy; and, somewhat in the manner of Saint-Simon, a palace of industry, a permanent exposition is to regulate economic life. What this "science" is, in what sense economics is science, is never, needless to say, systematically explained by Proudhon. He dabbles happily in Hegelianism and its phraseology, but the total sum of his philosophy of history and nature comes to the already met postulate that "science" now enables men to live freely, without the superstitions and economic misery of the past. That science and technology go hand in hand is not readily admitted by the proponent of the thesis that mankind has reached the age of science. The machine and the division of labor are the permanent sources of misery. The establishment of railway lines in France is the beginning of economic perturbations and the cause of the ruin of the agricultural workers.[35]

"Though very much a friend of order, I am in the full meaning of the word, an anarchist," wrote Proudhon.[36] And the avowal helps us to understand what anarchism is, for the two parts of the statement are really complementary. The "order" is the stability of beliefs and of economy of a pre-industrial household. If the anarchist dislikes compulsion and authority of any kind, ranging from the old types to the ones created by industrialization—the authority of the centralized state, of factory discipline—then by the same token he is quite ready to erupt into violence against destroyers of this "order." The most pacific of men, who reproved Marx for his dogmatism and lust for bloody revolution, Proudhon was drawn at times to programs of violent uprisings, to plans for arrest of the "reactionaries," forcible dissolution of convents and monasteries, and expropriation of bankers and industrialists. Democracy and government by the majority held little appeal for the anarchist convinced by the plebiscites of Napoleon III that the majority of people were idiots and universal suffrage a delusion.

It is customary to ask what a given thinker or school "stood for." In the case of anarchism, the question is extremely difficult to answer. Anarchism has excellent critical sense: the logical corollaries and weaknesses of competing creeds, especially socialistic, are pointed out with great perception. The inherent authoritarianism of the Marxist doctrine was seen by Proudhon with the acumen displayed later by Bakunin in characterizing Marxism as, essentially, state capitalism. The authoritarian implications of Etienne Cabet's Communism, Saint-Simon's elitism, and the hollowness of democratic slogans amid an ignorant and destitute population were all lucidly exposed by Proudhon. Proud of being French, he was at the same time an inveterate enemy of militant nationalism and an advocate of disarmament. Yet what is *his* response, *his* plan for the solution of the social problem? Here anarchism falters, for it is much more a feeling, a sentiment of protest rather than an ideology. Proudhon's *mutualism* envisages a network of productive associations of producers. The political state withers away while the autonomous associations happily trade with each other. But mutualism is as hazy in its administrative detail as it is paradoxical on its economic side. The enemy of savings banks and insurance, believer in "demonetization" of money, Proudhon calls upon, horrible to say, a centralized institution, a national bank to provide cheap and then free credit for his associations. Land is to be excluded from mutualism, because the private property of the peasant is to be guaranteed and passes by inheritance. The problem of politics and administration in the mutualist society? No such problem will exist, since public and private conscience, formed by the "science of right," will suffice to maintain order and guarantee liberties. This is the constant answer of anarchism to such impolite questions.

The anarchist *sentiment*, which underlay much of Chartism, never crystallized into a definite philosophy. Proudhon epitomizes the step forward from the mass of anti-industrial and anti-state prejudices, the inheritance of the peasant and craftsman psychology into a distinguishable, if hazily detailed, philosophy. From his socialist predecessors Proudhon is distinguished by his belief in revolution. The echoes of the older tradition, the search for a patron, Rousseau's "legislator" to put the new system into effect at one blow, are not entirely missing: at times Proudhon is not above putting his hopes in Louis Napoleon, or even Louis Philippe. But the main stress is on emancipation by the enlightenment and if need be by a revolution on the part of the proletariat. The anarchism of Proudhon becomes perhaps the most influential branch of socialism among the French workers. The incomplete victory of industrial values, when coupled with political instability, did not let the anarchist sentiment die out among the French proletariat, and the progress of industrialization reproduced this feeling under the new form of syndicalism.

One explanation for the victory of the industrial spirit in England and the persistence of anti-industrialism in other societies is suggested unwittingly by a man not credited with great theoretical insight:

> not only at the end of the last century but even today no other country attained the degree of development of capitalism and concentration of production in agriculture that we observe in Britain. Despite the development of capitalism in the countryside, other countries still have a quite numerous class of small and medium property owning producers in the countryside whose future would have to be decided in the event that the proletariat takes power.[37]

It is the existence of the peasant in society, the unerased peasant background of the proletarian, that makes him susceptible to anarchism, which in its modern form is the revolt against industrialized life and its corollaries, the state and urbanization. In England, through several circumstances, the peasant was practically eliminated; elsewhere the peasant problem often remained as the breeding ground for the appeal of anarchist and syndicalist philosophies.

And of Marxism. For while the theory of Proudhon, of Blanqui, or of Bakunin is as antithetical to Marxism as it is to liberalism, the anti-industrial anarchistic sentiment that underlies their doctrines can often find its *effective* expression in revolutionary Marxism. The latter as *protest* has almost everything that explicit anarchism can offer: it attacks the state and the possessing classes and reaffirms the dignity and the sole value-producing capacity of human labor. But Marxism has something else that is missing in anarchism. Anarchist feeling is too formless, too much divorced from the dynamic of economic development, to create objective conditions and organization capable of absorbing the economic facts of life. The anti-authority premises of anarchism hardly allow it to form an efficient political movement to compete for power.

The anti-industrial tradition in which French socialism not only had grown (as had all other socialisms) but also persisted thus enabled Marxism to play the leading revolutionary role in French politics, albeit Marxism in France appeared at times closer to syndicalism than to the doctrine of Karl Marx. By the same token, the persistence of the anti-industrial ethos has been in France, and in other countries under similar circumstances, a fertile soil for the revolutionary movements of the right. The persistence of this psychology in society is thus both the cause and the effect of radical and antidemocratic forces of both the left and right.

Marxism is the type of socialism that believes in industrialization, but can live as a revolutionary movement of importance only in symbiosis with a widespread anti-industrial feeling. As such it is unique among socialist systems of the nineteenth century. We might exhibit a case that is *almost* an exception to demonstrate the point. Among the leading socialist thinkers in France at the time, Louis Blanc provides a striking example of modernity. In reading his *Organisation du Travail*, first published in 1839, one receives the impression of a style, argument, and method more characteristic of an English Fabian or a German revisionist socialist of the end of the century than of any of the socialist effusions of the time in France, England, or elsewhere. There is no opposition to the state, very few of the tiresome tirades about religion and science. Believer in large-scale industry and probably the first exponent of the collectivization of land—not to provide escape from industrialization in the form of little, self-sufficient colonies, but precisely to apply the full advantages of large-scale planning and technology to agriculture—Louis Blanc strikes one as being quite modern in his preoccupations. But if Blanc writes in the spirit of what later became known as "democratic socialism," his analysis of the future of capitalism does not transcend contemporary radical opinion. The theory of "immiseration" is stated as clearly as in Marx. "But who would be blind enough not to see that under the regime of unlimited competition [*concurrence illimitée*], continuous fall of wages is a necessarily general fact, and not an exception."[38] That big capitalists will eventually devour smaller ones is as certain to Blanc as it is to Marx.

But even Blanc, who in some ways anticipates Marx and in other ways the revisionists of Marxism, suffers in return from the early socialists' illusion that a mechanical contrivance, a model institution, can in itself effect a political and economic revolution. His National Workshops, run by the state, are to demonstrate the superiority of socialism over capitalism. In a very Fabian way, he writes: "the state step by step will become master of industry, in place of monopoly we will have as the result of [our] success the defeat of [capitalist] competition, association."[39] But the state that is to plan the economy is not the kind of state that later in the twentieth century could perform planning and social welfare. The worker who is to be secured employment has but little liking for division of labor and industrial discipline, to which he is now assumed to submit out of a sense of social obligation rather than because of want or fear of unemployment. In the context of a society in which industrial values have not been assimilated, Blanc's socialism is almost as utopian as Fourier's.

The great synthesis performed by Marx, a synthesis based not only on theories and movements, but also on intuitive appraisal of social and political psychology of various classes, has given his doctrine an unusual power of survival and influence. After 1850 there will be many societies and countries where similar economic and political conditions will bring forth ideas and sentiments similar to those found in Chartism or in Saint-Simon or Proudhon. But the would-be innovators and revolutionaries will be presented with a doctrine and movement that already expresses some of their aspirations and revolt. *Complete* opposition to industrialization or its opposite, *complete* acceptance of industry and the state, will amost always confine the influence of Marxism to that of a small sect, while other types of socialism attract the majority of the working class. But in societies where anarchism has ceased to be a practical response and trade unionism of the English type has not yet been firmly established, Marxism will in fact become the vanguard of socialism.

— 4 —
The Diverging Paths:
Democracy and Marxism

Let us return to one utopia produced by the onset of the Industrial Revolution that has in a large measure been realized: the liberal utopia. It is the dream of society where men are imbued with virtues appropriate to industrialism, where they do not long for status, brotherhood, or the intimacy of a small community or organization, but where they set their sights in terms of income (i.e., the quantity of goods and services they can command), and where they will move from one end of the country to the other, from one profession to another, if they can materially gain thereby. It is a society where men are too busy cultivating their materialistic garden to get profoundly excited over doctrinal differences, be they in politics or religion. Science is equally and unexcitedly accepted as part of daily life. No beating of the head against the wall of facts of industrial life: division of labor and the factory system are equally accepted, and a rising standard of life makes them less and less of a nuisance. The citizen accepts the state, not because of Hegel, but merely by paying taxes and accepting its regulations. Where is democracy in this scheme? It is simply a by-product of the acceptance of industrialism, education, and a high standard of living, of the withering away of superstitions, and of the irrational longing for the "status" and "property" of the disappearing agrarian society. Again, it is not the General Will or any metaphysical business that inclines, say, 45 percent of the people to submit to being ruled for a time by persons elected by 55 percent; it is the realization of the essential *sameness* of political values pervading the whole society. A man is entitled to vote not because of any moral or Christian equality but because an advanced material and educational level makes the majority of people qualified to exercise intelligent citizenship.

In the first half of the nineteenth century, this dream would have appeared to the conservative and radical alike a nightmare, a contemporary version of Orwell's *1984*. To young Marx, it would have appeared *inconceivable under capitalism*. Yet when the co-founder of Marxism was on his deathbed in 1895, the liberal utopia seemed close to realization. Historical hindsight shows 1895 exhibiting some other portents too, but to a social observer in the year when Engels died and Vladimir Ilich Lenin joined what was to become the Bolshevik Party, liberalism, granted all its imperfections and limitations, appeared on the road to a triumphant fulfillment in the West and eventual spread elsewhere in the world.

The economic and social atmosphere in Western Europe has made irrelevant both the earlier types of capitalism and anticapitalism. Industrialization brought a higher standard of living. The state had begun to concede to the worker the right to organize and to press for his economic postulates, just as the ballot had given him the power to press his political aims. The capitalist found himself being curtailed by the state with its rudimentary social legislation, with its beginnings of progressive income and inheritance taxation. Again, the situation in the 1890's, which looks so old-fashioned and capitalistic from our vantage point, would have struck an observer looking back to fifty years before as incomprehensibly collectivistic. What radical in 1850 would have believed that the capitalists would submit without a death struggle to the progressive income or inheritance tax, social insurance, curtailment of political power through universal suffrage, or extension of the state's economic activity? Yet the seeds of all these measures or their beginnings are plainly visible in the 1890's. By the same token, what conservative would have believed in 1850 that a democratic electorate would tolerate vast inequalities of inherited wealth and income, or indeed the perpetuation of the industrial system? Both liberalism and the worker have changed. One has shown itself not exclusively based on extreme individualism and the inflexible belief in economic "laws"; and the other's psychology has been shown to be not exclusively grounded on anti-industrialism. The corrosive influence of economic improvement softened the doctrinal rigidity of the two opponents. The apparent triumph of liberalism, even if that liberalism had changed and softened, called for a new synthesis. The old battleground between capitalism and socialism, the battleground of industrialization, seemingly disappeared forever.

In dealing with Marxism during the period, we no longer deal with the thought of two men or with small groups of devotees. Marxism is now an international movement, the major inheritor of all the strains of socialism that were previously discussed. The doctrine has hardened into a dogma. The small groups of sympathizers and correspondents have developed into parties, some with mass followings. In the international socialist movement, Marxism is clearly the dominant tendency. The heavily intellectual doctrine becomes the official expression of the aspirations of workers throughout the world. The catholicity of the doctrine has surpassed even Marx's expectations. In it the German worker will express not only his economic grievance but a political protest against militarism and the Junkers, the Polish worker his protest against national oppression, and the Russian against absolutism and the lack of rudimentary political rights. To the intellectuals and large segments of the middle class, Marxism provides a "scientific" theory of society, a way out of social inequities through a rational organization of community, a much more practical expression of the instinct that led people to follow Saint-Simon, Fourier, or Owen.

Was the spread of socialism and especially Marxism a demonstration that the triumph of liberalism and the stability of capitalism were an illusion, or was it in fact an indication that socialism is the logical culmination and fulfillment of the other two? This is the question that dominates theoretical Marxism in the nineties. In the original canon there are arguments for both answers. But Marxism is now an international movement and a dogma buttressed by vast literature, theoretical journals, and the like. Whatever interpretation is given, its exponent will be reluctant to admit that the answer must be a relativistic one, that, taking the original premises of Marxism, it has completely different meanings in England and in Russia, that the logic of the argument would lead to revolutionary action in one case, to constitutional and democratic means in another, and to the abandonment of socialism in still another. Conflicting views of Marxism become engrossed in the exegesis of the scriptures. The doctrine becomes encrusted with heavy layers of historical, economic, and other commentaries to the point where its original outlines become almost unrecognizable.

We are here interested in one aspect of the problem: the uses of Marxism. To what groups, interests, and sentiments in the given society does the conglomeration of theories known as Marxism appeal, and why? And the obverse of the question: What instincts and interests does Marxism instill in those who consider themselves Marxists? How does Marxism "make a difference" between an average worker and the worker who considers himself a Marxist? To men who find themselves in absolute control of a society and who think of themselves as Marxian socialists? To a secular analyst, it is not necessary to connect answers to these questions with what "Marx really meant." The conglomeration of theories, facts, and predictions that is Marxism has a life of its own, and some of its uses and effects were as unanticipated by its authors as was the kind of world in which it was to score triumphs and suffer defeats.

The English Exception

Like the failure of the dog in Conan Doyle's story to bark, the failure of Marxism to take root in England provides a key to the mystery. The country which alone of European societies reached an absolute preponderance of industry over agriculture by the end of the nineteenth century, which pioneered in the development of modern industry and of social and political institutions appropriate to it, should have been, by a literal application of the Marxist analysis, the first place to have a Marxist revolutionary movement and a socialist revolution. Yet actually the Marxist situation in England had passed before

Marxism was formulated. Neither the theory nor the practice of Marxism found many adherents in the country in which Marx and Engels were residents. The Social Democratic Federation, founded in the 1880's, and the activities of a handful of English Marxists, like H. M. Hyndman, toward the end of the century, provide the very small exception that proves the rule.

The luxuriant growth of Marxist movements everywhere in the 1890's and the first decade of the twentieth century is not paralleled by anything in England. Of all the many strains and theories that went into the building of English socialism, the influence of Marxism was the slightest. We do not get in England even the phenomenon observable in similarly industrialized countries (for example, the Low Countries and Scandinavia), i.e., a socialist movement that is *officially* Marxist in name and paraphernalia, but non-Marxist in behavior. In the revival of socialism in England among the generation, roughly speaking, before World War I, all kinds of socialist theories and movements are propagated. The weakening of England's economic position in the world, her loss of economic dynamism, bring forth socialist recipes ranging from the evolutionary socialism of the Fabians to the faint echoes of anarchism and syndicalism represented by Guild Socialism. But interest in Marxism, whether by the intellectual or the worker, is practically nil. The ability of Marxism to assimilate and give political expression to various strains of socialist thought and movement is conspicuously absent in Great Britain.

What produced the modern socialist movement in Britain? The same thing that led to sizable socialist movements elsewhere: the worker's search for a party and movement that would represent his interests and give a theoretical formulation to his aspirations and grievances. The success of industrialism in allaying the first anarchic response of the worker, the work of education and democratic institutions in allaying his sense of "alienation" do not permanently remove the opportunities for socialism. A mature industrial society will be faced with socialism in two distinct, though often merging, forms. One will be in the inevitable tendency of the modern industrial state to grow more complex and more collectivistic, assuming, because of the factors of sheer size and technology, a greater and greater role in the field of economy and social relations. This is socialism inherent in the very process of industrialization and democratization beyond a certain state. In that sense, but not in the way he meant, Marx's prediction of socialism's emergence from capitalism is correct.

But this is socialism only in a limited sense of the word. It is socialism from the perspective of nineteenth-century economic individualism, the kind meant by a liberal chancellor of the exchequer when he said in the 1890's: "We are all socialists now." It is conceivable to have all kinds of collectivism and bureaucratic planning of economic life without the slightest advance toward social and economic egalitarianism. And the other kind of socialism is produced exactly by a certain egalitarianism fostered by industrialism and democracy. The rise in the standard of living kills off the earlier, anti-industrial type of socialism, with its anarchistic undertones. But the slackening of economic dynamism of an industrialized society, or a prolonged economic crisis, bring forth the kind of socialism that, in much purer form than other socialisms, is anticapitalist. Anticapitalism is no longer an expression of hostility to the whole complex of industrial and political institutions; it is a specific protest against large conglomerations of economic power and wealth in a society which no longer believes in unlimited opportunities for success and economic advancement for everybody. The proletarian of earlier socialism is the trade unionist of the later phase. The perspective of overthrowing the "system" and reverting to some real or imaginary pre-industrial situation no longer has any appeal for him. But the presence of class barriers, the lack or the slow pace of economic improvement puts him in the state of mind receptive to the kind of theory that presents socialism as merely a step forward from democracy, the reduction of existing inequalities, and the subjugation of economic to political power, which is already mainly democratic.

It is easy to see how badly Marxism fits the bill. The revolutionary appeal of Marxism rests on the worker's sense of grievance and alienation from society as a whole, the kind of grievance that had little relevance in England even of the 1890's. To assert that the electorate is being hoodwinked by the capitalists in power is not the same as to assert that the state is the executive committee of the exploiting class. The class-war appeal loses its emotional tone if you have to argue that because of the democratic franchise the class enemy is at your mercy. And under those conditions, the other side of Marxism, its technological enthusiasm, its indoctrination in the necessity of the industrial system, has likewise very little meaning. The industrial worker has reached the position where he is neither uncomprehending nor exultant over the facts of technology. Trade-union activity and political action are viewed by him as the means of both translating the technological progress into a higher standard of living and avoiding or tempering unemployment.

English socialism was thus likely to flow into other forms. It is misleading to view the problem of Marxism versus English socialism in terms of the dichotomy, revolutionary versus evolutionary socialism. The picture of the years before World War I is filled with major strikes, and with socialist theories which were quite revolutionary in their implications and at times sounded like echoes of the earlier anti-industrial opposition. The tenor of English politics of the period—the possibility of civil war in Ireland, the constitutional crises, and the social and fiscal legislation of the liberal administration of 1906 to 1914—created a situation which to contemporaries was fraught with revolutionary possibilities. But the response of the English working class was the creation of a labor movement and party, which, though led by socialists, did not commit itself to socialism until 1918. And even then this socialism was to be amalgam of egalitarianism and social welfare, with the nationalization of the major means of production as one of its main practical postulates. English socialism arose when the society was indeed far from a liberal utopia. But the saturation with industrial values was already sufficient to make both parts of the Marxist synthesis irrelevant to the British worker.

It is instructive to see both the essence and the extent of this adjustment. The oldest element is the fact of political democratization, the right of the worker to vote, the distracting

practical effect of political activity upon the revolutionary
utopias and dreams of reconstructing pre-industrial society.
The revolutionary spirit, the blend of romantic protest and
social utopianism, does not easily survive involvement in the
prosaic business of actual politics. The spread of parliamentarism, the extension of suffrage, had been viewed by Marx and
Engels with what was almost a nostalgia for the bad old days of
their youth, when the state was definitely "they"—the upper
and middle classes—and the worker had no right to suspect that
perhaps he was also a wielder of political power. Marx's
comments on the Gotha Program of the German Social
Democratic Party of 1875 reveal a conflict of attitudes: one, a
tone of pride at socialism becoming embodied in a real mass
party; the other, a tone of irritation at the almost inevitable
prospect of the watering down of the revolutionary spirit by the
trappings of legalism and "constructive" social legislation.
Equally threatening, though more distant, was the likelihood
of the seduction of socialist leaders by ministerial posts and of
the workers' "acceptance" of the state. Though the German
Social Democratic Party "purified" its program of the
Lassallean elements in 1891, the logic of legal political activity
was in fact to justify some of Marx's apprehensions.

In the case of British socialism, the absorption in actual
politics was, of course, a much more potent antidote to
doctrinalism and revolutionary romanticism. Even Chartism
had already found its outward focus in political demands. The
much more democratic situation toward the end of the century
imperiled even more the revolutionary protest of socialism.
The road to revolution became a series of elections and
legislative enactments. The final aim of socialism could not be
awaited with the impatience that is the springboard of
revolutionary action if indeed its postulates were being
accomplished step by step. Democracy, an adjustment to
industrialization, emasculated socialism of its revolutionary
enthusiasm.

The other element of adjustment is inherent in the growth of
English trade unionism. The union in its genesis is a product
of anti-industrialism. To the early liberal and Marxist alike, it
is the outcome of the "illusion"of the worker that through a

conspiracy he can mitigate the effect of economic laws, raise his wages, improve his conditions of living in defiance of the market. To the historian of trade unionism the early unions represent something else: a desperate, often illegal attempt by the proletarian to regain status through association, to reproduce, often through odd ceremonies and vocabulary, the feeling of "belonging," to restore the previous peasant and craftsman existence—a defense against not only economic but also social individualism imposed by industrialization. To the liberal, unionism, once legalized, would wither away with the worker's realization that it was impotent to change his bargaining position. To Marx, unionism, as tried by some Chartists, would also lose its early illusions and become the weapon of the worker in class warfare. Yet unionism grew, after initial setbacks and persecutions, but in a way which confounded both early hopes and fears. Like the cooperative movement, trade unionism, originally the product of the impetus to erect an artificial barrier or preserve against industrialism, did become in time an integral part of the more mature industrial system, an agency through which the worker arrived at his compromise with the system, and, up to a point, a school of industrial and democratic values.

The growth and character of English unionism in the 1860's and '70's alarmed and disgusted Marx and Engels. To them it seemed to foster the petty bourgeois character of the more prosperous segments of the working class and to transmute the class struggle against capitalism into minor skirmishes for higher pay and shorter working hours.

The conservative type of unionism, uniting essentially the aristocracy of the working class, was considerably changed by the rise of "new unionism" and the organizations of unskilled workers in the 1880's. But the result was still far from the Marxian vision of spontaneous organizations of the working class, exuding class warfare and basically and impatiently opposed to the bourgeois state. Trade unionism as it looked to Lenin in 1902 *was* in fact the spontaneous form of organization of the worker, but the trade-union mentality was the negation of the Marxian revolutionary pattern.

The atmosphere of unionism is in fact representative of the

mentality of the worker. But in its English version this class mentality settles at a point equidistant between what Marx and the liberals had predicted. It is neither a revolutionary reaction against the alienation and poverty inherent in the industrial system nor the loss of the feeling of class separateness and individualistic economic endeavor. The class mentality is that of the acceptance of separateness, but not of alienation; of the acceptance of the industrial system, but not of capitalism; of individualism, but not of economic insecurity postulated in the earliest laissez faire. The complexity of the worker's adjustment parallels that of the English capitalist, who is no longer the ceaseless entrepreneur and revolutionizer of economic life, self-righteous and unyielding in his prerogatives and ideology. The more involved economic reality traps and minimizes the sources of the revolutionary confrontation of the worker and the bourgeois state. The revolutionary optimism that Marxism exuded earlier, when the acute antagonism between capitalism and the working class had seemed to augur similar developments everywhere, gave way in the 1890's to a parallel apprehension: what if a similar rise in the standard of living and progress in representative institutions were to bring to the workers in other European countries, despite their present penchant toward Marxism, a similar trade-union mentality?

The defense of Marxian orthodoxy, of the essential correctness of the visibly disproved tenet of the continuous impoverishment of the working class under capitalism, became for the Continental socialists something of a psychological necessity in view of the English experience. The contrast between Marx's formulation of the misery of the workers under capitalism and the defense of this thesis by his disciples half a century later is quite striking. Marx expressed in an overly theoretical form what most of the contemporary radicals and advanced workers around the middle of the century firmly believed; but the German and other Marxists faced the exactly opposite task of telling the working class that what their senses told them was an illusion or a temporary freak. The German worker's genuine dissatisfaction with his country's political system and with capitalism as a form of organization of economic life had to be supplemented by the unreal feeling that

somehow his economic situation was getting worse. Indoctrination was called upon to help class consciousness. The self-
imposed task of orthodox Marxists on the Continent became,
one feels, not so much struggling against capitalism and
authoritarianism as guarding the worker against falling for the
"illusion" of economic progress and peaceful democratization.
The threat posed to Marxist orthodoxy by historical facts was
dismissed by Engels, shortly before his death, in an ingenious
prognosis: despite all the growth of the socialist parties and
democratization of political life, Marx's revolutionary prediction still holds true; it is now the capitalists who will strike
first to prevent a peaceful transition to socialism. Yet how
much sophistry and real apprehension of the extinction of the
revolutionary impulse is in this view as contrasted with the
primitive but self-assured and elemental appeal of the
Communist Manifesto.

English socialism, by contrast, was never faced with a similar
task of fitting reality into the uncomfortable confines of a
theory. It never attempted to decide the correct pattern of the
unfolding of history or the correct interpretation of the views of
two deceased thinkers by vote of party congress. Socialism in
England is fed by theories, some revolutionary, others
evolutionary; some moralistic and religious in their anticapitalism, others pragmatic and utilitarian in their tone. But
when the sum of influences jells into a movement and a
parliamentary party, it reflects the acceptance of liberal society
and the tendency to "stretch it" into socialism, the reflection
not so much of any theory or group of theories but of the
instinct of the British working class.

The attenuation of anti-industrialism as the basis for
socialism—and hence the irrelevance of Marxism under
English conditions—is best studied by observing the content
and influence of two schools of socialist thought of the
generation before 1917: Fabianism and Guild Socialism.
Fabianism is a socialist descendant of Utilitarianism, the
acceptance of liberalism with a collectivistic proviso. Guild
Socialism is the last cry and formulation of anti-industrialism,
the rejection of the state, an attempted escape from the fact of
centralized economic and political life into vague schemes of

workers' control and of guilds. Fabianism, for all its intellectual origins and attitudes, became the dominant tendency in English socialism. From it runs a fairly straight line to the Beveridge Report, the welfare state, and the philosophy of the Labour Party of today. Guild Socialism, for a period before and immediately after World War I, found some echoes in the sections of organized labor, but it vanished as a major influence and plays no part in contemporary English socialism. It failed to turn trade unionism in the syndicalist direction, and it left a much greater imprint on literary and intellectual life than on the ideas of the "lower part of mankind," which, whether in a democratic or nondemocratic society, ultimately decide the future of political movements.

Fabianism flows from the *Fabian Essays,* published in 1889 by a remarkable group of writers and reformers engaged in socialist propaganda. There is no echo in them of the theories of Karl Marx or of the presence in English society at the moment of Friedrich Engels. There is a small deposit, but very small, of what might be called the aesthetic protest against capitalism and industrialism, which will loom much more importantly in Guild Socialism. The early Fabians included Bernard Shaw and H. G. Wells, and there is something of Fourier in Shaw and an element of Saint-Simon's scientific utopianism in Wells. More generally, there is in the *Fabian Essays* a common-sense objection to the cultural and spiritual aridity of late Victorian life and an exasperation with conventionality and conformity and with the drab reality of the dominant lower-middle-class standards. This protest can be found vividly in H. G. Wells' novels of lower-middle-class life, with their revolt against the all-encompassing materialism and "propriety" of middle-class civilization and its choking effect upon human individuality. Unlike the earlier aesthetic critiques of industrialization and bourgeois values by Carlyle and Ruskin and the later ones by Chesterton and Belloc, this element of protest in the *Essays* is not a basic rejection of the new scale of standards by thinkers standing apart from politics and simply grumbling about materialism. Rather, the protest denotes a genuine disappointment at the unfulfilled promise of the new civilization; it is a critical re-examination of industrial civilization, symptomatic of the slackening of material progress, rather than of a fundamental hostility to the civilization.

The main theme of the *Essays* and indeed of Fabianism as it grew up was that its brand of socialism was simply the logical continuation and fulfillment of industrialism plus democracy. It is not an attempt to *épater les bourgeois,* but to convince them as well as the working class. The vision of industrial evolution is in the spirit of unemotional Marxism. The growing concentration of industry and business, and the depersonalization of the ownership of the means of production, makes their assumption by the state the next logical step. But despite some hints to the contrary, the take-over from the capitalists is generally assumed to come through "honest purchase" rather than expropriation. The expanding sphere of collectivistic action by the state as well as by the municipalities is quoted as a proof that the tendency is already evident and inevitable.

The approach to the realization of socialism assumes the reality of the democratic process. In fact, the Fabians were to use propaganda and education rather than any attempt at "mass action." The road, according to Sidney Webb, must be (1) democratic, i.e., "acceptable to a majority of people and prepared for in the minds of all"; (2) gradual, causing no dislocation; (3) not regarded as immoral by the mass of the people, and thus not subjectively demoralizing to them; and (4) "In this country at any rate constitutional and peaceful."[1] This is socialism that has accepted the premises of liberalism but no longer believes in the realizability of the liberal utopia. There is no wide-eyed enthusiasm over the powers of science and technology, no great concern with religion or the aristocracy. Fabianism is an unenthusiastic, matter-of-fact acceptance of industrialism and a plea, but again with very little emotionalism in it, for socialism.

Nothing illustrates the frustration of anti-industrial type of socialism in England better than the fate of Guild Socialism. In the years preceding World War I, Guild Socialism forged to the fore of socialist thought. In perspective, the period before the war represents a striking but short-lived rebirth of socialism grounded in the anachronistic protest against the over-whelming elements of political and economic reality: the state and centralized industry. It is no accident that the same period witnessed the questioning of the intellectual and political basis of liberalism. The rationalist tradition encountered a critique at the hands of Bergson, William James, and Freud. The reality of representative democracy was scathingly analyzed by Ostrogorski, Michels, and Pareto. The variety of criticisms of the foundations of liberalism was at once a proof that the intellectual underpinnings of liberal civilization in the West had passed their heyday and a tribute to the extent of achievement of the liberal utopia. A critic in the spirit of Hegel would see the varied movements of the generation before 1914 as a proof that the liberal synthesis had been established and that an inevitable challenge was forthcoming. A Marxist would observe the slackening tempo of economic expansion and the end of the revolutionary role of capitalism and would note the appearance of movements and theories questioning the basic premises of capitalism as the result of these changes. A secular explanation sees liberalism running "out of steam," unable to impose the pattern of industrialization and modernization, which had seemed to have come of itself in the West, on the world at large and on international relations.

In the English context, Guild Socialism is a rather distant echo of the general perturbation. The very name chosen by the movement indicates that what was implict in the original anti-industrial socialism is made explicit in this socialism as it fights a retreating action against the state and "wagery": a certain medievalism of outlook, the hankering after a society where everybody has his "place." From its beginnings, it was a hopeless political venture. The vision of the state transformed into a conglomeration of guilds, unions of workers, and professions, each running its own affairs, joined by something "non state," whether called the Commune or the Industrial Guilds Congress, has only to be put into words to show its utter unpracticality. The very need that Guild Socialists like S. G. Hobson and G. D. H. Cole felt to formulate their political schemes in detail shows the enervating influence of the British conditions upon anarchism and syndicalism. In France, Italy, and Spain, syndicalism of the period was widespread, but its exponents did not usually feel called upon to spell out what they would put in the place of the hateful realities of the state and capitalism. It is a sad day for syndicalists and anarchists when they feel compelled to produce positive proposals and organization charts!

The protest underlying Guild Socialism again links it to the critique of capitalism from the conservative viewpoint. The social passion of Guild Socialism pits it against the inequalities and competition of capitalist society. It harbors aesthetic grief over society's loss of organic unity and over the disappearance of the instinct for workmanship in pre-industrial crafts. These have been the traditional materials with which Christian socialism has been constructed. In Guild Socialism there is an additional echo of the revolutionary excitement of Continental syndicalism, of the worker now enmeshed in modern industry but still antagonistic to industrialism as such. We are reminded once more how anti-industrialism, if widespread in society, is the breeding ground of indiscriminate radicalism, how the former syndicalists often found their way into postwar Communism, but also how a residue of syndicalist ideas found a place in National Socialism and Fascism. The struggle against concreteness, the urge, in one's irritation with the facts of the industrialized state and the "apathy" of the working class, to plunge into irrationalism, are not entirely absent in Guild Socialism. There is even a furtive approach to mystical nationalism. The state makes a reappearance, in S. G. Hobson, to express the spirit of the community and "the abiding truths" of the national interest as against selfish interests of particular segments of the community.[2] G. D. H. Cole, in one of his earlier books, toyed with the Rousseauistic conception of the state and with that "elusive but fundamental reality which he [Rousseau] named the General Will."[3]

But how awkward and unconvincing does the phraseology of "higher" interests and of the "real" state sound against the pattern of prosaic economic pursuits and aspirations of the actual industrial worker. The points of real appeal in Guild Socialism—its protest against the class system; its plea for more

power for the unions and for social and economic democracy—
flow more naturally into other socialist movements. Barring an
economic or political catastrophe which disrupts the habits of
a century of industrialism, the worker's response to the
slackening of economic dynamism of liberal society takes the
form of laborism. World War I, with its shattering impact on
the domestic and especially what there was of the international
liberal order still does not constitute that catastrophe. The
British labor movement becomes more consciously socialistic,
but it finds its socialism in the Fabian version rather than in
other forms. What there is of Communism in interwar England
comes mostly, insofar as the workers are concerned, as a
reflection of the much oversimplified notion of Soviet Russia
as a "workers' state." In retrospect, the weakness of Marxism in
England had been ordained by the same forces and habits that
made for the insignificance of anarchism and syndicalism in
the working-class movement and for the acceptance of liberal
collectivism by society as a whole.

The Continental Pattern

The epoch-making intellectual achievement of the English
technologists and their like, who prepared the Industrial
Revolution and have afterward worked out its consequences in
technology and the material sciences, is not so much that they
gained a new manner of insight into the nature and working of
material things, as that they were, by force of circumstances,
enabled to forget much of what was known before their time; by
atrophy of the habitual bent for imputing anthropomorphic
qualities and characters to the things they saw, they were
enabled to interpret these things in terms of matter of fact.[4]

Veblen's characteristically involved statement contains its
own insight about the mechanics of adjustment to industrialization. The ability to forget is important not only, as Veblen
thought, in reference to the habit "of construing material
phenomena in occult, magical, quasi-personal, spiritual
phenomena." It is also the ability to forget the previous artisan
and peasant existence. In England, the working class was
already demonstrating this ability at the end of the nineteenth

century. On the Continent, the tremendous development of industrialism, in the strict sense of the word, was not accompanied at an equal pace by the institutional and social appurtenances of the process.

But the ability to forget has yet another dimension. In a study of Marxism, it is easy to fall into the temptation to believe that the reality of politics is expressed exclusively in terms of "economic forces" and indices of industrial production. One may neglect the emotional factor in the adjustment of the worker to the political system. In England, the labor movement has always had some difficulty finding an appropriate group of martyrs to symbolize its opposition to the bourgeois order. The "Tolpuddle martyrs"—the group of laborers who in the 1830's were sentenced to transportation for illegal union activity—figure rather faintly compared with the hundreds of executions that followed the suppression of the Paris Commune of 1871. The long delays and legal obstacles that preceded full recognition of the role and functions of English trade unionism are again not of the same order as, say, the suppression of the German Socialist Party under Bismarck.

The facts of economic improvement or deterioration are but part of the story of the adjustment to "industrialization." The early irritants of loss of status and factory discipline may become dulled with the passage of time and the rise in the standard of living. The workers will not be able to forget their earlier grievances and express their present ones, if the state stands as the symbol of authority, apart and against them, if, for all the right to vote, there is an unbridgeable gap between them and the machinery of the bourgeois state. In England, the self-professed task of the Socialist Fabian society was, first, propagandizing not so much the working class as the middle class about the necessity of socialism and, second, infiltrating the civil service with collectivistic ideas. This, under Continental conditions at the beginning of the twentieth century, would have been the height of naiveté. The French worker viewed his *patron* and the German worker the imperial civil servant as class enemies. Though England in 1900 was less advanced in social legislation than Germany, though France was a republic, the two Continental centers of socialism had elements in their political and social systems that gave more than superficial reality to the concept of the class war, and to the persistence within the working class of hostility toward the state and the ruling class on a scale unmatched in the country that originated the industrial system.

What Veblen wrote in 1915, trying to explain the dangerous character of German nationalism by the lag of social development in comparison with industry and technology, may be used (and not only in regard to Germany) to explain the acceptance of Marxist rather than laboristic socialism by a community with a high *technical* culture:

> As a cultural community the Fatherland is at present in an eminently unstable transitional phase. Its population is in the singularly untoward position—untoward, that is, in the present immediate bearing—that they have come out of an obsolescent cultural situation so recently as in effect not to have forgotten what is necessary to forget, at the same time they have not been in contact with the things of the modern world long enough or intimately enough to have fully assimilated the characteristically modern elements of the Western civilization.[5]

The "obsolescent cultural situation" has already been defined many times in our earlier pages as simply the lack of adjustment to industrialization in some important political or social respect. It hardly needs to be added that, taking England as a model of such adjustment, large areas of Europe in 1900, or in 1915, were in an "obsolescent cultural situation," and that the survival of anti-industrial and antistate attitudes against the background of the centralized state and rapidly industrializing economy was creating favorable conditions for the flowering of Marxism. It is tempting to play with categories and types. At one extreme is a society industrialized in spirit as well as in fact (England), where socialism, when it appears, assumes the character of laborism. Further down is a country (Germany) where socialism is cast in the official Marxist mold, but where the rapid pace of industrial advance makes the mentality of the workers, if not the phraseology of their leaders, less and less responsive to the slogan of the class war. France before 1914 can be used as a model of a country where the anti-industrial protest is still so strong that even the official Marxist ideology of the socialist movement serves as a veneer over the essentially anarchist and syndicalist mentality of the radical element of the working class. At the other extreme is, say, Spain, where the low level of industrialization makes the worker express his radicalism in anarchism and syndicalism pure and simple rather than in their subdued version of revolutionary Marxism.

If this pattern is examined, and if all the qualifications are allowed for, with an eye to the "catching on" of Marxism as a movement rather than as a theory, two things will be apparent: first, the tremendous ability of Marxism to fuse into itself, and to become the organizational expression of, other forms of socialism, mainly anarchism and syndicalism; and, second, the unstable character of the Marxist appeal to the working class. It is most effective at a specific period of the given society's development. But no sooner does Marxism replace anarchism and syndicalism as the official ideology than the same forces that had made the worker abandon the mere spirit of opposition to the state and industry, the mere principle of the workers' association as a substitute for any more comprehensive philosophy of politics and society, make him chafe under doctrinaire Marxism and push him toward a more pragmatic and evolutionary type of socialism. The ideal society for revolutionary Marxism is the one that is "arrested" in its response to industrialization; where large-scale industry and urbanization make simple anarchism obsolete and syndicalism unavailing from the point of view of the radical worker; where the relative newness of industrialization has not entirely killed off the peasant mentality; where a large part of the population consists of peasants tilling their small holdings; and where the political process and class divisions, whatever the official form of the state, do indeed give the worker the impression of the state as the "executive committee of the exploiting class."

We may observe the "in-between" character of Marxism by focusing for a moment on two writers of the period who attempted to rephrase socialism in terms of what they conceived to be the logic of social development and the character of class consciousness of the worker. At first glance, no two writers seem so many worlds apart as Eduard Bernstein and Georges Sorel. The German, a graduate of orthodox Marxism, a man who then attempted to modify Marxism to fit in with the genuine democratic creed, is the epitome of liberal values and the humanitarian approach to politics. The Frenchman, a proponent of irrationalism, without solid moorings in any political movement, later on an admirer of Lenin, a man whose writings found discordant echoes in syndicalism, Fascism, and Nazism, epitomizes the breakdown of the liberal values, the hankering after myths and violence—politics, in brief, as a form of excitement. The titles of their books, *Evolutionary Socialism* and *Reflections on Violence,* emphasize the contrast.

And yet how both of them turn to Marxism and invoke its thought in support of their quite contrasting conclusions! Neither is a "complete" Marxist, but each grasps one element of Marxian systhesis and disparages the other. To Sorel, Marx is the anarchist, the ancestor of syndicalism and the spontaneous revolutionary movement of the workers. To Bernstein, Marx is *primarily* the social democrat and humanitarian. If one discounts the revolutionary phraseology of Marx's younger days, obsolete under the conditions of socialism in twentieth-century Europe, one finds, holds Bernstein, the real Marx, real scientific socialism. If one discounts the deposit of the earlier socialist theories and utopias, retorts Sorel, one finds the real Marx: the revolutionary, the proponent of the violent take-over by the workers. Both the democrat and the believer in violence find in Marxism what they are seeking. Both the acceptance of industrialism and the democratic state and the rejection of industrialism and contempt for democracy which is syndicalism invoke Marx.

Bernstein and Sorel testify to how much the Marxist synthesis was made possible by the mid-nineteenth-century conditions under which it was generated, and how the breakdown of this synthesis fifty years later compels the Marxists to seize one or the other side of Marxism, for industrialism and anarchism can no longer be combined. Either, like Bernstein, you accept the logic of the doctrine as leading toward an industrialized state and democracy, or you seize the spirit of revolution and forget about the "stages of material development." Sorel portrayed with almost comic nostalgia the breakdown of the original Marxist analysis and the seductive power of industrialism and democracy:

> In a society so enfevered by the passion for the success which can be obtained in competition, all the actors walk straight before them like veritable automata without taking any notice of the great ideas of the sociologists: they are subject to very simple forces, and not one of them dreams of escaping from the circumstances of his condition. Then only is the development of capitalism carried on with that inevitableness which struck Marx so much, and which seemed to him comparable to that of a natural law. If on the contrary, the middle class, led astray by the *chatter* of the preachers of ethics and sociology, return to an *ideal of conservative mediocrity,* seek to correct the *abuses* of economics, and wish to break with the barbarism of their predecessors, then one part of the forces which were to further the development of capitalism is employed in hindering it, an arbitrary and irrational element is introduced and the world becomes completely indeterminate. This indetermination grows still greater if the proletariat are converted to the ideas of social peace at the same time as their masters, or even if they simply consider everything from the corporative point of view; while Socialism gives to every economic contest a general and revolutionary colour. Conservatives are not deceived when they see in the compromises which lead to collective contracts, and in the bargaining between employers and labour the means of avoiding the Marxian revolution; but they escape one danger only to fall into another, and they run the risk of being devoured by Parliamentary Socialism.[6]

And Sorel's source of apprehension—bad old capitalism is gone and with it may go the real revolutionary spirit of the workers—is Bernstein's source of hope: "The movement means everything for me" and what is *usually* called the final aim of socialism "is nothing." The "movement" for Bernstein is the movement toward democracy; for Sorel, toward revolution. The German wants to extirpate in the workers the last of revolutionary intoxication, imbue them with the feeling that they will get everything they want by swimming with the tide of industrialism and democracy: "The conquest of political power by the working classes, the expropriation of capitalists, are no ends in themselves but only means for the accomplishment of certain aims and endeavors."[7] The Frenchman wants to preserve the struggle against the state *as such,* against the capitalist as the instrument of the worker's enslavement and alienation: "Syndicalists do not propose to reform the State . . . they want to destroy it, because they wish to realize this idea of Marx's that the Socialist revolution ought not to culminate in the replacement of one governing minority by another minority."[8]

Bernstein's *Evolutionary Socialism* (1899) and Sorel's *Reflections* (1906) are works by intellectuals, shaped, no doubt, by their personal predilections and idiosyncrasies. But they reflect much more than that, as witnessed by the great éclat that greeted them at publication.

Bernstein's Marx is the Marx of the German worker who has forgotten his anarchistic antecedents. His increasing well-being, the social legislation and protection by the state, the power of the unions—all these change the character of class antagonism on which German Marxism at first had grown. But the ideology remains in name, for it is the focal point of the still vivid anticapitalism and the resentment of the arrogance of the ruling class and essentially nondemocratic government. But why a violent revolution if successive elections to the Reichstag bring a greater and greater socialist vote and open up the prospect of a peaceful victory of Marxism? What Bernstein wrote must have been felt by many: "As soon as a nation has attained a position where the rights of the propertied minority have ceased to be a serious obstacle to social progress, where the negative tasks of political action are less pressing than the positive, then the appeal to a revolution by force becomes a meaningless phrase."[9] If the German worker had not "forgotten" as much as his English counterpart, then, Bernstein believed, he soon would. And because in one sense he was still a good Marxist, he believed that he was describing the universal tendency of the working movement in the civilized world.

Sorel, never formally a Marxist, writes and speaks for syndicalism. The latter in its French version can be translated simply by "workers for themselves." The state, what is to be done the day after the revolution, how industries are to be run by the workers—these are problems on which syndicalism does not spend much time. Its French version reflects the specific French political and social conditions and the "memories" of the French working class. The roots of syndicalism lie in Proudhon and Blanqui. Its appeal to the *camaraderie* of the proletarian spirit and its protest against the *embourgeoisement* of the worker that is implicit in the more prosaic versions of socialism reflect the spirit of estrangement from the whole complex of the middle-class state. There is in Sorel a yet more extreme note—the rejection of the whole rationalistic and democratic tradition which Bernstein tries to read into Marxism. It is no longer a question of finding a refuge from the all-devouring state and industry: it is a masochistic delight at the forthcoming collapse of the whole mass of false values, the worship of action, admiration for all kinds of irrationalist theories showing up the "professors" and socialist bureaucrats. It is like much of *early* socialist thought, the instinctive reaction of the petty bourgeois striking up heroic poses in the face of the material forces that threaten his status and dwarf his self-esteem; but this instinct is now harnessed not to the scientifico-religious utopias of the pioneering socialists, but to the potentialities of the mass movements of the workers.

Sorel and Bernstein stand at the point of highest interdependence between socialist theory (and especially Marxism) and the Continental working-class movements. There is nothing yet of the ambiguity of the postwar situation, when one branch of the socialist movement will become an extension of the Soviet state and "its" ideology the result of decrees laid down in Moscow. The period before the war is one of *genuine* internationalism in the Marxist movement. The Second International, founded in 1889, is dominated by the Marxist parties; Marxism is acknowledged, in one way or another, to be the chief socialist tradition. Bernstein's revisionism, directed primarily to the awkward orthodoxy of the German Social Democratic Party, is also directed to the international socialist movement. Thus, its implications would read into international socialism the same meaning that Bernstein would read into the domestic form: it is the true heir, under twentieth-century conditions, of the cosmopolitan, democratic, and humanitarian tradition of nineteenth-century liberalism.

The pathetic strivings of the Second International to lay a basis for a world-wide pacifist movement to curb the rising tide of nationalism and militarism, to block the approaching war, are well known. Sorel's book provides a somber commentary on this count. Its exaltation of violence and irrationalism, its constant use of military figures of speech, augur the movements that will combine the socialistic appeal with racial and nationalist arguments. It is the sum total of Western bourgeois civilization which is to him odious: not only its state, its materialism, its industry, but its international order and rationalism.

The fears of Bernstein and the hopes of Sorel are alike symptomatic of the breakdown of the original Marxist synthesis—socialism coming in obedience to economic laws and fulfilling all the promises of rationalism; an international order and humanitarianism. This rationalistic optimism is missing in both writers. To Sorel, socialism will come only as the result of the abandonment of rationalism and a resolute stand against material progress: "use must be made of a body of images which, *by intuition alone,* and before any considered analyses are made, is capable of evoking as an undivided whole the mass of sentiments which corresponds to the different manifestations of the war undertaken by Socialism against modern society."[10] Bernstein's abandonment of Marx's automatism of economic laws is equally pronounced, though it leads him to quite different conclusions: "Social conditions have not developed to such an acute opposition of things and classes as is depicted in the *Manifesto.*"[11] Socialism, then, does not *have* to come in the way that Marx imagined it would. It can come only through democracy: "democracy is a condition of socialism to a much greater degree than is usually assumed, i.e., it is not only the means but also the substance."[12]

An irrational myth on one side—"the whole of Socialism in the drama of the general strike"—a refinement of democracy and liberalism, on the other: such are the paths recommended for a reinterpretation of Marxism.

And yet, if the original synthesis of Karl Marx had broken down in the face of the facts of the world of 1900, he might well have reproached his interpreters with failing to provide a new and more realistic road to socialism, with being as much under the spell of the "inevitable" patterns of development within their own societies as he had been under the spell of the conditions of Western capitalism in the 1840's and '50's. It was naive, he would have rejoined to Sorel, to ignore the logic of development of material forces, to imagine that socialism can come as an act of will, and to believe that the peculiarities of French and Italian capitalism, and hence of the working movement in these countries, represent a universal pattern. It was equally naive of Bernstein to discard Marxist determinism while implying the acceptance of liberal determinism, to think of an uninterrupted growth of material well-being and democracy as leading rather easily to socialism, to believe the English pattern to be, essentially, the universal one.

It is easy to see, in historical perspective, how the contrasting interpretations of socialism were grounded, as the original had been, on the confusion of a particular socio-economic situation with a universal pattern and how they tried to preserve as universally valid an ideology which has drawing power under particular circumstances at particular times. Bernstein and Sorel rejected *literal* Marxism in favor of one part of the doctrine because one said, in effect, "Where are your terrible economic crises and the worsening lot of the worker?" and the other, "Where is your socialism after more than fifty years of capitalism?" But the success or failure of Marxism does not depend on its passing the test of historical prediction; it depends on the existence of conditions in which the questions and answers that Marx give appear both important and convincing to the working class.

This was not the case in Germany, or even in France. As mentioned before, the Marxist doctrine was like an ill-fitting suit of clothing worn over the actual working movement in both countries; if German socialism had outgrown it and was chafing under it, the French one had never quite fit into it. When Bernstein came out with his revisionist bombshell, he was gently reproved, so the legend has it, by an "orthodox" colleague, who said that, although they all felt the way he did, it was highly indecent to question the orthodoxy in public! In France the official Marxist tenor of the socialist party, created out of previous groupings in 1905, had to contend with syndicalism of the working movement. The C.G.T. *(Confederation Générale du Travail)*—the French trade-union congress—in its official declaration at Amiens (1906) spelled out its syndicalism in definitely non-Marxist terms:

> But this task [of immediate practical protection of the worker] is but one side of the work of syndicalism: it prepares complete emancipation (*l'émancipation integrale*) which can be realized only by an expropriation of capitalism, it recognizes the general strike as a means of action and it considers that the union, today an organization of resistance, will be in the future the unit of production and distribution, the base of social distribution.[13]

It is natural that the trade-union movement should be more pragmatic, more related to the worker's nonphilosophical interests, and usually less radical than the corresponding socialist movement. It is thus all the more interesting that the French unions found themselves, by and large, on the left of the political movement and the German ones on the right.

The problem must be posed, though it cannot be discussed at length here, of the relationship of Marxism to the development of trade unionism. One pattern has been observed in Great Britain, where a party and a philosophy of socialism emerge from the structure of unionism, which represents the more active part of the working class, if it is not synonymous with it. In France, the much less numerous union movement (in proportion to the total industrial force), as represented by its major organization, the C.G.T., officially eschewed Marxism and professed syndicalism; and yet, because of practical exigencies, namely, the impossibility of expressing syndicalism in organizational political terms, it tolerated what might be called a liaison between the politically conscious worker and Marxism. In Germany, the relationship was more that of an uneasy marriage between the worker's party and his professional organizations. The relatively sudden and rapid onset of industrialization in Germany determined a correspondingly sudden and rapid growth of unionism and of political socialism. From their very beginning, the unions grew under the auspices of socialist theory, first that of Lassalle and then that of Karl Marx. While much is made of the differences between the two thinkers and of Marx's antipathy toward his colorful contemporary, the fact remains that Lassalle's socialism was essentially Marxist, even if it went further in explicit recognition of the role of the state and pragmatic use of unionism. German unionism was thus at an early stage divorced from its anarchistic roots. The socialist ideology grounded in Hegelianism and the large-scale character of German capitalism combined to uproot the remnants of anarchist feelings and to account for the weakness of syndicalist impulses in German trade unionism.

Was German *capitalism* helped in its rapid growth because the German worker, after industrialism hit Germany, never experienced a prolonged phase of "pure" anarchism and syndicalism, but found himself under a doctrine that, perversely acknowledged (and still does) the state and the benefits of industrialism? Or, on the contrary, was the character of German *socialism* determined by the rapid growth of German industrialism, by the visible benefits of the state and large-scale industry? There is, one feels, a great deal of logic to both hypotheses. Intense syndicalism is both a cause and an effect of a rather unenterprising small-scale capitalist development. A comment on French unionism may illustrate this rather involved point:

> Only in France, Italy and Spain were there strong syndicalist movements, and only in France was it the prevailing doctrine of an important trade union movement. . . . The slow rate of economic development, the continued prevalence of small workshops, the lack of entrepreneurial daring gave French workers the feeling that they had little to expect from gradual processes. Such were their employers and such workers' expectations from the state of the economy, that revolutionary change was easier for many to envisage than day by day gains in their conditions of life and work. A revolutionary solution held greater attractions and risked less than in countries where

capitalism was more dynamic. Even as they expressed their alarm over the spread of the Taylor system and the speed-up in France, C.G.T. leaders wished they could exchange their own unenterprising anti-union employers for no less anti-union but more enterprising employers of the United States. With such employers, they thought, French Unionism would itself take on greater force.[14]

We end up with a truly paradoxical picture: a vigorous growth of capitalism helps the growth of Marxist socialism among the workers; but, also, a speedy extinction by Marxism of syndicalist and anarchistic feelings among the workers can be a contributing factor to the flourishing development of capitalism! The lesson of Marxism has been absorbed by the worker: he works more efficiently since he accepts the inevitability of industrial labor and its appurtenances; his class hostility does not find expression in sabotage of the industrial and political system that he expects to inherit. The prospect of an *eventual* revolution removes the need for the strike, except as a struggle to win concrete professional benefits. One paradox leads to another: if capitalism is set within democratic or even semidemocratic conditions, the Marxist socialist movement will grow because of its undoubted organizational superiority over competing socialist movements. And under conditions of universal suffrage it may eventually come to power. But will this victory of the Marxist *movement* be the victory of Marxism, as Marx postulated? If the state has been conquered constitutionally, where are the state and the ruling class to be smashed? If, in the very process of gaining power, the working class, because of the lesson of Marxism and the rising standard of living, has learned to accept the industrial system, labor discipline, and centralization of economic life, where, in fact, is the revolutionary impulse? What remains, in effect, to revolt against? The contradictory parts of original Marxism are held together by one thing: the conviction that the growth of capitalism, of the industrial system, leads to the worsening of the worker's position. If that tenet is disproved, economically as well as politically, the very growth of the Marxist *movement* will lead to the worker's acquiring what Lenin called trade-union mentality; to his socialism being (for all the doctrinal references to the class war and revolution) essentially evolutionary and laboristic.

Revolution killed off by the growth of the Marxist movement, Marxism becoming the school of the middle-class values for the worker—these were the terrible possibilities faced by the leaders of the German Social Democracy. Ever since the party at its Erfurt congress in 1891 had purified its official doctrine of the Lassallean accretions, it had been considered *the* Marxist party in Europe, the official representative of the legacy of Marx and Engels. It was to the German socialists that the budding Marxist movements in Eastern Europe looked for leadership and guidance. It was the almost uninterrupted growth in union and party membership, in election votes cast for the socialists, that warranted optimism that Marxist socialism was the wave of the future. German socialism, like the rest of German society, patted itself on the back for its "theoretical" quality, as contrasted with the vulgar pragmatic of British socialism and the irrational adventurism of the French movement. For all the theoretical acumen displayed in the plethora of well-footnoted books and articles, for all the verbal fireworks with which the German socialists protested their contempt for bourgeois values and imperial institutions, the social democratic Karl Marx began to look suspiciously like Sidney Webb.

Bernstein's argument would have accepted and approved the similarity. German socialism, according to him, would have reaped the dividends of doctrinal flexibility and realism by attracting greater middle-class support in its struggle against the imperial government; it would have benefited from a more realistic and politically attractive policy on the peasant problem; and it would have had a greater possibility, even before a full electoral victory, of affecting German politics. The formal history of revisionism is well known: the party condemned Bernstein's thesis, reproved him, and clung to orthodoxy. The whole issue led the theoretical discussion farther and farther toward stretching the economic facts on the Procrustean bed of the original doctrine. Karl Kautsky's attempts to show that although the theory of "immiseration" may be *literally* incorrect, it is true in a *relative* sense, and that although the *natural* tendency of capitalism is toward the worsening of the worker's lot, a countertendency keeps it temporarily in check, are fine examples of the ideological calisthenics with which the leaders of the party attempted to keep the revolutionary spirit alive, if at a low intensity. The ingenious attempt of the left wing, represented by Rosa Luxemburg, to maintain Marx's theory of the catastrophic breakdown of capitalism by attributing the survival of capitalism to the exploitation of the noncapitalist segments of world economy, e.g., through imperialism, also falls in the same category.

It is customary to view the whole struggle within the German Social Democracy in terms of personalities: mild and democratic Bernstein, professorially unrealistic Kautsky, and revolutionary-minded Rosa Luxemburg, all struggling for ideological dominance in the spirit of German theoretical pendantry. An alternative is to refer the whole issue to the conservative habit of the party bureaucracy, which forced them to hang onto the doctrine with which they had grown up and with which they felt comfortable. But what underlies the conflict, the desperate refusal of the center and left wing of the party to acknowledge the facts, is an instinctive feeling that orthodoxy, with its absurd "immiseration" theory, is the last barrier preventing the worker's accommodation to the system and his *embourgeoisement*. And, under German conditions, if you give up revolution, do you guarantee that you will obtain democracy and representative government? We are discussing the period of irrationalist theories and movements, the period of the growing strength of nationalism, with its attendant phenomena of militarism and imperialism. It is ironic that the main Marxist party and movement, by its insistence upon an outworn theory, by saying in effect *"credo quia absurdum,"* ranges the Marxist tradition in the irrationalist camp and prepares the ground for its role as a theology in the Soviet system.

Orthodoxy versus revisionism in Marxism has its immediate meaning in the concrete tactics and problems of the German Social Democratic Party. A historian has outlined the theory under which the doctrine and reality reached a stalemate in the official posture of the German Marxists between 1900 and 1917:

> In terms of the divergent groups composing Social Democracy, Kautsky's theory may be viewed as a proposal for a truce under which the trade unionists and revisionists would give up their attack on revolutionary theory and their effort to come to terms with the ruling class, while the ultra radicals would cease their drive for a revolutionary tactic. The theoretical concept with which the truce was to be sealed was that of the passive revolution. Under it Social Democracy would move neither toward further acceptance of the existing order, nor toward action to hasten its collapse. It would organize and agitate, and maintain its moral integrity while waiting for the ruling class to destroy itself. Thus the effort to reconcile antagonistic political and intellectual tendencies led Kautsky not so much to a synthesis as to a stalemate.[15]

It is easy, with our historical hindsight, to project from this tragicomic predicament of the German Marxists—their inability to see things as they are because Marx had said they should be otherwise—a sequence of events from the German Socialists' acceptance of the war, through their growing impotence in the Weimar Republic, to their all too easy destruction by Hitler. It is also easy to urge, depending on one's point of view, that either of two extremes, Bernstein's liberalism or Rosa Luxemburg's revolutionism, would have brought better results than the "muddle of the middle" in which the party stuck. But theoretical formulas are not magic incantations capable of changing political reality.

Industrialization in Imperial Germany had gone far enough to strip the actual socialism of the working man of its revolutionary component, but not far enough, on its political and social side, to make this socialism mostly pragmatic, democratically and liberally minded. A society in which feudal concepts were still rampant, in which a large part of the population remained in peasant status, and which was not a democracy, did not offer a completely plausible setting for Fabian socialism. "The 'social problem' that was so puzzling to our fathers, how to organize a capitalist-socialist society, is in reality solved at the end of the nineteenth century. It means that its principles are laid down. Their execution will constitute the difficult task of the technique of statesmanship," wrote a representative of "academic socialism."[16] This was an illusion. But so was Rosa Luxemburg's expectation that the collapse of the liberal and capitalist order would of necessity result in a revolution both democratic and socialist. History was to show that Marxism could come to power not as the heir of democracy or as the receiver of bankrupt liberalism, but only under the same conditions that had made it the ideology of the working class, *as the heir of anarchism.*

Had the international order not broken down with World War I and the international implications of early liberalism been shown illusory, the story might well have been different. The cardinal point of liberal internationalism was well stated in the *Communist Manifesto.* "National differences and antagonisms between peoples are daily more and more vanishing, owing to the development of the bourgeoisie, to freedom of commerce, to the world market, to uniformity in the mode of production and in the conditions of life corresponding thereto."[17] Had Marx and the liberals been right, then the spread of Marxism might well have followed Bernstein's prescription and Kautsky's expectations: socialism as the logical successor and culmination of liberal democracy. But the destruction of liberal internationalism, the fatuity of the rationalistic dogma of the liberal utopia exposed by the holocaust of the war, again made Marx the revolutionary and anarchist a more convincing prophet than Marx the liberal and democrat. A new synthesis of Marxism—at the time of its formulation, the creed of a small body of fanatics issuing from a backward and despotic society—was to become the dominant strain of revolutionary socialism. When in 1918, at Lenin's prompting, the Bolsheviks decided to change their official title from Social Democrats to Communists, they were, like Marx and Engels in 1847, eschewing the nonrevolutionary and parliamentary connotation of the term "socialist." But there was a more profound, though at the time not entirely perceived, element of continuity with the original thought of Marx and Engels. That thought had been revolutionary; it had combined wonder at the material forces transforming men's life with protest against the destructive effects of industrialization. The same combination reappears in Communism and explains the sources and main locations of its appeal.

A New Marxist Synthesis—Leninism

The history of all countries shows that the working class, exclusively by its own effort, is able to develop only trade union consciousness, i.e., it may itself realize the necessity for combining in unions, to fight against the employers and to strive to compel the government to pass necessary labour legislation, etc.[18]

Lenin, when he wrote these words, set the basis for the Bolshevik party and for the movement which within fifteen years of the writing of *What Is to Be Done* was to seize the Russian Empire and inaugurate a new phase in the development of Marxism. In retrospect, it is truly amazing that a turgidly written pamphlet concerning an obscure conflict between two minute groups of Russian Marxists came to be the foundation of an ideology and a movement that was to conquer Russia and become a leading force of the century. It is as if an article written in 1944 concerning a dispute between two branches of the American Trotskyites were the foundation of the political movement in power in the United States in 1960, and thirty years later the basis of the ideology officially enthroned over one third of the population of the world.

What Is to Be Done is the basis of Bolshevism. It is the argument of Bolshevism, the formulation of the concept of the party, so essential to Communism. It is the *style* of Bolshevism—the tedious, repetitious, pedantic argument that makes the original works of Marx and Engels shine like great literature in comparison. One is drawn to wonder how the Russian revolutionary movement, initially so romantic, nurtured on so much literary inspiration, came to be expressed in a document having all the external romance and excitement of a doctoral dissertation! And the problem is more fundamental: how a movement capable of inspiring people to both heroism and cruelty, to tremendous feats of construction, and to an appalling subservience, can have as its set of scriptures a dismal collection of undigestible scholasticism. Why of all branches of *literary* Marxism was the Russian one destined to be the dullest, seemingly most drained of the feelings and emotions that excite people to revolutionary action; and why of all Marxist *movements* was the Russian one to emerge as the heir of the most elemental and violent of revolutions? Why has the same movement been the beneficiary of assorted revolutionary strivings all over the globe, of economic grievances of the worker, of the peasant's desire for more land, of national and anticolonial aspirations, of the intellectual's search for order and creed?

Those are the questions that can be addressed to the version of Marxism known as "Leninism," which in its simplest formulation is found in *What Is to Be Done.* The work is ostensibly a variation on one main theme: Marxian class consciousness, political class consciousness, socialist consciousness, call it what you will, can come to the workers only from the *outside.* As spelled out in the opening statement, by themselves the workers can reach only trade-union consciousness, the desire to improve their economic status and to obtain better working conditions, etc. Although the argument is directed at German revisionism and its alleged Russian followers, there is this basic agreement between Lenin and Eduard Bernstein: the forces of history are not making of the workers a *revolutionary* class; the spontaneous organization of the workers leads them not to revolution but to the struggle for economic and professional improvement. Why, then, is Bernstein a "revisionist" and Lenin an "orthodox" Marxist? Because Bernstein believes in the workers' party following the inclinations of the workers and bowing to the inherent laborism of the industrialized worker, whereas Lenin believes in forcible conversion of the worker to revolutionary Marxism. Wrote Lenin in 1902: "subservience to the spontaneity of the labour movement, the belittling of the role of the 'conscious element' of the role of Social-Democracy, means, whether one likes it or not, growth of influence of bourgeois ideology among the workers."[19]

Let us observe, in passing, how fixedly, for the moment, the eyes of this Russian revolutionary are on the West, on England and Germany. The Russian worker in 1902 is far away indeed from the status and feelings of the English or German trade unionist. But looking ahead to further industrialization of Russia, Lenin has no doubt that the great danger to the revolutionary élan, to revolutionary Marxism, is the slow but continuous and inevitable ebbing of the revolutionary impulse of the worker, his acquisition of trade-union mentality, of a savings account, of the feeling of amelioration of his status, which makes the desperate revolutionary reaction at first less urgent and finally unrealistic and unnecessary. "Hence, our task, the task of Social Democracy, is to *combat spontaneity,* to *divert* the labour movement, with its spontaneous trade-unionist striving, from under the wing of the bourgeoisie and to bring it back under the wing of revolutionary Social Democracy."[20]

"To combat spontaneity . . ." The literal statement sounds almost ridiculous, doubly so in the circumstances of its first formulation. Who is to divert the growing working movement in Russia from its natural course? A handful of revolutionaries—some of them in Tsarist jails—operating through a newspaper published abroad. But the statement contains the essence of Leninism, the perception that the *natural* development of material forces and the *natural* response of people to them will, in time, lead far away from Marx's expectations about the effects of industrialization on the worker. You do not jettison Marxism because it failed to predict the psychology of the worker in an advanced industrialized country, says Lenin. You "improve" and advance this psychology in the revolutionary direction by means of a party. A remarkably illogical performance. You reject the major premise of your ideology, yet you claim strict orthodoxy. Your argument is rationalistic and materialistic, and yet you set out, almost in Sorel-like fashion, to propagate the myth of revolution, the necessity of which, you have just asserted, the workers will feel less and less!

The approach in *What Is to Be Done* reveals a very significant factor in the reception of Marxism in Russia. To

Lenin and his contemporaries *Marxism means revolution.* Marxism as a reaction against the factory system, as a philosophy of materialism and economic determinism—these are secondary considerations both to Lenin and to his opponents. It is in the meaning of Marxism as a *specific road to political revolution* that they are chiefly interested. To the Russian intellectual, the philosophy of Karl Marx came not as an aesthetic protest against the industrial revolution, not even as a sudden vision of a better and more just society; it came primarily as the culmination of a century's search for a concrete and convincing philosophy and strategy of revolution. It is striking that missing from Lenin's pamphlet is a discussion of the issue that divided the Western Marxists at the time and that really lies at the bottom of the problem of spontaneity versus revolutionary consciousness: Is or is not the worker's standard of living worsening under capitalism? Both Lenin and his opponents are really interested in the "secondary" reflection of the problem: What kind of activity will enable the workers to carry off a revolution? The whole theoretical discussion of "immiseration," which fills up the life of the Western Social Democrats, is almost entirely missing in the Russian debate. Bernstein, Kautsky, Rosa Luxemburg, and Bebel quarrel about the historical trends, Lenin and his opponents about *tactics.*

And this explains how Lenin in 1902 can consider himself a materialist and yet reject spontaneity; how he can plead for a conspiratorial, centrally controlled revolutionary party, and yet feel that he is a democrat. For the conditions of Russia of 1902 make the revolutionary interpretation of Marxism as convincing, for all the logical paradoxes of the doctrine, as it had been in Western Europe of 1848. Industry is growing by leaps and bounds in the Russian Empire, but the necessary political component of industrialization is lacking even more than it had been in France or England of 1848. The contrast is stressed again and again by Lenin: "The Western-European Social Democrats find their work in this field facilitated by the calling of public meetings, to which *all* are free to go, and by the parliament in which they speak to the representatives of *all* classes. We have neither a parliament, nor the freedom to call meetings."[21] If the normal rudiments of parliamentary institutions are missing, if political activity is banned, then also missing is the vital element of the confrontation of the Marxist dogma with political and social reality which makes a Western socialist at least visualize the problem, and which by its absence enables the Russian Marxist to swallow the doctrine as a whole and to ponder only its tactical implications.

In a sense the Russian intellectual of Lenin's time lived in a jail. A comfortable jail if he did not choose to revolt, but a jail nevertheless, which separated him from the normal activity of his Western counterpart. Reality—the reality of an advancing industrial society, of vigorous artistic and scientific activity, encompassed in a political system which was by definition and in fact an autocracy—was in itself so fantastic that the paradoxes and incongruities of a revolutionary theory did not have the jarring impact they had in the West, but paled into insignificance against the urgency of revolution. For a century now the Russian intellectuals had sought a theory that would both explain and remove the humiliating political backwardness and impotence of their society: a revolutionary analysis, and a prescription of action. To the small groups that had been assembling illegally, Fourier, Saint-Simon, and Proudhon all provided material for analysis and revolutionary theories, but little for an effective political movement. Scientific and social theories, often politically neutral when enunciated in the West, were under Russian conditions transmuted into *philosophies* of revolution. Marxism, when it appears on the Russian scene in the 1880's, appears as a philosophy of total liberation: it is science, philosophy, and a general guide of action. It inherits much of the impulse that drove people into Saint-Simonian and Fourierist cults. It inherits much of the original political excitement that, after the liberation of the serfs in the 1860's, drove many politically conscious Russians into the ranks of the Populist movement.

The synthetic function of Marxism in gathering into itself various revolutionary and intellectual movements and impulses is nowhere as well documented as in Russia at the beginning of this century. To a socialist, as to a revolutionary disappointed in the fruitless terrorism of the "People's Will" of the 1870's and '80's, Marxism comes as a superior, systematic, and scientific revolutionary creed and method. The other non-Marxist or even nonpolitical sources of modernism, which in the West tempered the appeal of the doctrine, were in Russia almost nonexistent. Political liberalism prior to 1905 was prosecuted as vigorously as Marxism, or even more so, because the Tsarist regime feared esoteric intellectual doctrine less than the claims of "respectable people" for constitutional rights on one hand, and the terroristic activity of the heirs of the People's Will on the other. It was thus the autocracy that was the real barrier to the spontaneity of modern social development, which has in the West encroached upon the Marxist appeal. It is, then, no paradox but a fact—amply explained by the circumstances of the formulation of Leninism at the beginning of this century—that Russian Marxism can proclaim itself democratic and yet demand an elitist party of revolutionaries run in a dictatorial manner; that it is materialistic and rationalistic but wants to *impose* its ideology upon the workers. Again, as in the case of early Marxism, the combination of incompatibles into a single doctrine can be understood only in terms of specific circumstances of a specific society that make the paradox not only possible but convincing.

The struggle against the development of "trade-union consciousness" among the workers was but one aspect of Lenin's struggle against "spontaneity." Three years before his famous pamphlet, he had completed *The Development of Capitalism in Russia*. In his concluding remarks, he observes that the development of capitalism in Russia has been slow and adds astutely: "And it cannot be but slow, because no other capitalist country has preserved to such an extent institutions of the old, incongruous with capitalism, hampering its development, infinitely worsening the conditions of the producers who 'suffer both from capitalism and from the insufficient development of capitalism.'"[22] And he criticizes the Narodniks, the Russian Populists, for not understanding the development of industrialism and capitalism, for moralizing instead of applying Marxist criteria to the problems of politics and economics.

Secondary as the economic side of Marxism was to Lenin *at*

the time, it was already important enough to make him reject the populistic side of the Russian revolutionary movement. There is very little in Lenin of the strain that saw revolutionary hope in Russia's happy preservation from the evils of full-fledged Western capitalism. The strain that held the hope of socialism in the *mir* (the Russian peasant commune), which in an obscurantist fashion derided the West for its "materialism," finds in him but little echo, though Marx in his old age had, rather surprisingly, discoursed on this theme. The revolutionary movement, Lenin holds, must acknowledge in a hard-boiled fashion that capitalism is finally coming to Russia, that though it operates there under conditions different from those in the West, it is both illusory and harmful to imagine that Russia can "skip" the stage of capitalism.

More basically, Communism as fashioned by Lenin reflected, in addition to the revolutionary impulse, his and his contemporaries' impatience with the torpor and backwardness of Russian society and their feeling of the need and inevitability of modernization. The elements of difference and local charm that strike the Western reader in the Russian novel of the nineteenth century were anathema to Lenin and, by and large, became so to his movement. In Marxism he found the ideal of technology and science regulating society. His admiration of things German was not confined to the German Socialist Party before 1914, but included "German" efficiency, science, and talent for organization. In that sense, Germany represented to Lenin what Stalin later meant when he pleaded for a combination of Communism with the "American method": rejection of the whole complex of introspection about Russia's backwardness, rejection of intermittent self-contempt and glorification of Russia's "difference" from Western Europe, of the Russian soul, etc. In the same vein, the Soviet leaders felt constrained to condemn Pasternak's *Doctor Zhivago.* It was scandalous in their view not only because it is apolitical and not written in the style of "socialist realism," but also because its tone and concerns are out of keeping with modernized and industrialized Russia—its nostalgic and melancholy *motifs* clashing with the brave new world of Communism. Lenin's impatient Westernism, his longing for an emancipation from the interminable philosophical discourse and for *doing* things, is fully discernible before the Revolution of 1917, and illuminates in what sense Marxism "made a difference" in this revolution.

It follows that the struggle against the danger of trade unionism is to him no more important than the struggle against another type of spontaneity. Almost contemporary with the organization of the Social Democratic Party of 1898 was the birth of another revolutionary organization, the Socialist Revolutionaries. The latter, in effect, though not without an infusion of Marxism in their ideas, picked up the tradition of the People's Will, of revolutionary socialism looking to the small peasant rather than to the worker as the base for a future democratic society. The essential anarchism of the Social Revolutionaries and the practice of terrorism by its left wing represented to Lenin a danger as great as the reformism of the "Economists" (the would-be Russian followers of Bernstein) and the alleged proximity of the Mensheviks to the middle-class spirit. The Socialist Revolutionaries represented *par excellence* the reaction against industrialization that we have already encountered. The official democratic and socialist terminology of the movement ill concealed the essential anarchistic, anti-industrial reaction of the peasant *both* against the economic process that was disrupting the traditional economy of the countryside and against the political and class system that denied him more land. The Socialist Revolutionaries were, like all Russian parties and movements, led and staffed by intellectuals. But their ideology and political behavior up to the point when, after the revolution of 1917, having clearly become the leading party in terms of popular support, they were first split and then eliminated by the Bolsheviks, show clearly all the characteristics of anarchist, anti-industrially originated movements: organizational instability, inability to integrate the facts of the modern state and economics into ideology, and susceptibility to the extremes of nationalism on the one hand and anarchistic terrorism on the other. A Western study of the party's history and ideology shows well the instability of both its program and organization and its consequent defeat after the theft of its revolutionary appeal by the Bolsheviks.[23] In an industrializing society, with rapid growth of industry projected against the still overwhelmingly peasant character of the country and its backward political system, it fell eventually to the Socialist Revolutionaries to prepare the necessary anarchist and revolutionary background on which Marxism could achieve power.

The other aspect of the struggle against spontaneity was, then, Lenin's struggle against the *uncurbed* and *undisciplined* revolutionary impulse itself. Individual acts of terrorism, to a Marxist, are not only personal indulgence in heroics, which cannot affect the forces of history, but under the Russian conditions they resulted, as Lenin was sensible enough to see, in the alienation of large segments of public opinion rather than in coercion of the government into concessions. To base your revolutionary activity *merely* on the peasant's aspirations—and again the Marxist instinct of centralization and technological progress supplements the revolutionary's impulse—was to base it upon an essentially disorganized and vacillating element, susceptible both to the most primitive anarchism and to the most reactionary appeals of nationalism and religion.

It is a magnificent analysis of the deficiencies of various kinds of spontaneity that emerges from Lenin's heavy prose. The workers, if left to themselves, will eventually develop trade-union consciousness and will neglect the revolution for higher wages and better working conditions. The middle class will stop their revolution when they have constitutional rights, i.e., when they can play at parliaments and parties and preserve their property. The peasants? God only knows what the limits are to their aspirations! They will want to confiscate the lands of the gentry, but preserve their inefficient cultivation by the individual household and communes. They will press for all sorts of decentralization of political authority, thus making impossible any socialist economy, but will respond to the appeals of Russian chauvinism (or of other nationalisms in the non-Russian areas of the Empire) or religion. The conclusion should have been that there was no social basis in pre-1914 Russia for a *socialist* revolution.

It is here that the instincts bred into Lenin by immersion in Marxism prevent him from reaching the logical conclusion and enable him to come out, really unconsciously, with a fantastic solution. If all the widespread revolutionary pressures within the population still do not add up to socialism, why not create a party that, for all its allegiance to literal Marxism, will be able to appeal to and capitalize on the disparate revolutionary aspirations of various classes? A party that at different times and with varying intensity will still be able to associate itself with the claims for better working conditions for the workers, with the basic demands for democracy and a constitution, with the peasant's hunger for more land, and with an oppressed minority's desire for autonomy or independence; a party not limited and confined to these aspirations but using and pushing them as the means of achieving socialism? In *What Is to Be Done,* this idea is still only sketched and somewhat incoherently presented: "To bring political knowledge to the workers the Social Democrats *must go among all classes of the population,* must despatch units of their army *in all directions,*" and again, "We must go among all classes of the people as theoreticians, as propagandists, as agitators, and as organizers."[24]

But the organizational pattern is already clearly implied: to be that flexible and yet ideologically monolithic the party *has* to be elitist and centrally directed. It has to be a party of activists and not of mere sympathizers. The quarrel over a phrase that split the Bolsheviks and the Mensheviks in 1903 expressed not the ridiculous pedantry of contentious dogmatists but the issue of an inherently elitist and dictatorial concept of the party as the assimilator and guide of revolutionary impulses versus the party as their mere reflection. The Mensheviks, in their way as doctrinaire Marxists as Lenin, balked at the former.

It is always tempting to see a great historical figure as a genius developing the victorious formula for revolutions and wars in a flash of intuition. Actually, the concept of the party was only sketched by Lenin in 1902-1903. Its full formulation came through long years of theorizing and activity, not without hesitations and retreats, which led to November 1917. And the concept itself owes as much to the political acumen of Lenin's mind as it does to its narrowness, to his conviction that Marxism must mean revolution above everything else and that only Marxism can be the guide to revolution. A lesser but more sensitive man would have seen the paradoxes inherent in the Leninist solution. The party thus devised proved to be a workable concept under conditions of political suppression, but could hardly have survived had the Revolution of 1905 been followed by a really constitutional and free political life in Russia. The Bolsheviks proved to have the ideal organization and the ideal ideology to capitalize on the political and economic anarchy into which Russia was plunged after March 1917. Had the war and defeats not come, or had they come after another decade of vigorous industrialization, expansion of parliamentary customs, and the growth of the rural middle class, again it is most likely that the Bolsheviks would now figure in history as an insignificant fanatical wing of the Russian socialist movement.

The "ifs" and "buts" can be multiplied. What is important in this study is to observe the relationship of Marxism to Lenin's concepts. Lenin instinctively groped for the *uses* of Marxism under Russian conditions and found in it the road to revolution. There is enough democracy in Marxism to have enabled a Russian revolutionary to associate himself with the need for freedom felt by all Russian society before 1914. There is enough of the raw appeal of anti-industrialism and anarchism in Marxism to have enabled the Bolsheviks in 1917 to respond, and not insincerely, to the peasant's aspirations and to seize the leadership of the urban proletariat. What under normal "spontaneous" conditions of economic and political development would have been the fatal shortcoming of the doctrine proved under the anarchic conditions of 1917 to be the key to victory.

Lenin groped for the kind of party that Marx defined in the *Manifesto:*

> The Communists, therefore, are on the one hand, practically, the most advanced and resolute section of the working class parties of every country, that section which pushes forward all others; on the other hand, theoretically, they have over the great

mass of the proletariat the advantage of clearly understanding
the line of march, the conditions, and the ultimate general
results of the proletarian movement. (p. 334)

Under democratic or even quasi-democratic conditions the
workers will feel that they themselves have the "advantage of
clearly understanding the line of march" and that they do not
need the kind of party that tells them what they "really" want as
distinguished from their immediate and trivial demands. The
Leninist party is, then, practicable under conditions peculiar
to any society in transition, where the class interest of the
workers, in fact, the industrialized working class itself, has not
hardened into a definite mold, and where the process of
industrialization and modernization has all the confusing and
bewildering effects that it had in the West when Marx wrote the
Manifesto. The Leninist party becomes not only the repository
of dialectical wisdom; it becomes the dialectic itself. It is the
party that decides whether the "objective factors" make the
given society ripe for the bourgeois or socialist revolution,
whether capitalism has reached its full potentialities or not,
whether the given country, having passed the stage of
socialism, has entered the Communist stage. It is the party that
"decides" that the workers want to join the broad democratic
front (though the mass of the workers may be happily unaware
of the existence of the problem, not to mention the desire) or
whether, contrariwise, they want to strike on their own against
the bourgeois parties. The concept, to those who have
witnessed the behavior of the Communist parties in the West, is
quite fantastic. It is as if one were to get rid of the unpleasant
and unforeseen variations in the weather by vesting the power
to decide whether it rains or snows in a committee allegedly
endowed with the essence of wisdom about meteorology.

The full implications of the pattern became obvious only
after the Bolshevik's seizure of power and their attempted imposition on the socialist movement in the West and elsewhere
of the formula that had procured them victory. But the framework is set in *What Is to Be Done.* The pamphlet marked an as
yet overly intellectual statement of Leninism. The use
of ideology as a technique of acquisition of power be-

came clearer to Lenin as successive developments in Russia proceeded to offer both opportunities for and setbacks to revolutionary socialism. Thus the Revolution of 1905 provided a demonstration of the vitality of two issues that became incorporated into the victorious formula of 1917: the soviets and the peasant question. The revolution, in fact, demonstrated the indifference of life to stilted formulas: it was not a "bourgeois-democratic" revolution, nor was it a socialist one. It was a tremor of revolutionary excitement, which seized the Empire: peasant outbreaks, revolts of the sailors, and nationalist outbreaks in the non-Russian parts took place alongside and uncoordinated with the workers' revolutionary activity in the major industrial centers. For the first time, the raw materials of the effective revolutionary appeal were vividly demonstrated: the national aspirations of the non-Russians, the worker's propensity to form committees of action-soviets as the means of struggle, and—the master cause of all unrest, of all anarchism seeping into Russian society—the peasant's incoherent but steady protest against the social and political order, and his demand for more land immediately. Less than two generations after his emancipation, the peasant began to respond with political protest against the half-oppressed, half-emancipated status in which the measure had left him, against his exposure to, but not assimilation by, industrialization.

To Karl Marx, the peasant problem was, of course, one with which socialism would not have to deal at all. With his eye on the British economy of his time he assumed that capitalism would obligingly solve this problem as it would solve the problem of the artisan: by elimination. Large landed estates, run scientifically in accordance with advanced industrial techniques, would fall into the lap of socialism as easily as the great industrial and banking combines. The peasant, that curious figure defying class classification, radical and reactionary at once, attached to his property, enemy of the state and science, would not, in any appreciable quantity, be around by the time the expropriators are expropriated. Already the German Social Democracy had discovered that the German peasant, unlike his English brother, not only refused to die out but viewed with considerable distaste any socialist proposals to turn him into an agricultural worker.

By 1906 in Russia, it was fairly clear that the overwhelming mass of Russian peasants would never opt, either by election or revolution, for a program that would envisage their elimination as individual householders and cultivators, and that for all the alleged communistic propensities of the peasant and his traditional attachment to the *mir*, his radicalism included anti-property feelings on the subject of landlords, church, and state estates, but stopped short of the logical application of the same principle to his own holding. To the Marxist, the preservation of the peasant's small holdings or of their collective version in the *mir* was almost inconceivable. The small peasant bars the road to industrialization. The *mir*, in which some superficial Western observers professed to see a preview of the Soviet collective farm, was, of course, nothing of the sort. It was an obsolete form of communal organization of the peasantry in the Great Russian part of the empire, kept by the Tsarist government after the Emancipation for the purpose of preserving control over the peasant. To liberals and Marxists alike, the worship of the *mir* by the Slavophiles and the Populists was obscurantist nonsense. The *mir* was economically inefficient, inhibited better methods of cultivation as well as initiative and social mobility of the peasants. In retrospect, its belated retention helped to preserve in the peasant this peculiar combination of conservatism and radicalism, which under economic or political stress breaks out in anarchism.

It would take us too far to go into all the involved discussions of the peasant question that occupied Lenin and his Bolsheviks, the Mensheviks, and the Socialist Revolutionaries up to the Revolution of 1917. In April 1917, involved formulas and Marxist scruples all disappeared in the flash of intuition that Marxism indeed can come to power on the wave of anarchism; the painful formulas were superseded by Lenin's slogan: "Land to the peasants."

But as early as 1906 Lenin had been groping his way toward a formula with a concrete revolutionary appeal to the peasant. The Bolshevik program was explicit on the confiscation of all church-owned, landlords', and state lands, on giving the peasant the right to dispose freely of his plot. In a much more subdued tone, almost in small print, it was stated that *after* the democratic revolution the socialist party should strive to replace private property in land by national ownership.[25] Literal Marxism on the land question was unavailing in view of the Socialist Revolutionaries' and other Populists' hold on the peasant. Thus Lenin in practice appropriated the Socialist Revolutionary program on the peasant question, while he retained, for what seemed the distant future, the Marxist aim of socialization of the land.

How the ideas of *What Is to Be Done* cease after 1905 to be bookish concepts and become endowed with life is equally demonstrated in Lenin's attitude toward soviets. The intellectual enemy of spontaneity could not at first take kindly to the spectacle of *ad hoc* committees of the workers thrown up by a revolutionary situation or a general strike, committees subject to no common ideology, occupied exclusively with the conduct of the struggle at hand, and uniting people of the most diverse political opinions. This practical application of syndicalism, for that was what the soviets in 1905 and initially in 1917 were, must have appeared to Lenin as being quite far from the idea of disciplined revolutionary action by the workers in obedience to the call of the socialist party. To digress, it is impossible to overestimate how much Lenin revered the German Social Democrats and dreamed of the Russian Marxists' coming to resemble in organization and power their German brothers. This worship, which collapsed when the German Socialists meekly acquiesced in the Kaiser's war, kept Lenin, before 1914, from the complete and conscious repudiation of parliamentarism that was implicit in his theories and activity as early as 1902-1903. Yet the experience of 1905 demonstrated the revolutionary viability of the soviets. It must have become obvious that revolutionary socialism under Russian conditions could operate more successfully through the fluid structure of the soviets, whose very looseness and improvisation favored the kind of disciplined party which the Bolsheviks were, or were to become, than through formal, regularly elected parliamentary bodies, where under the most favorable conditions the Bolsheviks would be in a minority. The full realization of the role of the soviets again belongs to 1917. Lenin's slogan "All power to the soviets" becomes one of the key factors in enhancing the Bolsheviks' popularity and influence. In a volatile, unstable organization, which a soviet of workers or soldiers represents, the decisiveness and unity of the Bolsheviks, their lack of scruples in following the political mood of the moment give them an enormous advantage even over other revolutionary parties.

What is the sum of the effects of the Revolution of 1905 on Lenin? It is not unfair to characterize it as the growing realization, though he does not admit it to himself or to others, that a revolutionary situation in Russia would not follow any neat socialist preconceptions, but would be, in essence, an anarchist revolution. For the Marxist party to succeed, political authority would have to collapse; the instruments of coercion (i.e., the army) would have to become demoralized; the mass of the peasantry would press for their immediate interests; and political power would become parceled out among a variety of local organs—the soviets. The elaborate agrarian programs and parliamentary schemes would be of no avail. What would count would be the sensitivity and responsiveness to the variety of revolutionary impulses stirring up the society. The task of the socialist party, in Lenin's view after 1905, becomes not so much to "combat spontaneity," but to *manage* revolutionary spontaneity without becoming subservient to it.

Again, the realization is neither full nor decisive until 1914. The pattern of literal Marxism—industrialization, the bourgeois democratic revolution, and only then the socialist revolution—is persuasive enough to make Lenin reject Trotsky's thesis that in Russia the historical process might be telescoped and that a socialist revolution might follow the bourgeois one immediately, rather than after an interval. Until the war and the collapse of the liberal international order and, in his eyes, the abdication of the Western socialists, Lenin cannot embrace the thesis of "permanent revolution," and the fact that he does not do so is a tribute to his realism. The Revolution of 1905 was followed by two major reforms, which, if they had had time to work out for more than a few years, would have made the permanent revolution of 1917 most unlikely.

The constitutionalism introduced after 1905 was of the

lamest sort; and the parliament, the Duma, was very far from being a true legislative and representative body. Yet the rudiments of parliamentary procedure and civil rights existed, and they began tempering the revolutionary protest and channeling it into concrete political demands. More important, Prime Minister Stolypin instituted agrarian reforms, which looked forward to the break-up of the *mir* and to allowing the capitalist process to take its course in the countryside. Like his predecessor Witte, Stolypin believed in bureaucratically inspired industrialization as being the only solution of Russia's predicament. The break-up of the commune and a vast program of peasant resettlement would enable "nature," i.e., capitalism, to take care of the peasant-land problem. Eventually a class of individual, prosperous peasants would replace the inefficient, discontent-breeding communes and would become the rural middle class. The financial burdens on the peasantry, dating from the Emancipation, were lifted, and incentive was given to the peasants to become "separators"—to take their land out of the communes. The scheme, in the few years it enjoyed, proved to be a success.

It is unlikely that the sum total of the reforms and the social engineering by the Tsarist bureaucrats would have undercut social discontent or the appeal of socialism. But the reforms were providing this institutional and social framework for industrialization, which, as we have seen, channels the revolutionary protest into reformism and strips the socialism of the worker and peasant of its anarchistic and hence revolutionary character. The Marxist in Lenin had to greet these developments with an ambivalent feeling: from one point of view they were according to the script. Capitalism in Russian society was becoming stronger, less hampered by the pre-capitalist remnants. Yet by the same token the prospects for revolutionary socialism were becoming less hopeful. Trotsky's permanent-revolution theory frankly implied that the socialist revolution would emerge from backward rather than advanced capitalism. But Lenin was never ready to depart from even the *letter* of Marxism unless there were concrete revolutionary dividends to be gathered up. The acceptance of the practice of permanent revolution was thus postponed until there was in fact permanent revolution in Russia.

One is struck again by the fact that a certain narrowness of mind—perhaps one might call it the lack of speculative imagination—was a contributing factor in Lenin's greatness. Before 1914, he could believe that he was a good social-democrat, with equal emphasis on both sides of the hyphen. In 1917, he became, for all purposes, an exponent of anarchism. All this time, his belief in the canon of Marxism remained undisturbed. This quality, which becomes inherent in Communism, cannot be traced exclusively to personal characteristics. It is the product of thorough immersion in Marxism under conditions of society where the logic and the conclusions of the doctrine are *not* shown to be mutually contradictory. In 1917, without the slightest hesitation or introspection, Lenin was to grasp that although the letter of Marxism includes democracy and ordains socialism to proceed from advanced capitalism, the spirit of revolutionary Marxism is the exploitation of the anarchism inherent in backwardness.

The breakdown of the international liberal order illustrated by World War I was the signal that the synthesis of democracy and Marxism implied in the position of the German Social Democracy—especially in that of Karl Kautsky, who had been to Lenin before 1914 a theoretical guide and exemplar almost on the order of Marx and Engels—had equally broken down. In his most unoriginal work, *Imperialism,* written in exile in Switzerland in 1915, Lenin "demonstrated" the necessary tendency of capitalism, in its later stages, toward monopoly and then imperialism. While the argument of the book is borrowed from J. A. Hobson's book of the same title, and the Marxist interpretation from Hilferding and Rosa Luxemburg, the book in conjunction with the war arrives at the most catastrophic and hence, for a Marxist, optimistic view of the evolution of capitalism. The prosperity of capitalism, its ability to raise the worker's standard of living in the West, its democratic features—all these apparent refutations of Marx are but temporary delays of the inevitable doom, purchased by the ruthless exploitation of colonial and backward areas. The postponement of Marx's prognosis is but temporary, for imperialism is bound to end up in vast conflicts among the imperialists: "From all that we have said about the economic essence of Imperialism it follows that it should be characterized as transitory, or to be more exact, dying capitalism."[26]

The apparent contradiction of Marx by the facts is thus explained away. There is no reason to soften the revolutionary rigor of Marxism by reading into it democratic and parliamentary postulates. The war is the dying pangs of capitalism. In their struggle for investment markets, the capitalists have to arm the proletariat. The expropriation of the expropriators will now become an international phenomenon, with the war-weary workers turning their arms against their capitalist masters, transforming the imperialist war into civil wars for socialism. The war enables Lenin to dispel the last doubts about the incompatibility of Marxism with an outright revolutionary position. The undercurrent of doubt, the perhaps subconscious questioning of the prophecies of the master can now be laid aside. Marxism means revolution. Those Western socialists who participate in the war activities of their states or who prattle about pacifism are traitors and opportunists.

It is impossible to explain the concentration, decisiveness, and drive of Lenin and the Bolsheviks in 1917 except by the enthusiasm of believers whose doubts about their canon had collapsed and who saw in their faith an infallible guide to success. In a few days after his arrival in Russia in April 1917, Lenin was able to dissipate the last social democratic notions of his colleagues and to undercut any attempt at a reunion with the Mensheviks. Though the Bolsheviks had existed as a separate party since 1912, no one had previously excluded the aim of a reunion of all the Russian Marxists. But soon after his arrival Lenin wanted the party's name to be changed to "Communist," so as to consecrate the break with the past tradition of doubts, democratic scruples, and reinterpretations. He was to get his way only after the November Revolution, though by that time the whole democratic tradition had already been rejected in fact.

The revolution which in March 1917 overthrew the Tsar and vested power in the provisional government is classified in Marxist semantics as a "bourgeois democratic revolution." In reality, it very soon became much more than that. The whole structure of authority, the rudimentary and growing social and political institutions of industrialization, were swept away. The veneer of authority vested in the provisional government concealed the essential state of anarchy, political as well as social. As Sir John Maynard wrote: "In explanation of what happened in rural Russia, let me again emphasize the virtual disappearance—outside of the *Mir* and the Canton Committee—of all authority. Tolstoy had counselled his countrymen that each should say: 'For me there is no state.' They had taken his advice and the State had vanished into air."[27] The soviets in the cities and soon among the armed units even at the front shared in this anarchic process. In brief, Russia found itself in a state of anarchy with just a shell of parliamentary and modern political institutions imperfectly concealing the chaos. The political party closest to anarchism, the Socialist Revolutionaries, became the most popular movement in the country. Even after the November coup of the Bolsheviks in the election to the ill-fated Constituent Assembly of January 1918, the Socialist Revolutionaries demonstrated that their combination of anarchism and agrarian socialism commanded the sympathy of the majority of the electorate. But anarchism, while it is the mood of revolution, cannot become the organizational principle of it. The Socialist Revolutionaries, with their interminable dissensions, with opinions among the leaders ranging from constitutionalism and the desire to continue the unpopular war to direct revolutionary action and defeatism, demonstrated the historical incapacity of anarchism to provide viable political and economic formulas.

The slogans—All power to the Soviets! Land to the peasants! End to the war!—thrown by Lenin on his return revealed his identification of revolutionary Marxism with anarchism. The party built upon the denial of spontaneity and upon the principle of centralization and military discipline was in the best position to use the spontaneous revolutionary impulse of the people without itself being carried by it. Until the end of the Civil War, the Bolsheviks not only used anarchist slogans and practices; they became in all respects, *save the internal organization of their party,* anarchists. It was by deepening the anarchist character of the revolution, by sabotaging any attempt to erect a temporary shelter for constitutionalism, that the Bolsheviks sought power. The Mensheviks, or most of them, clung to the literal interpretation of Marxism, to the impossibility of erecting socialism in Russia without first going through the democratic phase. No Marxist inhibitions held Lenin back from advocating the complete smashing of the state by parceling out power to the soviets; from assuring the Bolsheviks the support or at least the benevolent neutrality of the peasants by inciting them to seize the landlords' estates and force the "separators" back into the *mir;* and from encouraging the dismemberment of the empire by a radical advocacy of national self-determination and of defeatism in the face of the German advance. It is customary to attribute all these moves to political acumen rather than to ideology. But the latter provided a wonderful reassurance to the Bolsheviks that in sponsoring anarchism they were in fact promoting socialism. Unbelieving apostles, it has been said, are usually unconvincing. Because of Marxism, Lenin's party could and with conviction did become, in revolution, anarchists, just as with revolution and Civil War barely completed they could turn around and begin to stamp out the anarchy, begin to build modern history's most centralized and absolute state.

An observer as sympathetic to revolutionary Marxism as Rosa Luxemburg could not, in her comments on the Bolshevik revolution, restrain her misgivings about its anarchist character. The Bolsheviks, she observed, in their desire to propitiate the peasant, officially nationalized land, but in fact let the peasants seize and cultivate land in small units. More fundamentally, Lenin erred in instituting revolutionary terror, which denied democracy and the freedom of activity even to other socialist and revolutionary parties. But her criticisms failed to perceive that revolutionary Marxism *has* to be essentially anarchist in character. It has no chance unless the structure of authority and the habits proper to organized industrial society break down, and it forsakes its opportunity if it sticks to the democratic and centralistic parts of the Marxian canon.

The immersion of the Bolsheviks in anarchism is best

demonstrated by Lenin's *State and Revolution,* written on the eve of the Bolsheviks' *coup.* For all the self-conscious denials that his theory of the state is anarcho-syndicalist rather than Marxist, Lenin propagates the views for which Communists in 1921 and 1922 were, at his command, to be read out of the party, the views which in 1921 were to inspire Kronstadt sailors to rise against a Bolshevik regime already on the road to centralization and bureaucracy. The state is to be smashed away, the bureaucracy and professional civil servants abolished; egalitarianism is to rule supreme—all this, not in the distant state of Communism, but at once under the dictatorship of the proletariat.

> All officials, without exception, elected and subject to recall *at any time,* their salaries reduced to "workingmen's wages"—these simple and "self evident" democratic measures, which completely uniting the interests of the workers and the majority of the peasants, at the same time serve as a bridge leading from capitalism to socialism.[28]

And what, if not anarchism, is this statement:

> With such *economic* prerequisites it is perfectly possible immediately, within twenty-four hours after the overthrow of the capitalists and bureaucrats, to replace them, in the control of production and distribution, in the business of *control* of labour and products, by the armed workers, by the whole people in arms. . . . *All* citizens become employees and workers of *one* national state "syndicate." All that is required is that they should work equally, should regularly do their share of work, and should receive equal pay.[29]

These words of August 1917 should be read in conjunction with the plea for a centralized (i.e., hierarchical) party of *professional revolutionaries* in *What Is to Be Done.* They should be read in conjunction with what Lenin had to say immediately after the revolution when he confessed unabashedly that it was impossible to replace the capitalists and bureaucrats in "twenty-four hours." Every factory, he was to say in 1919, every industry, represents the concentrated experience of capitalism which we do not have. He was not as yet to say, as Stalin was to explain eleven or twelve years later, that socialism had to acquire the experience and, incidentally, the methods of capitalism. But Lenin was ready to sneer at those who accused the Bolsheviks of inconsistency or hypocrisy, now that the Communists' anarchism and belief in the people were visibly cooling off: "As if one could undertake a major revolution, knowing in advance how to conclude it! As if this knowledge could be drawn from books!"[30] And he went on to talk about the need for military and civilian specialists.

Here, then, is Leninism. Is it an ideology? Or is it a political temperament and an eclectic technique enabling one to respond to power situations, at one point to be a social democrat, at another an anarchist, at another a bureaucratic enforcer of state power and capitalism? The sum of theoretical innovations by Lenin is meager; his views on Marxism are usually applications to Russian conditions of some German Social Democrat's interpretations. Yet it is Lenin's *use* of Marxism that stamps him as a new and, in a way, original synthesizer of the original doctrine and the Russian revolutionary conditions. In 1917, Lenin was capable of grasping the revolutionary sense of Marxism, its portrayal of the peasant's and the proletarian's psychology of opposition to the state and the forces of modernism, and applying it to the problem of seizing power.

His socialist opponents, who saw Marxism only as a series of political prescriptions based on economic stages of development, were inhibited from seeing that a Marxist revolution was possible in Russia precisely because capitalism had *not* fully developed in the country, precisely because Russia was *not* ready for socialism. The same instinct after the Revolution and even during the latter stages of the Civil War caused Lenin to begin to discard the anarchism and egalitarianism needed for popular support during the struggle for power. Whence came the realization that real national self-determination, real regional autonomy, and really independent trade unions were against the grain of Communism? It is easy to equate them with unideological attachment to power and the very human unwillingness of rulers to weaken their authority. But the almost immediate, sharp reversal of party policy would have been impossible without the psychological mechanism instilled by Marxism in its devotees, which makes them prone to anarchism in the time of revolution, to centralism and inegalitarianism after power has been won. It was Lenin's achievement to construct a party that could best instill in its members the separateness of the two parts of the task: one, the conquest of power; the other, the use of power. This lack of susceptibility of the Communist party to democracy, to the desires of the people whom it represented, to their own slogans, was not only freely acknowledged but boasted of by the Bolshevik leaders. Said Zinoviev, then the spokesman for Lenin, at the Eighth Congress:

> The whole basis of our disputes with the so-called "economists," the Mensheviks . . . was based on [their] confusion of two concepts, the party and the class. Those people did not understand that the party is different from the class and the class from the party; that the party should be the leading part of the class, that it sets aims which the working class does not understand completely today but will understand tomorrow.[31]

It would have been impossible to make this avowal of what in common-sense language is simply duplicity without the strong sanction of and unbounded belief in the ideology. Otherwise Zinoviev's statement, which in various versions has been the leitmotif of the Communist leaders from 1902 up to our own day, would have been a species of self-destructive cynicism verging on the most extreme naiveté.

Thus on the morrow of the Revolution "the aim which the working class does not understand today" is the exact opposite of the aims it understood and supported in the Revolution: the building of the stong authoritarian state; industrialization, which will require methods more severe than those employed by early capitalism; and the consequent erection of a totalitarian structure. The totalitarianism inherent in building an industrialized society under Marxist auspices was brought on by the very success of the revolutionary slogans. Not only the workers but many of the Party members were carried away by the slogans they had been proclaiming. It took Lenin's party some time to realize that Marxism in power is the exact opposite of Marxism in revolution and that the first task of the victorious Communist party is the extirpation of revolutionary democracy and anarchism in its own ranks.

— 5 —
The Other Side of Marxism

With the Bolshevik Revolution and the almost miraculous survival by the Communist regime of the attacks by diverse domestic and foreign forces, a new era was opened in the history of the Marxist movement. Prior to November 1917, Marxism had always been in opposition or in revolution; now a party proclaiming itself to be an orthodox Marxist movement achieved power in a great country. Enough has already been said about this feat's being achieved under conditions quite contrary to Marx's expectations and in the spirit that we have classified as anarchist rather than Marxist, if by Marxism is meant a scrupulous adherence to the main strictures of Marx and Engels. But once the Civil War and the danger of the immediate overthrow of their regime was over, the Bolsheviks were faced with an unprecedented task. Even the external characteristics of this task were back-breaking: the economy thoroughly ruined, the promising industrial development prior to 1917 almost totally undone, the ruling party a garrison amidst a hostile or indifferent population, the idea and the reality of the modern state barely visible against the canvas of universal lawlessness and disorganization. And the fundamental issue: How to build socialism? Where to begin and with what? The idea of a universal socialist revolution in the wake of the Russian one, of the help extended to the young socialist state by its more advanced partners was shown by 1921 to have been a mirage. To the Communists fell the historical task of showing what the other side of Marxism was, demonstrating socialism in action, proving that Marxism could not only carry off a revolution but rule and develop a society.

Stalinism

To "practical people" in 1921, socialism was a vague concept associated with street fighting, strikes, and fantastic theories. Communism in its Russian version was identified with a group of wild revolutionaries, whose very appearance and behavior marked their separation from the main stream of European culture and development. Anarchism, atheism, terror, and destruction of private property—these were the things for which the Bolsheviks were known. Could those people organize the state, collect taxes, fit their country with a modern economy and civil service? Where was a guide to enable them to set and develop the intricate mechanism of the modern state and economy? Even sympathetic observers who applauded the revolutionary romanticism of the movement, its aura of struggle, of bold innovations, even of terror, felt pity at its predicament: How would these revolutionary heroes become prosaic legislators, tax gatherers, and managers? How would they stay in power, not to mention the lifting up of their barbarous society to socialism?

A revolutionary optimist in the West would have predicated success upon one thing: the Revolution, having freed the people from the shackles of capitalism and the remnants of feudalism, would have created a new and unprecedented grass-roots democracy and popular participation among the people of Russia, and almost with no direction or compulsion the whole nation would bend its energies to the task of creating a better life. A more moderate supporter of the new Soviet state would "realistically" expect the regime to cool off in its revolutionary fervor and, after an interval, to rule in the usual way, in the immemorial fashion of revolutionary groups who, having seized power under the banner of a utopian creed, after due time revert to the "usual" ways of politics and economics. The beginnings of the New Economic Policy, inaugurated by Lenin in 1921, were greeted by the "realists" as proof of their wisdom: the regime was settling down, forsaking the extremes of Marxism, and allowing a modicum of private property and initiative. The political aspect of the regime? Here historical experts knowingly discoursed on the eternal forces of Russian history: the people's susceptibility to despotism, their instinct for "collectivity," which made them endure the despotism of the Bolsheviks as cheerfully as they had that of Peter the Great. (The comparisons with Ivan the Terrible became more fashionable with the period of Stalin's terror.)

What the realists, the revolutionary sympathizers, the historical experts, and those who saw in the Bolsheviks simply the embodiment of Antichrist all agreed upon was that the thing least important about the Bolshevik state was its alleged connection with the obscure and impractical theories of Karl Marx. Yet, paradoxically, it is Marxism and its importance in the development of the Soviet Union which makes the preceding judgments superficial. Had the foreign observers taken the trouble to study the ideology and the extent to which both the leaders and the rank and file of the Bolsheviks were grounded in it, they would have realized the cohesive function of the doctrine, the extent to which it held the party together, and the degree to which it determined the character of postrevolutionary Leninism as well as the main traits of what we call Stalinism. It is difficult for us in the West to admit and understand how real, live human beings can be affected in their behavior, in their concept of self-interest and duties, by something somebody scribbled a century before; and it is most difficult to conceive of people in power, with a multitude of choices, being directed by the imperatives of an ideology. This is the basic reason why so many have seen the development and policies of the Soviet Union as an enigma inexplicable by anything in historical experience. It is this pragmatic bias, in reality, the unreflecting acceptance of *our own ideological premises* as having universal validity, that must be overcome to assess the development of Communism.

The theory of and habituation to Marxism were all that the Bolsheviks had in the way of economic and state-building experience. To the most unfriendly observer, the magnitude of the task, and the administrative and economic skill displayed by the Bolsheviks in restoring their country's economy and in laying the administrative foundations for the prodigious transformation of the whole society that took place under Stalin are extremely impressive. The Bolsheviks were imbued with administrative and economic instincts without which the later transformation of Russian society would have been inconceivable. One is drawn to think of another group of fanatics who, faced with concrete material tasks, displayed engineering and managerial abilities unsuspected in their original obscurantist creed: the Saint-Simonians. It is as if the selective function of Marxism had been to draw into the Leninist party the people who, under the cover of their revolutionary doctrinairism, possessed in the highest degree the managerial and administrative instincts required to erect the modern industrial state. Projecting into the Stalinist period the picture of the Communist, one sees him in Marx's words:

> Fanatically bent on making value expand itself, he ruthlessly forces the human race to produce for production's sake; he thus forces the development of the productive forces of society, and creates those material conditions, which alone can form the real basis of a higher form of society, a society in which the full and free development of every individual forms the ruling principle.[1]

Is this Marx's description of the socialist? No, this description—and how well it will fit the self-proclaimed task of the Communist party under Stalin—is of the capitalist.

Before the Communists could turn to the task, which can unabashedly be characterized as the construction of Marxist capitalism, they had to dispose of revolutionary Marxism. One may think of Marxism as a "two-stage" ideology. The revolutionary stage drops off after the revolution. The democratic undertones of Marxism are disposed of, revolutionary anarchism is extirpated, and the task of construction in spirit and by means antithetical to the revolutionary stage is begun. The process is neither smooth nor automatic. It comes in a series of realizations, first by Lenin, then by Stalin, that a faithful application of the principles under which the party had been carried to power would, in the postrevolutionary era, hamper and make impossible the construction of socialism. It comes almost as the process of natural selection: those Bolshevik leaders who had become most imbued with the democratic and anarchist slogans of the revolution, those who temperamentally were most averse to the negation of the revolution that now must take place, get broken and then eliminated. The process becomes associated with the struggle for power, where the fighters and orators who made the revolution possible have to yield to the administrators.

And the political transformation has its social and artistic accompaniment. The revolution and the postrevolutionary era extending until the late 1920's is characterized by the outburst of social and artistic exuberance that always follows in the wake of a great historical transformation. Unrestrained individualism and nonconformity in personal and artistic behavior, unconventionality and inventiveness in the arts follow November 1917. As the new order crystallizes and the main task of society becomes to industrialize, the shackles of conformity, orderliness, and socialist respectability are imposed upon the arts and social mores. It is as if all the varied forces which had assured that the bourgeois culture and mores of the nineteenth century became subjugated to the task of industrialization—nonconformist moral precepts, intellectual and artistic fashions of Victorianism, the overwhelming materialism of society—now became concentrated in the interpretation of Marxism that the party was imposing upon Russian society.

In retrospect, then, this is the picture of the interpretation of Marxism imposed upon Russian society by Communism. While it is possible to attribute the terror, violence, and pathological aspects of the process to the tyrannical personality of one man, or a group of men, it is impossible to deny that the essential authoritarianism of the process is implied in the logic of Marxism and in the concept of the party which boasts that it "sets the aims which the working class in their totality does not understand today but will understand tomorrow."

On the morrow of the revolution, the masses—to use this unlovely expression of the Communist vocabulary—want socialism. But they do not "understand" that socialism can come only to an industrialized society. They "understand" even less that industrialization means a strong centralized authority, the strong state. Who does not understand, said Stalin in 1930, when he could afford to be frank, that it is one of the creative paradoxes of Marxism that, although we Communists are for an eventual demise of the state, we are for the present for the dictatorship of the proletariat, "which is the strongest and the most powerful form of government of all that have existed?"[2]

Had the masses understood that, the Bolshevik revolution would in all likelihood not have taken place. The state was to be smashed, popular initiative and participation were to take the place of the professional civil service, the necessary economic and political coordination was to be the result of free and spontaneous coordination of autonomous, democratically elected regional authorities. This promise of revolutionary Bolshevism, one of the main points of its popular appeal in an anarchically minded society, was solemnly embodied in the first Soviet constitutional documents. The letter of the law followed closely the modified anarchism of Lenin's *State and Revolution*; the unwieldy constitutional structure seemed to offer the widest scope to local autonomy; during the very first years of the Soviet regime, no *formal* links connected the Soviet republics of Russia, Ukraine, and Byelorussia. Individual workers' unions and the unions as a whole arrogated to themselves considerable powers over the industries. Short of the temporary requirements of the united effort against counterrevolutionary forces, the constitutional structure promised to offer the widest scope for local and professional autonomy. With the rather considerable exception of members of the former exploiting classes, democratic rights were guaranteed to everybody, again with temporary limitations for the period of the Civil War. If we add the peasants' appropriation of the landlords' and the state's estates and the egalitarian mood and practices of society, we get an official structure just this side of anarchism.

Yet from the very beginning this picture has been a mirage. The *real state* in Soviet Russia—the agency not only for political and economic coordination and legislation but also for the vast schemes of social engineering and of coercion of society—has always existed in the Communist party. The "bourgeois democratic" state has, in effect, been smashed; but, in ironic fulfillment of Karl Marx's dictum of the state's being the executive committee of the exploiting class, the executive organs of the Communist party became the state. The decentralization, national and regional autonomy, and autonomy of various social classes were and have been the façade behind which the real political process in Soviet Russia has been taking place within the Communist party. If the party was to be monolithic and united, then all the constitutional autonomies and separations of power were not to matter one iota. If the party was to be run dictatorially, as turned out to be the case, then all the guarantees and inviolabilities were not worth the paper on which they were inscribed. *The party became the state.*

The struggle for the centralized state was bound to take place within the party. The story has often been told of the attrition and then elimination of the last, lingering democratic instincts within the Bolshevik party. A few weeks after the November 1917 coup, a few Bolshevik leaders could still resign from Lenin's cabinet in protest against his concept and practice of one-party government. Yet these doubts soon disappeared, and the party unanimously supported the suppression of all parties, even of other revolutionary and socialist parties, and the curtailment of freedom of the press and of political life in general. The remnants of any democratic feeling in what used to be the Social Democratic Workers' Party of Russia evaporated with such rapidity that, in 1926 at the Fifteenth Party Conference, Zinoviev, fighting against Stalin for his political life, could yet describe as an "unheard-of libel" the accusation that he and the rest of the anti-Stalin opposition wanted to transform one-party rule into a "democratic republic." Lenin's party was not likely, in any case, to attract as members, people with overly democratic instincts.

Other groups and parties could be eliminated, but the ruling party itself remained, for a time, as the arena of contending principles. The party was—and on this all its members agreed—the vanguard of the working class. But in which

direction should the vanguard move? The acceptance of an
ideology as the ruling, if not the only, guide of action is always
a dangerous inhibition to the freedom of a political organism.
Personal conflicts, differing temperaments, must be expressed
in the ideological jargon. It is difficult for the contestants to
admit that there can be several alternative courses of action.
There *must* be only one "correct" line, and the proponents of
other views must be in error or, worse, in sin, or, to express it in
the Communist parlance, subject to other class interests,
viewing problems from the non-Marxist standpoint. What,
then, inhibited from the very beginning any democratic life
within the party (and it should be remembered that when
Lenin formulated his concept of the party in 1902 and 1903 he
explained its undemocratic features as imposed by the then
impossibility of free political life in Imperial Russia) was the
concept that the Bolsheviks were not a *mere* party: they were
the carriers of the true ideology and the correct interpretation of
history. It is as if the fathers of the American Constitution had
not been guided in their deliberations by the problem of
devising the most practical and workable constitutional
arrangement, but had operated from the assumption that on
every issue—even the most minute—there was only one correct
solution, which must be found in and justified by recourse to
the writings of, say, John Locke.

Whatever the personalities involved, the inherent ideological assumption of the Communist party made it of necessity a
totalitarian party. What is referred to as the period of party
democracy, until 1925-1926 when Stalin emerged as the
undoubted dictator, is really the period of groping *for the
organizational expression* of the totalitarian formula; and it is
unlikely that the result would have been less totalitarian, even
if the application might have been more humane or less
efficient, had Lenin lived on or had Zinoviev or Trotsky
emerged in ascendance.

It was this inner logic of the development of the party that
made it not only the instrument of the centralized authority of
all kinds—something which is implied in Marxism—but also
an instrument of totalitarianism, i.e., of suppression, and of
liquidation of any freedom of discussion, any free development

at all—something for which not Marx but Lenin's concept of the party and its application by Stalin must be blamed. It was, then, almost inevitable that Marxism, which, whatever one may say about it, is a rationalist and intellectual technique, would be elevated into a mystique and ritual and that disagreements or varying interpretations would become translated into the problems of orthodoxy and heresy. The product of nineteenth-century liberalism, the technique for modernization and industrialization, became the means of ritualistic incantations accompanying purges and brain-washing.

It is this aspect of Marxism in the Soviet Union, the horrible terminology of "left" and "right" "deviations," the paranoiac expansion of the study of class and personal motivations (if Zinoviev and Kamenev were against Stalin, it "really" meant that they had been against Lenin and that they were "really" ready to sell the Soviet state to the Western imperialists), that makes the importance of ideology in the Soviet context so difficult for a Western observer to discern. We long for a direct rather than a circuitous and ritualistic statement of the relationship of the aims and means. Why could not Lenin after the revolution simply say: "The revolution is over; the logic of the situation, which is also the logic of Marxism, means that we cannot have socialism without industrialization. We cannot have industrialization without a strong centralized authority, without experts, wide disparities of pay, and so on. Hence, we must forget all the nonsense propagated by us during the revolution about smashing the state, equality of pay, status, and so forth. Let us get on with the job." But before this degree of rationality and ideological introspection could be *almost* achieved by the party (and when it is completely achieved Marxism will cease to play any role in the Soviet Union) Communism had to go through debates, splits, purges, and terror.

The most immediate difficulty was that the party itself was thoroughly imbued with democratic and semianarchist ideology. Any drastic attempt to apply the logic of Marxism in defiance of its revolutionary spirit would have met, in the Communist party of 1919 or 1920, with repudiation by a vast majority of its members. It is instructive to study one aspect of the problem centering about the so-called Workers' Opposition. This group, as early as 1919, attacked the tendency to build the state bureaucracy, to employ bourgeois specialists, in brief, the whole attempt to create the machinery of state under Soviet power. The Workers' Opposition and the Democratic Centralists, another group akin in spirit, discerned as early as 1919 and 1920 (the period which, from the present perspective or even that of thirty years ago, appears as one of drastic economic egalitarianism in society and of relative democratic procedures in the party) the growth of the oligarchical principle in Communism and the related phenomena of official favoritism and bureaucratic mentality. This, to repeat, took place in the USSR of 1920, which, from today's perspective, looks like an anarchist paradise. Yet a considerable body of Communists was already chafing under inegalitarian conditions and dictatorial and bureaucratic methods in the party and the state!

What did the Workers' Opposition want? Their whole complaint is not so much a definite policy as a reflection of a malaise—the feeling in wide circles of the workers that something is wrong with the revolution, that the reality of Communist life is not in accordance with Communist promises. The specific proposals advanced by the opposition within the party look, in effect, toward syndicalism. It is difficult otherwise to interpret the leader of this opposition, Mme. Kollontay, as she phrases the demands:

> To form a body from the workers-producers themselves—for administering the people's economy. . . . All appointments to the administrative economic positions shall be made with the consent of the union. All candidates nominated by the union are nonremovable. All officials appointed by the union are responsible to and may be recalled by it.[3]

The practical effect would be the vesting of the control of the economy—more properly speaking, of government—in the hands of the workers' unions rather than the party. Mme. Kollontay, daughter of a Tsarist general, did not hesitate to recommend that the Communist party should become even more proletarian and that all the nonworking elements who joined the party since the November Revolution should be expelled.

> Appointments by the leaders must be done away with, and replaced by the elective principle all along the party line ... all the cardinal questions of party activity and Soviet policy are to be submitted to the consideration of the rank and file and only after that are to be supervised by the leaders.[4]

It is even possible to feel some sympathy with Lenin, head of a devastated and disorganized country, confronted with this millennial demand to introduce immediately a syndicalist utopia, until we remember that Mme. Kollontay's demands are but more detailed elaborations of what Lenin had said in *State and Revolution*. The Workers' Opposition argued from the premise of the Communist and proletarian dictatorship, with little thought of the rights of the nonproletarian majority of the people.[5] But the fulfillment of its postulates could only have meant the breakdown of the incipient structure of the Soviet state.

Not connected with the Workers' Opposition but another evidence of the anarchist mood and condition of the country was the uprising at the great naval base of Kronstadt. In 1917 the Bolsheviks had no stronger supporters than the sailors of the Baltic Fleet. Then, in 1921, the very same element rose against them. The sailors claimed freedom of activity for all the left socialist and Anarchist parties, full freedom for the peasants to do as they liked with their land, abolition of the special position of the Bolshevik party, and equal food rations for all.[6] Both within and without the party, the Bolsheviks were confronted by the danger that the same tide of anarchism that had carried them to power would now engulf them.

Two things became obvious within the context of the Russian situation between 1920 and 1922. The Marxist instinct of the Communist elite and their self-interest in preserving power went hand in hand in keeping Lenin and his group from giving in to the democratic and or syndicalist demands. At the same time, a complete about-face from the slogans of November 1917, frankness about the goals and methods of the Communist state (such as was to be exhibited by Stalin in the 1930's) not only would have been psychologically impossible but would have shocked the majority of their own followers to the extent that the leaders could not have kept power. It took all Lenin's prestige, as well as considerable chicanery, to defeat the Workers' Opposition at the party congresses. The Kronstadt uprising had to be drowned in blood.

What would have been the effect had Lenin said, in 1921, as Stalin was to say in 1930, that egalitarianism in wages was a petty bourgeois superstition and had nothing to do with Marxism and that the unions should not get in the way of industrial management? The man who approached this bluntness about the meaning of Marxism in postrevolutionary Russia was Lev Trotsky. It was he who employed "specialists" in the army and industry and talked with frankness about the economy's requiring complete subordination of the unions to the party. But this very bluntness and forthrightness, Trotsky's ability to see the sense of Marxism in every concrete situation, was probably the cause of his future weakness among the rank and file of the party and among its leaders, of the attribution to Trotsky of the dictatorial designs that Stalin was soon to carry out so successfully. The practical meaning of Marxism under the conditions of Russia of 1921—the building of the strong centralized state, the use of essentially capitalist methods and incentives to restore and then to industrialize the economy of the country—could not have been bluntly acknowledged or formulated, in the face of the anarchist and democratic sentiments intensified by revolutionary Marxism. An outright about-face would have led to other Kronstadts and would have magnified beyond control the turbulence of inner-party struggle.

It is ideological self-deception rather than conscious hypocrisy that led Communist autocracy to change thus into outright totalitarianism and made Leninism shade into Stalinism. Neither Lenin nor his associates could acknowledge to themselves that Marxism, Communism, now must mean something other than what it meant during the Revolution.

The old terms have to be preserved. Those who propagate the Bolshevik slogans of the past "must" be shown to be "really" counterrevolutionaries. The socialist of other varieties, exponents of popular discontent, must be demonstrated to be foreign agents, agents of the landlords, and Tsarist generals. "Objective historical reality" teaches the party that a Menshevik pleading for democratic rights is a counterrevolutionary and a worker demanding the fulfillment of the Bolshevik promises of 1917, an agent of the White Guards. The same element of part self-deception, part political acumen keeps Lenin from formulating clearly the issues separating him from the opposition in the party. The workers' unions are not yet fully subjugated, as Trotsky had desired, but are proclaimed, in a soothing formula, to be schools of Communism for the workers. At the same time the administration of the party is turned over to those who appear most capable of subduing its unruly and syndicalist wings and of turning it into a monolithic organization. The New Economic Policy of tolerance toward the remaining elements of capitalism and of relief for the peasant is proclaimed as a measure to restore the economy rather than a drastic departure from the promise of the revolution.

Inherent in all these measures, or in the way they were presented, was the attrition of the sense of political reality, an attrition characteristic of true totalitarianism. Lenin's party recognized that "the masses" might not share its aims or approve its policies of the moment, but it hoped it would win their support in the future. Stalin's party assumed and required immediate support of the dictator's policies. Lenin admitted that the masses might be swayed by petty bourgeois prejudices, and the workers by their "trade-union consciousness." These stilted formulas still contained an approach to real life that Stalinism was to reject, its simple assumption being that whatever the dictator had ordained was desired by the people.

The full flowering of Stalinism in Soviet society had to await the forging of the party into a monolithic organ of totalitarianism. This process occupied some years after 1922, when Stalin was installed as Secretary-General. Details about the elimination of Trotsky, then of Stalin's original partners,

Kamenev and Zinoviev, then of his later allies, Bukharin and others, do not belong in this study. It is important, however, to draw attention to one aspect of Stalin's rise to power that is not often given its due. It is easy to read the whole story in the Secretary-General's talent for intrigue and in his administrative maneuvers. But the initial stages of Stalin's ascendance cannot be divorced from the popularity of the program and ideological tendency he represented, and from the persuasiveness of his position. With the anarchist stirrings suppressed and the country recovering economically under the NEP, the Communist party was increasingly being infiltrated and officered, especially at the lower levels, by young and rather unsophisticated people who joined it after the Revolution. Such people were different in their habits and thinking from the older type of revolutionary worker. To them, the nascent bureaucracy, socialism-Marxism, meant a series of concrete jobs to be done rather than ideological wrangling. Stalin of 1924 and 1925 stood as the symbol of Communist "normalcy" and common sense, as the advocate of the restoration of the economy and administration, rather than of foolhardy social policies and dogmatism. Moderate policies toward the peasant, cautious industrialization, the maintenance of the international revolutionary appeal of Communism, but with the eschewing of dangerous foreign adventures for the young and feeble Soviet state—these were the points of Stalin's "platform." In contrast, his opponents in the crucial years were maneuvered into a position where they could be presented as wild-eyed fanatics: Trotsky as allegedly desiring to postpone the building of socialism in Russia until after Communist revolutions in more advanced countries; Zinoviev and Kamenev as allegedly desiring to oppress and coerce the peasants. It becomes understandable how the Secretary-General and his group could command an overwhelming majority at the Fourteenth Party Congress in 1925 and the Fifteenth Party Conference in 1926, the last occasions on which anything resembling free political discussion took place within the Communist party.

The focus of political power in the Soviet Union was already the Secretariat of the Communist party, which, from its insignificant administrative beginnings in 1919, was to grow under Stalin into the policy-formulating organ for the party, the state, and society, with its departments and divisions paralleling and supervising the major branches of party and state activity. The real state in Russia was thus no longer even the party as a whole but just its administrative machine. It was no longer only the constitutional organs of the state that atrophied in real importance. In the evolution of Stalinism, the same fate awaited party congresses, conferences, even the Central Committee. The "withering away" of all the democratic and anarchistic appurtenances of the revolution was thus a mere matter of a few years. The enthronement of the administrative organs of the party and Stalin's personal dictatorship are an ironic commentary on Lenin's promise of the Communist state where the people will rule themselves and where "accounting and control . . . are the *chief* things necessary for the organizing and correct functioning of the *first phase* of Communist society."[7] With the state, the organ of social coercion, reborn in its most intense form in the Soviet Union, the next phase of Marxism—the development of "those material conditions which alone can form the real basis of a higher form of society"—can now take place. In *State and Revolution*, Lenin credited to Bernstein and other "philistines" the view that centralism means "something from above, to be imposed and maintained solely by means of bureaucracy and militarism."[8] This is not a bad characterization of Stalin's centralism and its superbureaucratic character.

The problem that confronted Stalin and his advisers in 1927-1928, with the country's economy recovered to, roughly, the prewar level, with the state and party firmly in their hands, was the classical problem of Marxism: the transition to socialism and the method of industrialization under Russian conditions. Shortly before his death Stalin summarized the problem confronted by Marxism in Russia:

> What should the proletariat and its party do in a country—including our country—where conditions favor seizure of power by the proletariat and the overthrow of capitalism . . . but

where agriculture, despite the growth of capitalism, still remains so scattered among numerous small and medium owner producers, that there appears no possibility of raising the question of expropriating these producers?

And the alternatives which confronted him in 1927, though with his typical obfuscation he speaks as if the problem had been confronted and solved by Lenin in 1917, are also sketched:

The answer is not, of course, provided by the opinion of some pseudo-Marxists who say that in such circumstances seizure of power should be rejected. They propose to wait until capitalism has contrived to ruin the millions of small and medium producers, turning them into farm laborers, and has concentrated the agricultural means of production. . . . Likewise unacceptable is the view of other pseudo-Marxists who would, if you please, seize power and set about expropriating the small and middle producers in the countryside and socializing the means of production. Marxists cannot agree to take this senseless and criminal course.[9]

The whole passage is typical of Stalin's rewriting of actual history. The implication is that the whole problem was solved by Lenin's formula of voluntary collectivization and that this solution was, after 1928, put into effect by his faithful pupil Stalin. The fact is, of course, that the actual policy adopted by Stalin after 1928-1929 was that of the "pseudo-Marxists" who "set about expropriating the small and middle producers in the countryside." Collectivization was not voluntary; it was a euphemism for the subjection of the peasant to the most stringent control, and as such it was resisted by the mass of the peasantry and accomplished under conditions of extreme violence, necessary to break down passive and active resistance of "small" as well as "middle" peasants.

The peasant collectivization illustrates the meaning of Marxism under Russian conditions. The decisions to collectivize and the parallel course of rapid industrialization initiated after the Fifteenth Congress of the Communist Party in 1927 denote the second and decisive phase of applying Marxism structures to Russia. Marxism-Communism became equated with rapid and drastic industrialization. At its altar were sacrificed all the previous revolutionary, anarchistic, and democratic elements of the doctrine and practice of Communism. For a generation the imperative to produce, to expand the industry, to make Russia into a modern industrial state not only takes precedence over any other objective, but subordinates and absorbs everything else in society. The power motivation of the rulers and the urge to industrialize become practically identical.

The actual decision may be related to several practical necessities and features of the Soviet regime around 1927 and 1928. It reflects the fact that the NEP had restored the Russian economy to the point at which further economic expansion required thorough industrialization. It was not unconnected with the difficulty of obtaining grain from the peasants, pampered, from the Communist point of view, during the NEP. It was a reflection of the international situation: an industrially backward Russia would be at the mercy of the capitalist aggressors. It can be seen as the natural consequence of the dynamics of totalitarianism: the dictator and his group have consolidated their grip on the party and the country. Now comes the moment to build up their power externally.

All the preceding considerations, taken separately or together, do not begin to explain the drastic and violent character of the process. In view of the weak position of agriculture and the lack of capital, the decision to industrialize rapidly and to telescope into ten years what, in the West, took generations represented a vast gamble, which a regime thinking *solely* in power considerations and about clinging to its dictatorial position might have hesitated to undertake. When in 1929 Stalin decided that the planned tempo of collectivization was too slow and that the major part of the task must be accomplished before 1933, he was entering upon the most hazardous period of his rule. Famines, deportation of hundreds of thousands of peasants, lowering of the already pitifully low (from the Western point of view) standard of living—all those measures and effects strained the coercive powers of the regime to the utmost, and confronted not only the dictator but the Communist state with mortal danger. Years

later, Stalin confessed to Churchill that even the most
depressing moments of the Russo-German war did not
approach in devastation or in danger to the country the years of
the first Five-Year Plan and the crucial period of collectivization. Power considerations are insufficient to explain why the
regime at the height of its strength should plunge into a vast
socio-economic reform, the character of which, as well as the
methods by which it was executed, would bring the regime to
the brink of disaster. Ideological as well as power considerations, or more properly power considerations seen through an
ideological prism, provide the explanation.

To Marxism, industrialization means not only the creation
of heavy industries and their appurtenances—economic independence and military security—it means the creation of a
new national psychology. Just as the liberal in the nineteenth
century had believed that industrialization would create an
enlightened population fit for democracy and impervious to
the irrational and emotional appeal of class hatred or religious
and national fanaticism, so the Communist leader wanted the
assimilationist potential of industrialization to create the new
Soviet man—materialistic and pragmatic in his psychology,
automatically responsive to the command and propaganda of
his party. The elimination of the individual peasant household
did not simply reflect the desire to make agricultural
methods more efficient through large-scale cultivation and
thus to release millions of peasants for work in the new
factories. The millions of peasant households, each tilling its
small plot, were seen as the breeders of anti-industrial,
and therefore anti-socialist, attitudes. The peasant, with his
psychology of the small property owner and ingrained
traits of conservatism and radicalism, had to be transformed into the agricultural worker, as materialistically
and pragmatically minded as his industrial counterpart. Old
Russia, with its backwardness, mysticism, torpor, and inherent
anarchy, emanating not from any "Russian soul" but from the
anachronism of peasant society, would be replaced by a
modern, scientifically and materialistically minded state and
society.

Here, then, is the sense of Marxism in Russia, the

meaning of what has been called the third Russian Revolution of 1928-1933. The Marxist state, through compulsion and planning, was striving to achieve what an unplanned and undirected conglomeration of social and economic forces had achieved in the England of the first half of the nineteenth century. The ideology of Marxism was revealed as being much more self-consciously the technique of industrialization and science than its ancestor liberalism had been. Both had to ride roughshod over the sensitivities and feelings of the bulk of the population, which was forced into occupations and ways of life strange to it. The edicts of the dictator replaced, as the mechanism of change, the allegedly impersonal forces of the market and acts of parliament. This time, it was not the casual indoctrination of the middle class with industrial values but the forced imposition of these values upon the whole society in the name of socialism that provided the dynamics of the process. It is as if in some perverse fashion Karl Marx's oversimplified description of the state as the executive committee of the exploiting class, designed to give political and social sanction to the extraction of surplus value from the worker, has finally found its mark in the Communist state. But there is nothing perverse in this relationship: it is the meaning of industrial fanaticism that Marxism had inherited from early liberalism, which, now that the revolutionary and anarchist ballast of the doctrine had dropped off, was displayed in its full power.

The nexus *ideology-power* is best demonstrated in the attempted solution of the peasant problem. During the NEP, Stalin was displayed as, and gathered political credit for being, an advocate of moderate measures toward the peasant. In 1924 and 1925, the party under his leadership had granted the peasants the right to lease land and hire labor—strange doings, his opponents observed, for the regime committed to the ending of "exploitation of man by man." He was in those days an apparent follower of Bukharin, whose alleged injunction to the peasants to "get rich" was later quoted as evidence of a disgusting right-wing deviation. From the Marxist viewpoint, Bukharin's policies were far indeed from being a crime. Industrialization, then socialism, can come, Marx teaches, only

after agriculture, like industry, has become concentrated in
large units. Why should the Communist state not imitate,
within limits, Stolypin's formula? Why not let nature take its
course? The more enterprising, more capitalistically minded
peasants, the kulaks, would absorb more and more land. Their
less enterprising brothers would be forced off the land and
supply the industrial proletariat. The average unit in
agriculture would become larger and more efficient, industrial
labor would be forthcoming, and the future socialization
of land would deal with a relatively small class and not with
millions of individual households. But this course, acceptable
from the viewpoint of academic Marxism, cannot be accepted
by a Marxist party that wants to industrialize in a hurry and
does not want to lose any part of its power in the process. As any
class gains in economic well-being and becomes more
materialistically minded, it comes to desire more than just
economic rights. The prospect of the growth of the rural
middle class had always filled the Bolshevik with alarm. As
Lenin said: "Small scale production gives birth to capitalism
and the bourgeoisie, daily, hourly, with elemental force and in
vast proportions."[10] In 1927 and 1928 the peasants were
reluctant to sell grain to the state. Since they were not getting
enough money for it, they preferred to consume it or to feed it to
their animals. To let "nature to take its course" in the
countryside meant structuring prices and producing enough
consumers' goods for the peasants. If you appease the peasant
economically today, won't he demand political rights tomorrow?

Hence the adoption, as we have seen, of what Stalin was later
on to characterize piously as a "senseless and criminal
course"—driving the peasant by compulsion into the collective
and state farm. The slogan of extermination of the kulaks as a
class was a hypocritical cover-up for the coercion of all the
peasants; the party fell with a fury upon the countryside, upon
the vast social element that had baffled Marxism for
generations, had stood as the massive barrier to the industrialization of society, as the embodiment of what Marx so
pungently described as "the idiocy of rural life." The
immediate objectives of collectivization—release of millions

for industrial work, and the government's control over agricultural production—were attained, though at a terrible human cost. But a solution to the peasant problem in complete accordance with the desires of the regime eluded the despot and is still on the agenda of his successors.

The definition of the struggle repeated by Stalin during the first years of industrialization was one taken from Lenin: "Who will get whom." In Stalin's phrasing, it not only became the formulation of the Communist demonology—the forces of light (the Communist) fighting against all the real and imaginary enemies of Soviet power and industrialization (foreign capitalists, kulaks, saboteurs, all of them somehow connected, their malevolent and "wrecking" activity explaining the suffering and temporary reverses of the great industrialization). It also became the slogan of the historical task of Marxism in Russia, of socialism fighting against the immemorial forces of lethargy, popular apathy, and superstition to create a scientifically and industrially minded modern society. The aim was often obscured by the means employed: terror, propagation of the myth of wreckers and saboteurs, portrayal of the peasant clinging to his miserable plot as the class enemy. A strange way to achieve modernism and progress, and one that has caused believers in the "continuity" of Russian history to draw parallels with Ivan the Terrible, with his "Oprichnina," and with Peter the Great's brutal efforts to Westernize his country. But while it is shallow to forget, slight, or excuse by the magnitude of the task *that* aspect of Stalinism, it is equally unhistorical to ignore the other side of the coin: the realization of Marxian strictures about industrialism.

Here again a complete and drastic break had to be made with the egalitarian and anarchist part of Russian Marxism. In the twenties, Stalin courted popularity as the exponent of pragmatic, living socialism as against the stilted exegeses of his opponents. Were Engels alive today, said Stalin at the Fifteenth Conference of the party, he would undoubtedly say: "May the devil take the old formulas; long live the victorious revolution in the U.S.S.R."[11] With all power in his hand, no such frivolous approach toward the ideoogy was tolerated. At the Seventeenth Party Congress in 1934 Stalin "explained" that

Marxism is an enemy of the equalization of wages, that the latter has nothing to do with socialism but is in fact a petty bourgeois superstition! In the frank adoption of vast inequality of wages and salaries, in the adoption of capitalist incentives to production, there is not even a trace of the embarrassment with which Lenin was explaining the slight departures from equality in 1921 and 1922. Stalin said: "And so our task is to put an end to the instability of labor power, to abolish equalitarianism, to organize wages properly and to improve the living condition of the workers."[12] In the same speech in 1931, Stalin called for full authority of the industrial managers in the factory and for no union interference with management. In 1923, the then Commissar of Trade, Leonid Krassin, had called for similar attitudes toward industrial management. Krassin, an engineer by profession, was ridiculed and attacked as an "inclinator" toward capitalism and was soon removed from his position. Now Stalin proclaimed unblushingly the necessity of the most stringent capitalist methods of organization of industry. The trade unions by 1930 had been subordinated to the party to an extent surpassing Trotsky's most drastic ideas in 1921. And the subjugation of the worker to industrialism was demonstrated not only by the abandonment of egalitarian pretenses and of the worker's right to interfere with management, but by an industrial code meting out punishments undreamed of under the most extreme laissez-faire capitalism for absence from work, repeated lateness, or unauthorized abandonment of one's employment. Strikes become unthinkable, and wages are fixed by fiat from the planners.

It is easy to lose sight of the human elements of the transition. Forced industrialization meant heavy investments in the means of industrial production. These investments could be financed only by lowering the already low standard of living and by pushing into insignificance the production of consumer goods. The general lowering of living standards, the widespread famine in the Ukraine in 1932-33, and the general dislocation of the countryside throw into insignificance the turbulent effects of the unplanned industrialization of the West early in the nineteenth century. It is inconceivable that any regime, even one endowed with absolute power, would have survived this accumulation of human misery without some element of popular support. All accounts of the period stress the enthusiastic response of the Communists, especially the younger strata of the party, to the task of industrialization. The explanation of this response cannot be found only in "propaganda" or in young people's susceptibility to indoctrination. The enthusiasm of an elite group, amidst the sea of human misery that surrounded it in the crucial years from 1929 to 1933, can be explained only by the essential agreement between the ideology in which they had been bred and the industrial fanaticism which they were now exhibiting. The worship of the machine, lyricism over production figures, which later on became artificial and officially propagated myths of "socialist realism," are for the early 1930's a not inaccurate representation of the mentality of the Communist activist, who well might have felt that he was creating "those material conditions, which alone can form the real basis of a higher form of society, a society in which the full and free development of every individual forms the ruling principle." And like an early capitalist entrepreneur defending the employment of children in factories, a Communist official forcing peasants into a collective could feel that he was an agent of progress and an executor of benevolent laws of historical development.

In step with the introduction of capitalist incentives in economic life and the harnessing of the whole society to the task of industrialization, the regime felt constrained to enforce social and artistic mores consonant with the change. The revolution, like all revolutions, brought a breakdown in social conventions. The ideology then sanctioned the rejection of bourgeois "philistinism" in the spheres of family life and sexual relations. Essentially, Marxism has never condoned libertinism or bohemian attitudes toward morals. But legal restraints were always associated with the hypocritical standards of bourgeois society; and in the twenties divorce was made easy to obtain, abortion was legalized, and the whole sphere of personal relations and behavior was considerably freed from law-enforced conformity. The change is very pronounced in the decade of Great Industrialization. Abortion for other than health reasons is declared illegal. Divorce is discouraged by the courts and expensive to obtain. The penal code invokes heavy penalties for homosexual acts. The sanctity of the family tie is invoked both in official pronouncements and in Soviet literature. The Communist party has always required of its members dedication of their personal lives to the cause and a consequent high standard of personal behavior. But now the whole sphere of social behavior of every citizen is officially prescribed to be in accordance with the most conventional, most bourgeois pattern. Bourgeois respectability becomes the expected pattern of socialist behavior.

As in the case of morals, the arts, literature, and even science become increasingly subjected to the authority of the party. The depiction of the unusual or the morbid, stress on individual problems unconnected with the building of socialism, is in effect prohibited. It is not even convention, as in the case of Victorian England, but the state with its police powers that enforces the desirable pattern on arts and literature and commands the proper approach to science. "Socialist realism" depicts the Soviet man striving victoriously against nature and the class enemy for the attainment of collectivization and industrialization, in the process, submitting his personal interests and feelings to those of society and the party.

The Bolshevik revolution meant, and proclaimed, the rejection of Russia's past. Her history was sketched by the Marxist historians as a long story of obscurantism, oppression of the people by successive governments, a story only illuminated from time to time by "progressive" figures and movements. In this respect also, the thirties mark a sharp turn. The inculcation of Russian nationalism, both as a unifying political force and as an added incentive to the prodigious national endeavor, prohibits the presentation of the past as a story of unmitigated darkness. Russia's past is officially rehabilitated, and an excessively Marxist reading of the motives of such figures as Peter the Great and Ivan the Terrible is prohibited. In *Russian* nationalism the regime now sees one of its strongest supports. Political centralization is enhanced by the imposition of national domination, as Soviet chauvinism is by Russian.

The sum of the changes that can be found in the most diverse and minute aspects of society makes the USSR of the 1930's a thoroughly totalitarian and xenophobic society. It is, seemingly, worlds apart from what is meant by "Western" culture and from the traditional atmosphere of Marxism, which, though authoritarian in its conception, breathes some of the rationalistic and cosmopolitan spirit of liberalism. And yet the effect of the great changes is to inculcate in a large part of society the good bourgeois values of the nineteenth-century West: the importance of hard work, of saving, of measuring one's station in life by one's income and the quantity of material goods, etc. The alleged aim is socialism, and while one may become rich in the Soviet Union, one may not own a bank or a factory. But the end and the total effect of the reforms, made in the name of socialism and by means of compulsion that have no parallel in modern history, is to instill the attitudes and aspirations of a middle-class society. Even the external characteristics of the plutocratic West are revived: old titles in the army, decorations and uniforms even for civil servants. The constitution of 1936, adopted to celebrate the completion of the socialist phase of the development of Soviet society, gives the USSR a paper constitution which in its parliamentary structure and political terminology is an unabashed copy of the Western documents of the same type and abandons the populistic phraseology of the earlier Soviet constitutions.

The meaning of Stalinism is the triumph of the logic of Marxism over its revolutionary spirit: the creation of a powerful state and an industrial and scientifically minded society. Missing from the picture entirely is what Karl Marx imagined would be the result of that development: democracy. Marxism in Russia has shown its aptitude first as a technique of revolution, then as a technique of industrialization and modernization. It has not brought socialism or democracy, in the sense in which a nineteenth-century socialist defined these terms. It falls to another chapter to analyze the predicament of Stalin's last years and that of his successors: the dilemma of preserving totalitarian methods in a society that this very totalitarianism has made modern and materialistically minded to the point at which it chafes under the shackles of the police state and a now unreal ideology.

Historical "forces" and "developments" cannot obviate the fact that Stalinism has also meant terror, purges, and infinite abasement, on a national scale, of human personality. It is possible to view various types of relationships between this trio: Marxism, totalitarianism, industrialization. An apologist for Stalin as well as a detractor of Marxism will see a clear and logical connection between Marxism and totalitarianism. If the former ordains industrialization, then a whole nation has to be coerced into new ways. "It is too bad," says the apologist, "but see how much has been achieved." And to the detractor, Marxism, by its inhuman insistence on historical laws, and Communism, by its presuming to tell people what is good for them, already premise terror, purge trials, and confessions—in brief, Stalinism. Then there are a handful of non-Communist Marxist idealists for whom the tie-up is unnatural: Russia could have been transformed without totalitarianism: it is the essentially un-Marxist character of Stalinism, not Marxism, that explains Soviet totalitarianism.

The truth, as usual, is more complicated than any of these simple views would have it. It was sound historical instinct, but bad history, when Khrushchev in his "secret" speech in 1956 tried to divide Stalin into two persons: a faithful pupil of Lenin and a great socialist statesman in his earlier years (until 1934), and an increasingly paranoiac tyrant after that. It was sound historical instinct because Communism, in its conception, involves social compulsion that Khrushchev does not want to disclaim, the kind of compulsion that led, in 1929 and 1930 and afterward, to the death or expulsion of hundreds of thousands, if not millions, of peasants. It was also sound to realize that the terror of 1934, the decimation of the party, the filling of the labor camps with millions of prisoners, and the weird rituals of the purges were in no sense connected or justified by Marxian social engineering (as pro-Communist apologists had claimed before 1956), but represented the then unrestrained sadism of the dictator and the Byzantine atmosphere of his entourage and secret police. By 1934, the great breakthrough had been accomplished, the opposition in the party had been cowed, and no real or imaginary plots justified the blood bath into which the whole society was plunged.

But the analysis falls short of the truth insofar as it ignores the fact that the methods adopted after 1934 were inherent in the Bolshevik policies dating back to the earliest postrevolutionary period. One can grant that the task before Russian Marxism could not have been accomplished according to the precepts of Western constitutionalism or democracy. Of the alternative methods available for political consolidation and economic reconstruction, the policy chosen at every step was one that would vest the most additional power in the dictator and his entourage. It was not so much the attrition of the democratic instincts (of which they never had had an abundance) that led the Bolshevik party to the full excesses of Stalinism and the "cult of personality." It was, in addition to the much more fundamental attrition of the humanitarian instinct, the urge to present every decision, even the most unpopular, as coming from the "masses." The Communist party—or, in actuality, the dictator and the small group around him—acted as a kind of prompter on the historical stage, "reminding" the masses how they should act. Thus the campaign for collectivization was accompanied in the official language by the "sharpening of the class struggle in the countryside," i.e., by party-sponsored violence of the poorer peasants against the kulaks. The very pretense of democracy by the essentially undemocratic system was thus the major reason for the manipulation and exploitation of popular prejudices, passions, and fears, which made the Soviet state even more totalitarian than warranted by the premises of Communism in Russia.

The International Aspect

The idea of creating a new international Marxist organization to replace the Second International had been with Lenin since 1914. In 1919 this idea received organizational expression, and the Third International, the Comintern, was created. The Second International had been a loose conglomeration of socialist and labor parties, not all of them of Marxist or revolutionary character. Thus, the British Labour Party was a member, and the Russian Socialist Revolutionaries were for a time represented, as were the Bolsheviks and the Mensheviks. The Comintern, on the contrary, was to be a highly centralized, definitely Marxist, and revolutionary body. The participating parties from the beginning had to pledge conformity with Leninism insofar as their ideology and organizational pattern were concerned. The Second Congress of the Comintern, in 1920, laid down twenty-one qualifying conditions for membership, which included the need of "democratic centralism," i.e., the organizational structure evolved by the Bolsheviks, of a clandestine organization to be set up even where a Communist party was legally permitted, and of periodic purges to rid the parties of "opportunists" and "reformists." Formation of the Comintern marked the repudiation on an international scale of the social democratic tradition that the Bolsheviks had definitely repudiated internally by 1917.

The result was the general split of the international labor and socialist movement. The Second International, recreated after the war, continued the older tradition; and European socialism, as distinguished from Communism, became more and more pragmatic, more responsive to the circumstances of each given country's political and economic conditions than to the injunctions of Marxism. By contrast, the socialism of the Communist International was to become more responsive to the dictates of the policy of the only existing Communist state. It was inevitable in the nature of things that the Soviet Communist leaders would, from the beginning, play a dominant role in the Third International. It was almost equally inevitable (anything else would have taken an inhuman degree of self-restraint in the Russians) that, for all the assumed equality of all member parties of the Third International, the Soviet party would exercise dictatorial direction and that in due time the international Communist movement would be used as an instrument of Soviet policy. The history of the Comintern reflects the shifts in the internal politics of the Soviet Union, with the splits, purges, and other internal developments of the Communist party therein. What is of primary interest to us is how the Soviet Communists assessed the role and possibilities of Communism on the international scale and how their policies illuminate the nature and opportunities of Marxism in the interwar world.

World War I had marked the definite death of the liberal

utopia. The demise of the earlier type of liberalism was nowhere else more evident at the end of the war than in its international premises. To the man who was to formulate the economics of new liberalism, the collapse of the older type was obvious and vivid on the morrow of the Western powers' victory:

> What an extraordinary episode in the economic progress of man, that age which came to an end in August, 1914! The greater part of the population, it is true, worked hard and lived at a low standard of comfort, yet were to all appearances reasonably contented with this lot. But escape was possible, for any man of capacity or character at all exceeding the average, into the middle and upper classes, for whom life offered, at a low cost and with the least trouble, conveniences, comforts and amenities beyond the compass of the richest and most powerful monarchs of other ages.[13]

And the most characteristic aspect of the liberal ethos before 1914 is evoked by Keynes:

> But, most important of all, he regarded this state of affairs as normal, certain, and permanent, except in the direction of further improvement, and any deviation from it as aberrant and scandalous. The projects and policies of militarism and imperialism, of social and cultural rivalries, of monopolies, restrictions, and exclusion, which were to play the serpent to this paradise, were little more than the amusements of his daily newspaper and appeared to exercise almost no influence at all on the ordinary course of social and economic life, the internationalization of which was nearly complete in practice.

The economic side of the old system is recalled by Keynes in terms suggesting mid-nineteenth-century "fundamentalist" liberalism:

> Europe was so organized socially and economically as to secure the maximum accumulation of capital. . . . Herein lay, in fact, the main justification of the Capitalist System. If the rich had spent their new wealth on their own enjoyments, the world would long ago have found such a regime intolerable. But like bees they saved and accumulated, not less to the advantage of the

whole community because they themselves held narrower ends in prospect. . . . Thus, this remarkable system depended for its growth on a double bluff or deception. On the one hand the labouring classes accepted from ignorance or powerlessness, or were compelled, persuaded or cajoled by custom, convention, authority, and the well established order of Society into accepting, a situation in which they could call their own very little of the cake that they and Nature and the capitalists were cooperating to produce. And on the other hand the capitalist classes were allowed to call the best part of the cake theirs and were theoretically free to consume it, on the tacit underlying condition that they consumed very little of it in practice. The duty of "saving" became nine-tenths of virtue and the growth of the cake the object of true religion.[14]

How close to the early capitalist, or to Marx's view of the function of capitalism, is this picture? Like all evocations of the allegedly golden past, Keynes' description is perhaps too onesided and overlooks the fact that the change was not simply the result of one dramatic event, the war, but also the product of forces and tendencies already visible and growing prior to 1914. But this lyricism over the past, the conviction that old-fashioned capitalism was gone forever, was typical of the immediate postwar psychology; and the conviction was not limited to the revolutionaries. To a stout believer in the virtues of the old system, which Keynes was in 1919, the future was foreboding and revolutionary: "The bluff is discovered; the laboring classes may be no longer willing to forego so largely, and the capitalist classes, no longer confident of the future, may seek to enjoy more fully their liberties of consumption so long as they last and thus precipitate the hour of their confiscation."[15] And when we read this we are reminded, and the reader will forgive the insufferable repetition of this point, how much of Marxian apprehension there was underneath the liberal's economic optimism, and how much of the liberal's obsession with production and capital formation there is in Marxism.

The general feeling of the collapse of the old order and of the imminence of world revolution was most acute among the Bolsheviks following their own victory. In the beginning there was no idea of a possible conflict of interests between the

Soviet state and foreign Communist or revolutionary movements. The very first instinct of the Bolsheviks tells them that their own revolution cannot survive short of revolutions and seizures of power in the more advanced states. To the radical socialists in the West, in the wake of World War I, the intricacies of Bolshevism are unknown and unimportant: Soviet Russia is a "workers' state." In 1918-1919, even some trade-union leaders in Great Britain and socialists in France and Germany, later on very unrevolutionary indeed, talk about forming their own soviets. All Europe between 1918 and 1920 appears to the majority of Bolshevik leaders as Russia did between March and November 1917: the dissolution of the old order releases the revolutionary potential of society. Germany is several times on the brink of a Communist take-over. Soviet regimes spring up in Bavaria and Hungary. Never again was the idea of Communism to have so much popular appeal and revolutionary potentiality in Europe as in the very infancy of the then devastated and almost impotent Soviet state. And then the revolutionary wave passes and Western capitalism becomes stabilized.

The coexistence with capitalism, which history has imposed upon the Communists and which they have had to accept as at least temporary reality, created certain problems for both domestic and international Communism. These problems are not of the kind usually conceived of in the West as the dilemma of Communism. The usual phrasing erects a neat antithesis, as in the question: "Are the Soviet leaders sincere in talking about a world revolution and the triumph of Communism, or do they cynically exploit foreign Communists for the sake of the power of the Soviet Union and with no scruples about what happens in the process to the foreign Communists and the revolution?" As usual when we ask this question, we demand and expect in other people a degree of introspection into their motives and a logical clarity about them of which we concede ourselves to be quite incapable in our own actions. It is simple common sense to assume that from the very beginning the Soviet leaders had thought, and quite "sincerely," that what was good for the Soviet Union was good for world Communism. By natural selection, the foreign Communist parties eventually came to be led by people who also (though the psychological mechanism here is more complicated) became convinced, and "sincerely," of the truth of the same proposition. Doubts and conflicts, in the latter case, were bound to occur on a large scale only when some Communist parties achieved power in their own countries. The problem is not the world revolution versus the selfish state interest, or Communist idealism versus power cynicism. A more sophisticated and useful way of attacking the problem is to study the changing appraisal of foreign revolutionary possibilities by the Soviet leaders.

The earliest and most millennial period of expectations was, as pointed out, closely connected with the very weakness, vulnerability, and isolation of the Soviet state. It is psychologically quite understandable how to the average Communist, in the period of famines and the Civil War in Russia, a Communist uprising in Hamburg or Budapest seemed as urgently important as what was happening in his own country. A few years later a good Communist still might think of himself as being equally solicitous about the welfare of foreign Communists, but there was now a concrete and promising job of socialist construction at hand in Russia, and somehow the foreign Communists loomed less important.

This inevitable "pragmatization" of life paralleled certain domestic developments: in 1920, amidst appalling devastation and backwardness, the party could be terribly agitated by the question whether it was or was not according to the canon for a commissar to be paid more than a skilled worker. A few years later, whether one was for or against Stalin, for or against collectivization, no heat could be generated over the old problem, which now seemed simply irrelevant. Within a few years after the revolution, the earlier emotionalism over world revolution or any particular foreign revolution became unthinkable. It was characteristic of the political acumen of Stalin that he capitalized on this very natural evolution of feeling and, professing scrupulous regard for the international aims of Communism, suited his policies to the prevailing mood.

It was typical of the reaction of the opposition to Stalin in the early twenties, the reaction of a drowning man grasping at what is at hand, that they tried to make a point of the alleged sacrifice of world Communism by the leadership of the party. Some of them were asinine enough to complain to the Executive Committee of the Comintern about the behavior of their leaders. It is almost incredible that a man with Trotsky's intelligence, the earliest advocate among the Bolsheviks of rapid industrialization and modernization of Russia, could let himself be maneuvered into appearing as the enemy of "socialism in one country." In 1926 Stalin could ask what Trotsky's alternative was; he was able to upbraid Trotsky as an adventurer whose policies would plunge the unindustrialized Soviet state into a war with all Europe.[16] Trotsky's retort that one could build socialism in one country but could not finish building it while capitalism survived elsewhere would have been, at one time, regarded as a fine example of Marxist sophistication and subtlety. But to the assembled party and state bureaucrats, it was now just doubletalk.

The inevitable, complete subordination of the world Communist movement, like the crystallization of personal dictatorship in Russia, was a matter of several stages. The initial divisions and wrangling among the Soviet leaders found their echoes abroad. Thus Trotsky's disgrace had considerable repercussions: to foreign Communists his name approached that of Lenin's in glamor; more cosmopolitan in his outlook than his opponents, his disgrace was followed by the defection of the most individualistic among the foreign Communists. On a smaller scale, the same thing was to happen in the wake of the descents of Zinoviev and Bukharin, the successive leaders of the Comintern. By 1930, the Stalinist pattern was firmly impressed, as it was in Russia, on the most foreign Communist parties; their leaders for the most part were miniature Stalins: rough-hewn party bureaucrats with little of the intellectual *éclat* and individualism of the generation of Trotsky, Radek, and Bukharin. The parties became "bolshevized," as the official phrase went in the 1920's, i.e., not only did they become obedient to Moscow but they became small copies, ideologically and structurally, of the Communist party of the USSR. Like Pavlovian dogs, they are now not only obedient but conditioned to obedience: a bell would be rung in Moscow and soon an identical response would be coming from *Humanité* in Paris, *Die Rote Fahne* in Berlin, and the *Daily Worker* in London and New York.

The development in Russia was, in a sense, a natural if perverse product of the Russian conditions of Marxism. To impose the same pattern, the same mentality, upon the Bulgarian or British Communist as upon the Soviet one was, by definition, to impose a considerable artificiality upon foreign Communist movements, to isolate them from the main trends of their national life, to the point where even the revolutionary aspirations of their societies could not accommodate themselves freely in bodies that to all purposes appeared as agencies of the Soviet government rather than native expressions of revolutionary Marxism. The foreign Communist lived in a world much more artificial and ideologically crippling than even his Soviet brother did. In the case of a foreign and especially a Western Communist, the denial of spontaneity, on which Leninism was originally based, was carried to the extent of the suppression of one's political and social instinct, to an *unnatural* alienation from one's society. The natural impulses of Marxism—the sense of social injustice, materialist iconoclasm, and revolutionary impatience—had themselves to be restrained and doled out in accordance with orders from Moscow. The violent verbal behavior of Western Communism and its almost voluptuous self-abasement before the Soviet Union and Stalin are the reverse psychological effects of the constricted political lives that Western Communists had to lead. It is equally remarkable how at the times when they were allowed to act "naturally," to exhibit, within limits, "spontaneity" (as during the period of the Popular Front or during the Second World War and the Resistance), the sense of release made of the automatons and repeaters of stilted formulas brave revolutionary leaders and resourceful politicians, capable of seizing a popular following and strategic social and political positions. But the leash on which international Communism was held during the interwar period usually gave it but little opportunity to exploit the chances for revolutionary Marxism in any Western country.

The basic trouble lay in the heavy-handed application to very different societies of the same formula that had provided the victory of Communism in Russia. Lenin's party was assumed to be the microcosm of revolutionary forces in society, its leaders, because of their Marxist sophistication, always one step ahead of the actual revolutionary movement in their society. Marxism and "objective facts" teach that the peasants are likely to become stirred up; lo and behold, the party forges ahead in proclaiming and exploiting the peasant's grievances. In power, the Bolsheviks served themselves with the same formula. The Soviet leaders assumed the role of prompters in the historical drama unfolding to a script by Karl Marx.

But what gave the spectacle an *appearance* of reality in the Soviet Union was lacking in the world at large; namely, the prompter also being the producer and having complete control over the actors. A Soviet textbook that blithely proclaims that the class struggle became sharper in the countryside in 1929 and 1930 expresses partial truth: the kulaks were being persecuted and expropriated. Never mind the fact that the "peasant masses" fell upon the kulaks because they were being egged on and coerced by the party and the police, and not because of their heightened class consciousness. In Western Europe in the late twenties, the Communist parties had been told to intensify their revolutionary propaganda and attacks on the "socialist traitors." The "objective facts" and Marxism told the Soviet masters of the Comintern that the "masses" in Germany and elsewhere should become convinced of the bankruptcy of the system and turn to Communism as a result of the Great Depression. But the play did not adhere to the script. The German "masses," for instance, turned to fascism. The script was patched up: National Socialism was to be a brief interlude, not to be seriously resisted, for it was the last stage of bankrupt capitalism, to be followed by a spontaneous turn to Communism. But even the revised script failed to be acted out.

The question remains why, even in the West, in the face of the inherent awkwardness of the Communist formula and the inhuman subordination of the Communist parties to a foreign country, Communism still made considerable inroads in the interwar period; and why, after the war, during which the antithesis between Communism and patriotism had disappeared with the attack on the Soviet Union by the Germans, it became, for a while, the most popular movement in Italy and France.

It is best to confine our brief analysis to the interwar era, because the USSR was then not yet a super power. Still, the success of Western Communism during the period, with all the handicaps it labored under and the legal persecutions it was often subjected to, was not inconsiderable. In England, although the Communist party judged itself in luck to secure a seat or two in Parliament, it exerted a disproportionate influence in some of the unions. The French and German Communist parties commanded a considerable following among the working class. In Italy, under Mussolini, Communism gathered dividends from its talent for illegal organization. Indeed, small but well-organized Communist parties existed in all European countries. Even the slaughter of foreign Communists in Russia during the 1930's and the terrible spectacle of the purges did not seriously disrupt the organizational continuity or the blind allegiance of foreign Communist parties to "the Fatherland of socialism."

The answer must be sought in a whole complex of causes. Here we might pause on one that relates the historical role of Marxism to the qualified success of Communism in Western Europe. The breakdown of liberalism as the ascendant philosophy of the Western world led to the disruption or arrest of the process that in all its economic, social, and political effects we have called industrialization. Keynes's vivid words demonstrate the shock the system received from World War I. Though the economy of Europe appears stabilized, and largely by the old methods, by the 1920's the psychological appurtenances of the old order are decisively disrupted. Nothing will again instill or restore the belief that the liberal order of things—political democracy and capitalism—is the *inevitable* product of social evolution. Nothing will restore the illusion of the beneficent laws of the economy working out their designs with the least interference by governments. The whole network of political rationalism, always fragile and artificial, has been shaken.

We see in Western Europe in the postwar period, developments reminiscent of the turbulent period of industrialization in the 1830's and '40's, the era which, by the seeming logic of its developments, gave Karl Marx the illusion of the prompt and inevitable breakdown of capitalism and the revolutionary arousal of the proletariat. The onset of the Great Depression of 1929 seems the very fulfillment of all that Karl Marx had prophesied, the veritable *Gotterdämmerung* of capitalism and liberalism, no longer to be delayed or avoided by the now exposed panacea of parliamentarism and other political illusions. The breakdown of the habits imposed by the long period of domination of liberal ideology was thus followed by the breakdown of the liberal economic mechanism. First the international economic system, before World War I already strained by the development of economic nationalisms, and then the whole intricate economic machinery of the major capitalist powers broke down in a way that apparently conformed to the blueprint laid down by Karl Marx. All the remedies developed during more than three generations of the flourishing of Western capitalism were tried and found wanting.

What is it that Marx wrote in 1848?

Society suddenly finds itself put back into a state of momentary barbarism; it appears as if a famine, a universal war of devastation, had cut off the supply of every means of subsistence; industry and commerce seem to be destroyed. And why? Because there is too much civilization, too much means of subsistence, too much industry, too much commerce. The productive forces at the disposal of society no longer tend to further the development of the conditions of bourgeois property; on the contrary, they have become too powerful for these conditions by which they are fettered, and as soon as they overcome these fetters they bring disorder into the whole of bourgeois society, endanger the existence of bourgeois property.[17]

In the 1930's, for the first time, Marx's prophecies appeared to be justified. The higher the extent of industrialization of the given country and the more complex and advanced its capitalist structure, the deeper appeared the character of the economic crisis, the more profound the shock to the established mores of the older liberal creed.

It is not surprising, therefore, that the party that proclaimed itself the inheritor of revolutionary Marxism should have been in a position to capitalize on the developments consequent upon the great crisis. In retrospect, even the Great Depression does not vindicate Marx the prophet. The Depression was the breakdown of the social psychology as well as the mechanics of the older type of liberalism. The revolutionary situation created over much of Europe had, as we observed, many elements in common with the very revolution that brought liberalism into ascendance and capitalism as the ruling economic system. But, as we also saw, the popular radicalism generated by the Industrial Revolution was by no means of the prevailingly socialist variety. We noted in England from 1820 to 1850 the presence of movements and strains of thought of the proto-fascist as well as the proto-Marxist variety. The optimistic assumption of Marxism—the breakdown of capitalism leads to a socialist revolution—which was inherited by Communism, paradoxically proved to be in itself a remnant of nineteenth-century liberal optimism.

Now in the century of mass communication media, mass political movements, the anarchist feelings contained but not erased for generations by the discipline of industrialization and the ethos of liberalism erupted under the spur of depression, but by no means exclusively in the direction of socialism or Communism. The breakdown of middle-class values, the hostility toward banks and industry, the feeling of unreality about a constitutional and democratic system in a time of profound economic crisis, all these quasi-anarchist feelings can flow into revolutionary fascism as well as into revolutionary socialism. National Socialism, for all of its links with big business, which foolishly saw in it a defense against "radicalism" and its identification with extreme nationalism, actually had its roots in anti-industrial and anti-state feelings. The philosophy of "blood and soil," the obscurantist worship of race and of the peasant as its ideal representative, the echoes of syndicalism, virulent anti-Semitism—the Jew again, as to many radicals of the Industrial Revolution, the embodiment of materialist and "rootless cosmopolitan" viewpoints—this whole irrationalist complex of its popular appeal springs up from the undoing of the large part of the institutional and psychological appurtenances of industrialization. The same in a lesser degree can be said of Italian fascism. The social focus of earlier radicalism, including socialism during the Industrial Revolution, i.e., the lower-middle class threatened by the new economic forces, is now recreated in the spheres most susceptible to the appeal of fascist radicalism: the same strata, now including parts of the working class and the peasants, whom the depression has ejected from the seeming security and status by which a century of material progress had stilled their inherent anti-industrialism. Thus even the most catastrophic event in the history of Western capitalism justifies only Marx the sociologist of revolution, not Marx the prophet of socialism as the receiver of bankrupt capitalism and liberalism.

The fact that the decline and then the catastrophe of the old economic order did not give the Communists in Europe a more substantial success can be attributed, in the main, to two reasons. The first is the type of direction provided by Moscow. To capitalize on diverse sources of revolutionary feeling in diverse societies would have required of the local Communists the kind of sensitivity to local conditions and feelings that would have precluded in the first place their blind dependence on Moscow. The British Communists would have had to be, and *convincingly*, attuned to the now firm traditions of political democracy in England, the French Party *genuinely* responsive to the syndicalist and anarchist trends in the French revolutionary makeup, the Germans mindful of both German nationalism and the German working-class feeling of solidarity. But the logic of *spontaneous* response to the revolutionary possibilities in their societies, the logic that is ordained by revolutionary Marxism, would have made the foreign Communists unable to obey almost instinctively what the comrades in Moscow saw as the urgent tasks of the given Communist party.

Even when the Soviet masters of the Comintern appraised correctly (especially when it coincided with the interests of the

Soviet state) the most promising line of activity and propaganda of the given Communist party, the consequent behavior of the German, French, or Spanish Communists was usually too artificial, too transparently managed, to enable them to swim with the tide of revolutionary spontaneity in the way that the Russian Communists had done so successfully in 1917. Putting aside all moral considerations, such as the suppression of the instinctive feeling of national pride and the psychologically and intellectually crippling mechanism by which people have to rationalize the transmuting of their humanitarian and revolutionary motives into the service of a despotic foreign state, the dilemma of European Communism was and is (though as we shall see a major change was attempted after Stalin's death) a paralyzing one. To illustrate this dilemma: how far would the Bolsheviks have got in 1917 if, instead of responding readily to the rapidly shifting revolutionary moods, they had had to check their policies with a foreign center of Communism, if some organization or dictator sitting, say, in Vienna had to decide whether the slogan "All power to the soviets" was a "correct" or "incorrect" one, and if they had to arbitrate between Lenin and Zinoviev about whether to undertake the November uprising? The predicament of the European Communists was often a tragicomic one: a new policy would be sanctioned of, let us say, wooing the nationalist element in Germany. The greater the enthusiasm and devotion with which the given leaders pursued this aim, the greater the danger of their inability to shift at the next change of the party line, and their consequent purge. In fact, instead of the management of revolutionary spontaneity, the premises and operations of the Comintern, often led, insofar as European Communism was concerned, to the drying up of its spontaneous revolutionary response.

The other reason for the failure of Communism is perhaps more basic. As much as the Great Depression reopened the social wounds inflicted by the Industrial Revolution, it was unable to create in the most thoroughly industrialized societies of the West a "Marxian situation." The discipline of industrialism, the habits of democratic politics remained too strong in Great Britain, the Low Countries, and Scandinavia to allow a social dissolution reminiscent of Russia of 1905 and 1917, or Germany in the early 1930's. The ultimate defeat of early liberalism was followed there not by a reversal to an earlier, basically anti-industrial type of radicalism but by the development of a new type of liberalism, state- and welfare-oriented, perhaps sliding easily into what has been called laborism, but worlds apart from revolutionary Marxism. The development of Keynesian economics provided a new economic "science" to bolster the instinctive turn toward the state and the democratically dictated tendency toward economic equality. Communism in the most thoroughly industrialized societies of the West (and again, "industrialized" referring not only to the existence of an industrial economy but also to the existence of appropriate social mores and institutions) had no function to perform and no overwhelming appeal to exploit.

It is interesting to digress on some exceptions to the rule. Admittedly in the thirties and during and immediately after World War II, Communism had its pockets of influence and attraction in Great Britain and the United States. The nature of this appeal was related more—the distinction is difficult but important—to the real or imaginary accomplishments of the Soviet Union than to the relevance of revolutionary Marxism in the given society. The French or German worker "fell" for Communism largely because its exposition of revolutionary Marxism appealed to some of his basic instincts and needs. The British worker was more likely to opt for Communism because of the mistaken notion that the Soviet Union was a "workers' state" founded upon social and economic equality. The attraction of a Western intellectual was more often than not grounded on distaste for the "bourgeois philistinism" which surrounded him and the vision of a socialist society where—how fantastic in view of what was going on in Russia in the 1930's—bold experimentation and nonconformity were encouraged. There was more substance in the views of those who, struck by the collapse of the premises of liberal economy and the resultant economic chaos, looked enviously at the planning and the scientific and technological development of Soviet Russia. But despite some views to the contrary, frustrated bohemianism and dissatisfied intellectuals do not add up to the foundation of a revolutionary movement.

At the other side of the scale from the failure of Communism in the West lies its very considerable success in the colonial and semicolonial areas. The extent of this success became apparent only after World War II, with Communism engulfing large parts of Asia and becoming a powerful contender for many other underdeveloped countries. But the seeds of this success, then undoubtedly enhanced by the tremendous emergent power of the USSR, lie in the policies and principles adopted in the interwar period. As in other areas, the successes or failures of Communism reflect the peculiar circumstances of each country and each Communist party. But there are also basic differences between the appeal of revolutionary Marxism in the West and in Asia. And here there is no doubt that Marxism has provided a master revolutionary formula for the underdeveloped areas and that Communism had applied this formula, as it did not apply Marxism in Europe, with instinctive skill.

Proof of this lies not only in the Communist postwar conquests which resulted more from concrete Soviet help than from any inner "necessity." A more objective proof is the general use of Marxist categories, even in their vulgarized Communist form, by many typical, even anti-Communist, intellectuals from the colonial and semicolonial areas. It is found in the general revolutionary volatility of political movements in Asia and their affinity with Communism. There is something natural, and it would be foolish to disregard it, in the appeal of Marxism as a system of thought for an Asian revolutionary; there is something natural in the technique of the Marxist party for the political movements of the underdeveloped countries. In both cases, the Marxist phase may never coincide with the Communist one, or it may eventually be left behind, but it is almost inevitable. Marxism in such a society promises, even before the first modern factory is built, the road to modernization, the technique of emancipation from traditionalism, a rationalization of the disturbing forces of modern life as well as a protest against them.

The recognition that an economically backward country offers a more fruitful field for revolution than does an industrialized one is implicit in Lenin's interpretation of Marxism. This "discovery" of Lenin was anticipated in Marx's writings on Ireland, India, China, etc. While held back by his own theory from postulating *socialist* revolutions in these countries, Marx had the essential insight that societies in the process of transition have a considerable revolutionary potential and that the effect of colonial rule is in many ways equivalent to the beginning phases of industrialization. Although primarily preoccupied with the industrialized West, Marx had seen, long before Lenin's *Imperialism*, that colonial areas were the vulnerable areas of the capitalist world and that the road to socialism in Asia, just as in the oppressed European countries (Poland, Ireland), led through *national* revolution. From these rather marginal elements of Marx's revolutionary sociology, the Comintern, as early as a few years after the Bolshevik revolution, forged its scheme of Communist expansion in Asia. Two factors explain this strategy: the prospects of revolution in the West vanished for the time being, but at the same time it became clear that World War I had destroyed most of the appeal of liberalism as a proselytizing creed of modernization and that in Asia, at least, Marxism could in a fair way become its successor.

In conditions of underdevelopment *and* foreign domination, the inherent paradox of Marxism—the cult of modernization and technology, and the exploitation of the unsettling effects of industrialization—does not provide an obstacle to the spread of the doctrine. It is the foreign rulers who in the popular mind become associated with all the evils of the transformation: the destruction of old customs and ways of life, the ruin of the handicrafts, and agrarian poverty. Even the most primitive rudiments of industrialization, i.e., a slight improvement in sanitary and medical conditions, bring with them pressures of population upon land that, under conditions of primitive economy, create insufferable conditions of rural overcrowding, inefficient cultivation, and all the consequent economic evils. The leitmotif of nationalist propaganda against imperialism almost always has this twofold refrain which fits in with Marxism: like the capitalist in the nineteenth century, the colonial power is blamed for the economically destructive effects of the modernization at the same time that it is accused of keeping the colonial territories in backwardness and of denying them the benefits of modernity. The counterpoint of Marxism has, under Asiatic or African conditions, a natural affinity with nationalism. The keynote of Marxian propaganda can be presented with double effectiveness, because the "exploiter" is, or certainly was in the interwar period, a foreigner or a Westernized entrepreneur or landlord.

Into this naturally Marxist situation the Comintern injected the most effective revolutionary policy: the muting of other elements of Marxism, or their de-emphasis, in favor of revolutionary policy based on the encouragement of nationalism. The nationality policy inside the Soviet Union during the first decade after the revolution gave this policy a high degree of external plausibility. The opening of educational opportunities on a wide scale to the non-Russian elements of the population, the encouragement of cultural autonomy within the Soviet Union, the nationally heterogeneous composition of the Bolshevik leadership, all these developments obscured the already existing link between Soviet imperialism and international Communism. The incongruity between the revolutionary aspirations in the given society and the dictatorial sway over the given Communist party by Moscow, which was so jarring in the case of European Communism, did not exist on the same scale in Asia. Rather than fighting against the nationalism in the given party, the Soviet leaders more often than not had to restrain the Marxist fundamentalism of their Asiatic followers and try to teach them to appear as good nationalists. Radek said to the Chinese Communists in 1922:

> You must understand, comrades, that neither the question of socialism nor of the Soviet republic are now the order of the day . . . the immediate task is: 1) to organize the young working class, 2) to regulate its relations with the revolutionary bourgeois elements in order to organize the struggle against the European and Asiatic imperialism.[18]

An *oppressed* nationalism easily becomes an ally of revolutionary Marxism. In Asia, foreign domination or foreign economic exploitation created revolutionary possibilities and situations analogous in many ways to the conditions in Europe in the nineteenth century that gave rise to Marxism. The national revolution in Asia, after World War I and up to our own day, has taken the place of and often been synonymous with the Industrial Revolution. But the symbiotic relationship between Communism and nationalism was bound to be of a different order than the same relationship between Marxism and anarchism. In exploiting the latter, Marxism gave a revolutionary organization and theory to varied and largely formless forces of social protest. In their selfish collaboration with colonial and semicolonial nationalisms, the local Communist parties have allied themselves with and attempted to exploit specific parties or movements, each with its own organization and ideology.

After an interval, the nationalist movement, especially if it had a social basis in the middle class, would often perceive the incompatibility of its aims with those of Communism and would refuse to serve as an interlude in the unfolding of the Marxist scheme of history staged by Moscow. The local Communist parties found themselves partners of movements which, instead of being eventually absorbed or destroyed by the Communists in the manner of the Left Socialist Revolutionaries in the Russian Revolution, aspired to and were often capable of turning the tables on the Communists. Militant nationalism sometimes appeared capable of superseding the Marxist formula, of exploiting the traditionalist reaction and social disturbances due to modernization, and, contrariwise, of satisfying the craving for modernization and the breaking down of old customs and traditions.

The limitations of any overly deterministic pattern of linking the social development with prospects for Marxism are well illustrated by Japan. Here is a classical case, in many ways parallel to prerevolutionary Russia, of a rapid industrialization taking place in a society still pre-industrial in its social structure, with the land-peasant problem persisting in all its acuteness. Yet, for all the existence of strong Marxist movements, the economic tensions of the transition found their release not in a socialist revolution but in militant nationalism, which utilized the traditional symbols for economic and imperial expansion.

Elsewhere in Asia, between the two world wars, Communism appears to have unwittingly helped precipitate nationalist revolutions without eventually turning them to its own uses. The picture in China after the Communist-Kuomintang break and in the countries where national consolidations and modernization took place under nationalist and dictatorial auspices (as in Turkey, Persia, and, in a way, India) would have led to the conclusion that for all its greater sophistication in Asia, Communism failed there in its expansion as badly as it did in Europe. Just as the literal reading of Marxism—mature capitalism leads to a socialist revolution—proved false, so the sociological insight contained in the Communist exploitation of backwardness proved almost equally futile. One might have supplemented Lenin's dictum by saying that if in an industrialized society the spontaneous development of the workers leads them to acquire trade-union rather than revolutionary consciousness, so in an "underdeveloped" country the social development will lead the elite, perhaps after a Marxist phase, into nationalism rather than Communism.

This view had a degree of plausibility, but it should not be carried to the point at which we make every specific political situation the outcome of personalities involved, military and diplomatic factors, and plain accident. The interwar period was used for this analysis of international Communism because Soviet Russia was as yet not capable of installing Communism in a given country by sheer might, whatever the "underlying social forces" and "the stage of economic development." But even a superficial comparison of the role of revolutionary Marxism in the most industrialized segment of the world with its role in societies in the process of transition points out differences that cannot be completely explained by personalities, by the efficiency or inefficiency of the given police system, or even by the correct or incorrect "line" imposed by the Comintern.

Industrialization, if supplemented by appropriate political and social development, instills a network of habits and institutions that make the appeal of Communism, even under optimum conditions, as during the Great Depression, limited and temporary insofar as the mass of the industrial workers and society as a whole are concerned. In a country beginning the process of modernization, or at a point where modern industry coexists with peasant or colonial problems, the necessary barrier of industrial and middle-class habits and values has not been erected to replace the traditional ones and ward off the revolutionary forces engendered by the process of new economics and new ideas moving in. In underdeveloped societies, Marxism as the promise of rapid industrialization and escape from humiliating backwardness, as the beneficiary of the tensions and tribulations of modernity, is always a strong contender for power, even though the actual Communist party may be small or uninfluential.

The Russian Communists have tried with varying success to apply the formulas learned in their history to promote revolution abroad, first, as protection for their own vulnerable state, and then for imperialist reasons. In their domestic evolution, "life" has taught them that the practical meaning of Marxism in power is state capitalism and the instilling of essentially bourgeois values in the whole nation. To foreign Communists, they expound revolutionary Marxism not as an inflexible set of ideas but as tactics for exploitation of whatever there is in the way of revolutionary, anti-industrial potential in the given society. In societies where the lesson is relevant, the Communists are spared the ideological scruples and contentions of pre-1914 Marxism. In the quarrels and purges of international Communism, the motivating factor is no longer a disagreement on principles or about "what Marx really meant." The seemingly ideological arguments are but the invocation of scriptural authority for the disgrace of this or that leader and his group because of the failure of their "line" or their loss of favor in Moscow. If the average person feels the sanctions of religion more strongly after a moral transgression has involved him in misfortune, so a Communist feels that he has sinned against Marxism only if his anarchist or nationalist "act" has led his party to a defeat. The old ideological dilemmas and scriptural subtleties of the Plekhanovs, Trotskys, and Martovs, seeking the *one* right and legitimate formula for Marxism in Russia before 1917, are replaced by the recognition of the variety of the means to revolution.

Thus the man who was to be the most successful of Soviet Communism's pupils was at pains to point out that Marxism should freely use and associate itself with peasant anarchism, but it should not become lost in anarchism, which is but a *stage* in its revolutionary tactics. Speaking in 1927 about the peasant riots in Hunan, Mao Tse-tung must have had in mind the Lenin of 1921 confronting the anarchist slogans of the Lenin of 1917. In a didactic fashion, Mao asked: "Are we to get in front of them and lead them, or criticize them behind their backs, or fight them from the opposite camp?" And he continued:

> An agrarian revolution is a revolution by the peasantry to overthrow the power of the feudal landlord class. If the peasants do not apply great force, the power of the landlords consolidated over thousands of years can never be uprooted. There must be a revolutionary tidal wave in the countryside in order to mobilize tens of thousands of peasants and weld them into this great force. The excesses described above result from the tremendous revolutionary enthusiasm of the peasants. In the *second revolutionary stage* of the peasant movement, such acts are very necessary. In this *second stage*, an absolute peasant power must be established, no criticism of the Peasant Associations should be allowed; the gentry's power must be totally liquidated, the gentry knocked down, even trodden upon.[19]

Exploitation of peasant anarchism was for Mao, as it had been for Lenin, the means of enthroning Chinese Communism in power. Once there, Mao and his followers would move even faster than had the Russian Communists towards the erection of the centralized state and all powerful party. While clearly following the Soviet example, Mao attempted to introduce a significant variant: periodically, as during the Cultural Revolution of 1966-1969, the Communist state and society should be thrown into an upheaval so as to prevent bureaucratic ossification of the state apparatus and recoup the original ideological fervor. But unlike what was believed in the West by the New Left, such quasi-anarchist intervals were not intended to detract from the authoritarian character of the regime or to increase the element of popular participation. The political upheavals were essentially contrived affairs, directed from above, which may have temporarily weakened the hold of the bureaucracy over society, but were not allowed to challenge the power of *the* leader and his closest entourage. The Cultural Revolution then served Mao the same purpose as did the Great Terror for Stalin: it exalted his stature and power at the expense of the party. With the Great Helmsman gone, his successors, as did those of Stalin's, decided to discard their predecessor's dangerous experiments and reverted to the oligarchico-bureaucratic model of governance. The Sino-Soviet dispute should not be allowed to obscure the fact that if Chinese Communism is "different," as sometimes believed in the West, it is mainly so in having learned the use of Marxism as demonstrated by the history of the Communist party of the USSR and in attempting to go consciously and rapidly through the phases that the Russian Communists traversed more painfully and by improvisations.

Obviously the clash between the two Communist super-powers has already changed the international setting in which the story of Marxism has been unfolding. The pattern of absolute domination which Moscow had imposed on the international Communist movement in the Stalin era is clearly a thing of the past. And this in turn is bound to transform—in many cases has already transformed—the character of militant Marxism in individual countries. But though Communism has by now amply demonstrated its inability to create a new international order, it still threatens to destroy what remains of the old, and though wracked by schisms and national conflicts, it continues its bid to become the world's dominant ideology. That it is in a position to do so is due primarily to Communism's ability to harness for its purposes the two most vital elements of Marxism: its sensitivity to the revolutionary stirrings of a society where the traditional culture and traditional economy have broken down and have not yet been replaced by firm new structures, and its ability to inspire political fanaticism in the service of modernization and industrialization.

— 6 —

The Crisis of Marxism
and the Soviet State

The two most striking characteristics of the late Stalinist regime were its palpable absurdity and its apparent invulnerability. An unbiased foreign observer could not but experience a sense of unreality in reading the Soviet press of the 1940's and early 1950's, its front page almost daily preempted by the messages of greetings to and eulogies of the "genius-like" leader of the Soviet people and of all progressive mankind. Wherever one turned for other reading—a biology journal, a textbook on literature, a historical monograph—the name of J. V. Stalin was bound to crop up, as that of the supreme authority on the subject, the inspirer of the author's labors, the man to whom every scientific discipline, every art in the Soviet Union looked for guidance and owed its successes.

More amazing even than the vanity this required and the servility and fear inherent in such tributes was the picture of Soviet politics following World War II. It was reminiscent of a surrealistic landscape: a desert with the only discernible object amidst it a vast statue of the Leader. Government and party institutions had atrophied to the point of insignificance compared with the power of one man. Only one regular meeting of the Central Committee is reported to have taken place between 1945 and 1952. The Party Congress, required by its statutes to meet at least once every three years, was not to assemble until 1952, thirteen years after the previous one. Even the Politburo was summoned infrequently. The novelty was not that the government of Russia was entirely in the hands of the despot and whoever happened to be his favorite of the moment—that had been true since the early 1930's. The new element was that even a relatively high official, not to mention the average citizen, was completely in the dark as to how and why decisions were being reached, be it on matters of high policy or on the criteria for the permissible styles in literature and music. The secrecy which enveloped every aspect of policymaking was preposterous, even by the standard of the most repressive system. And by the same token, the pattern of repression went far beyond anything which might have been required by the most far-reaching concern for internal and external security on the part of the regime. The burden of fear imposed upon the average citizen in those years was as great, if not so often punctuated by widespread violence, as during the Great Purge of 1936-1939. His isolation from the outside world became more absolute than ever.

Similar irrationality intruded into the economic sphere. Granted that for long the regime's policies were based on the ruthless exploitation of the peasantry, yet the very extent of this exploitation and of agricultural policies in general was clearly counterproductive. With no material incentives for the producer, Soviet agriculture became the Achilles' heel of the entire economy. In the face of the post-war inflation of prices, the collective farmers were paid in 1952 less for grain, beef, and pigs than they had been in 1940. "The price paid for compulsorily delivered potatoes was less than the cost of transporting them to the collecting point, and this cost had to be borne by the *kolkhozes,* who thus in effect got less than nothing."[1] Most bizarre was the system of self-deception employed by the government in methodically falsifying crop statistics. Instead of reporting harvest figures in terms of the grain actually collected, the regime, beginning in the middle thirties, began to give out the so-called biological yields, i.e., *visual* estimates of the crops standing in the field. This fraudulent technique, practiced until after Stalin's death, resulted in overestimates of the actual harvest by as much as twenty to twenty-five percent. The actual figure of grain collected remained a state secret, and as such was withheld, one assumes even from many people charged with economic planning.

The war holocaust, in addition to the devastation of the western, then the most developed, region of the country, had claimed the lives of some twenty million Soviet citizens. One would have thought that the most urgent post-war priority would have been to treasure and utilize all available resources of manpower. But here again the paranoia of Stalin's despotism clashed with what would appear to have been rational policies. Millions continued or became freshly incarcerated in forced labor camps, many of them for no other crime than having been prisoners of war, and apart from the greatly increased rate of mortality, this vast army of slave laborers obviously could not be as productive as those working outside the "Gulag archipelago."

And yet the regime which presided over this vast maze of oppression, exploitation, and irrationality, far from tottering on the brink of disaster, was in fact domestically invulnerable, and its foreign policy was scoring an almost continuous success. At home Stalin's power was unassailable, abroad the USSR loomed as a colossus. The ubiquity of the police controls and the past experience of mass terror made any dissent inconceivable: when a man is conscious that he might be arrested for no reason at all, he has neither the time nor energy to protest and criticize, especially when he knows that his act of defiance would not become known beyond his immediate circle. Far from taking any practical steps to compel the USSR to live up to its wartime agreements and to undo the effects of its post-war usurpations, foreign statesmen were anxiously seeking ways to prevent or stop any future Soviet bid for expansion.

Such then was the paradoxical picture of the last phase of Stalin's rule: terror and deception rewarded by the erection of a powerful industrial state; lack of democracy and the most basic freedom leading not to a challenge to the tyranny, but to the consolidation of the Soviet Leviathan. In the world at large, Communism was still expanding, still appeared as a docile tool of Moscow. Few in 1948 thought that Tito's Yugoslavia might become a harbinger of a new era in international Communism, or believed that the rebellious Communist chieftain and his little country would be able to hold out for long against the

Soviet bloc. In any case, Yugoslavia's defection looked insignificant within the context of the ever growing Russian domination of Eastern Europe, the fact that the Communist parties were now serious contenders of power in Italy and France, and most of all, against the momentous victory of Communism in the world's most populous country. And the achievement of Chinese Communism seemed to offer a portent for much of the non-Western world. Over large areas of what we now call the Third World, the combination of Soviet power and the attraction of revolutionary Marxism made it more than possible that the modernization and industrialization of those countries would take place under the auspices of Communism and rebound to the greater power and influence of the Soviet Union and to the further demonstration of the debility of the democratic states and the ideologies they represented.

The more than twenty-five years which have passed since the death of the creator of the system have enabled us to acquire a more balanced perspective on Stalinism. We can now see that it was neither a foolproof recipe for tyranny nor the most effective vehicle of advancing the cause of Communism and Soviet power. Had Stalin, now senile and paranoid, lived a few more years, the system would have found itself in a crisis dwarfing that of the 1930's. Everything we know entitles us to believe that with him in power, the conflict with China would have come sooner and in a more intense form than it did under his successors. His skill in managing foreign affairs gone (witness the break with Yugoslavia, provoked quite needlessly, and largely because of the old man's vanity), the USSR might not have been able to avoid a confrontation with the West, and that at a time when the United States still enjoyed a vast superiority both industrially and in nuclear weapons. Internally Stalin's death bared, rather than caused, the strains and weaknesses which existed beneath the façade of monolithic totalitarianism. It is an oversimplification to argue on the analogy of the 1930's when a specific set of circumstances, both domestic and international, enabled Stalin to decimate the party, government, and army elite. Another purge of such dimensions, and which evidently was in the offing before March 5, 1953, could have had quite different consequences. Perhaps it was lucky for

Stalin and the Soviet regime, not to mention the millions of his surviving victims, that he died when he did.

The Party and the State

With the despot gone, his successors, though they now could breathe more easily, many of them having been marked for a purge, expected evidently a much more serious threat to the regime than the one which eventually materialized. The official communiqué announcing changes in the party and government high command described them as intending to prevent "disorder and panic." Divided as they were by the struggle for power, the oligarchs were evidently unanimous in deciding that the worst features of Stalinism had to be abrogated forthwith and that the regime had to move rapidly to relieve sufferings and to avoid the wrath of its people. Characteristic of the apprehension—perhaps even panic would not be too strong a word—which seized the leadership was its decision on March 24, 1953, to proclaim an amnesty for several categories of prisoners. Amnesties hitherto had been issued on festive occasions such as major anniversaries of the Revolution, and no one could miss the incongruity of this one coinciding with the period of official mourning for, as an official communiqué phrased it, "Comrade Stalin, whom we all have loved so much and who will live in our hearts forever." Among the "crimes" whose perpetrators were to be pardoned were such as lateness to work, alleged inefficiency in production, desertion (as proved by having been a prisoner of war), etc. And the amnesty decree also stipulated that all those draconic laws put in the criminal code in the 1930's were to be removed from it, the ministry of justice being given just thirty days for the task. And almost simultaneously, the vast network of the forced labor camps began to disgorge its prisoners.

Since humanitarian reasons could not have been the decisive consideration in the leaders' hurry to dissociate themselves from the worst features of Stalinism, what prompted their actions, i.e., of what were they afraid? For at least a generation there had not been anything resembling organized political opposition in Russia, the population had been cowed, and to an outsider the idea of a popular revolt in 1953 must have seemed incredible. But not so to the heirs of Stalin, as Khrushchev confessed, "[We] were afraid that the thaw might unleash a flood which we would not be able to control, and which would drown us . . . [which] would have washed away all the barriers and retaining walls of our society."[2] And the man who launched de-Stalinization follows this admission with a priceless understatement: "From the point of view of leadership, this would have been an unfavorable development."

Well, the Kremlin's worst fears did not materialize. But the statement demonstrates how Soviet leaders are prone to what might be called power hypochondria. And perhaps their apprehensions, although exaggerated, were not altogether unreasonable. The whole bizzare structure of repression and controls which was Stalinism depended in the last analysis on the legend of one man's infallibility and omnipotence. We do know that the news of the tyrant's death was followed by riots and revolts in some forced labor camps. And in the summer of 1953 came the workers' revolt in East Berlin, and portents of future troubles appeared in some other satellite areas.

By their own testimony, the new leaders obviously did not believe that in the thirty-five years since the revolution the Soviet people had become sufficiently imbued with faith in Marxism-Leninism to keep them from turning on the regime. No such fears were expressed or felt after Lenin's death, though then the Soviet Union was infinitely weaker and much more vulnerable to a domestic upheaval or an attack from abroad. But the party was still imbued with a real ideological fervor and a sense of mission. In the intervening period, however, the power of ideology had atrophied. And what now held the whole edifice of Communism together was Russian nationalism on the one hand, and instruments of repression, the secret police in Russia, the Red Army in the vassal states, on the other. But with the old sorcerer gone, none of his pupils, or even all of them together, could hope to manipulate those forces with his skill. The Soviet Union and world Communism could no longer be run through sheer terror, deception, and myth making.

With the machinery of mass terror dismantled, the regime set about erecting new "barriers and retaining walls" for its totalitarian structure. (It is ironic that the leading proponent of "socialist legality" became the long-term overlord of the secret police, Lavrenti Beria; but when very soon afterwards he fell victim to the intra-oligarchy power struggle, his liquidation and the purge of his followers in the security apparatus was still done in the old, i.e., pre-1953 style.) There was brisk competition among the leaders for devising a formula which would enable them to run the country in the essentially authoritarian manner, but at the same time secure the regime popular acceptance. Beria had made his bid in the name of "socialist legality," i.e., by lopping off the worst excrescences of Stalinism, but his colleagues' suspicions that he wanted to take personal credit for this policy and use it as the means of establishing his own "personality cult" brought about his downfall. It was then the turn of Malenkov to make his bid for supreme power, rather than being first among equals, by promising relief to the long-suffering Soviet consumer. But again his fellow oligarchs hastened to curb his ambitions. Unlike Beria, he was chastised and demoted rather than liquidated, a significant sign that by 1955 the Soviet Union was definitely moving away from the Stalinist pattern and practices.

It fell to Nikita Khrushchev to lead the Communist state into a new era. The key to his success lay in his ability to incorporate in his political "platform" the most attractive, from the point of view of the bulk of party membership, postulates of his two fallen rivals as well as a much broader and comprehensive program of reform of the Soviet system. The key provision of this reform was the attempt to breathe new spirit into the ideology, and by the same token to restore vitality to the Communist party. As against the narrow circle of his immediate colleagues on the Presidium, Khrushchev sought, and for quite a while enjoyed, the support of the broader range of party leaders, the local secretaries, and the managerial bureaucracy. This broader stratum of the oligarchy saw in Khrushchev's explicit de-Stalinization the promise not only of greater personal security (no longer would they be fired or worse at the mere whim of *the* leader *or* some of his favorites of the moment), but also of greater power and importance for themselves.

From being mere clerks, local party chieftains were transformed into people of consequence. They also had the added satisfaction of seeing those who had lorded it over them now "revealed" by Khrushchev as having been accomplices in Stalin's crimes. It was the support of this intermediate group of party leaders which saved the First (to mark the distinction from the bad old time, Khrushchev would not use the title "General") Secretary against the intrigues of his senior colleagues in 1956-1957, the conflict eventually being resolved by the ejection of the group headed by Molotov and Malenkov from the Communist Olympus in 1957.

For quite a while it seemed that the attempted resuscitation of Marxism was having a spectacular success. With Khrushchev's famous denunciation of Stalin in his "secret" speech at the Twentieth Congress in 1956, many even in the population at large must have felt that the horrors of the past era were not something which was inherent in the ideology or in Communism as such. Stripped of its Stalinist excrescences, Communism could be a dynamic creed which still had a great deal to offer to Soviet society and which could be dissociated from terror and excessive conformity. The party appeared to recover its vitality as the real moving force in politics. Its congresses were held at regular intervals and while obviously not the forum for decision making, they at least provided the Soviet citizen with some insight about the past and present policies. Another departure from the old pattern was the frequency of the meetings of the Central Committee. And on several occasions, proceedings of the Central Committee were made available to the public. The average party member, not to mention the bulk of the population, was still a passive rather than active participant in the political process. But unlike what had gone on before March 1953, he now had an inkling of what was going on.

To be sure, this pattern of open, or what might be called populistic-style, authoritarian politics could not continue indefinitely. Once the people became accustomed to not being afraid, some of them were bound to develop aspirations going beyond what Khrushchev's regime at its most liberal was willing to or could afford to grant, and this in turn was bound to alarm the party elite, including those who initially had been among Khrushchev's strongest supporters.

Beset by growing opposition within the oligarchy and by increasing troubles and setbacks of his foreign and economic policies, Khrushchev initiated in 1961 a new course which was bound to bring a new crisis. At the Twenty-Second Party Congress he attacked Stalin and Stalinism in terms which to many constituted a threat to the very basis of the Soviet system. This was followed by a series of measures which were bound to alienate not only the old guard on the Presidium, but also many in that wider oligarchy of party secretaries and functionaries who had provided the base of his political support. The Central Committee meetings, and toward the end of his reign even the Presidium's would be held in the presence of outsiders. From the point of view of the First Secretary, this was expected to inhibit any criticism of his policies by his colleagues and to secure their acceptance. But to a party bureaucrat, even if he were one of Khrushchev's strongest supporters, that procedure threatened to dilute the power and prestige of the ruling class, and looked suspiciously like Khrushchev's bid for popular support against the party hierarchy as a whole. The same sinister meaning was read in Khrushchev's slogan that the current phase of Soviet society was "the state of all the people." Another measure which contributed to the erosion of the First Secretary's popularity and support within the ruling group was the reorganization of the party organs he carried through shortly before his downfall: party secretariats at all levels, up to that of the union republics, were to be divided into two segments, industrial and agricultural. For the local party boss who had grown to consider himself a little king in his domain, this was the crowning blow. Had Khrushchev been able to show spectacular successes in the foreign relations and economic fields, it is possible that he could have overcome the opposition to his reforms and perhaps succeeded in drastically transforming the character of the Communist party bureaucracy. But in the wake of the Cuban missile fiasco, the ever noisier dispute with China, and bad harvests, his position became untenable. In October 1964 the majority of his senior colleagues staged another plot against him, and this time they found an overwhelming support in the Central Committee and were successful.

The Brezhnev-Kosygin regime which emerged from the October *coup* represented the triumph of conservatism and of the oligarchic principle within the Communist party. Khrushchev's improvisations were quickly undone. A stop was put to what the ruling group had for some time considered to be *excessive* de-Stalinization. In brief, the regime has resisted any attempt to tamper with the essentially oligarchico-bureaucratic system of political power. Mass terror and extreme intolerance of anything new and unconformist in the arts, science, etc., have not returned. But structurally the regime remains Stalinist in its essentials. It was even found desirable to restore Stalin to respectability. No longer a divinity, he has been placed upon a more modest pedestal as "an outstanding party leader" who regrettably had made some mistakes, but who in the main served the Soviet state well. Even the party nomenclature has reverted to the Stalinist style. There is again a general secretary, and, as before 1952, the highest body of the party is called Politburo, rather than Presidium, a symbolic gesture by the new leadership meant to convey "whatever our enemies say, we are not ashamed or contrite about our past."

In abandoning any search for innovation in domestic politics, the Soviet leadership has tacitly acknowledged that there is little place for Marxism in the USSR except as an official cult. There was a great deal of theatricality in Khrushchev's efforts to prove that ideology still had a vital role to play in the development of Soviet society, whether through his organizational pyrotechnics or his slogan (who remembers it now?) that in 1980 the Soviet Union would enter the stage of Communism. Now the most dramatic event scheduled for that date is the Olympic games in Moscow, while Marxism-Leninism, more than ever before, seems irrelevant to real life concerns of the rulers or the ruled.

Russian Nationalism and the Nationality Problem

One of the basic premises of Marxism was that the process of industrialization brings with it the waning of nationalism. History has confuted these predictions of Karl Marx; nationalism has been the central phenomenon of the twentieth century. Nationalism, i.e., the skillful exploitation of national grievances of various non-Russian ethnic groups in the tsars' empire, enabled Lenin's party to come to power and to establish the first Marxist state in the world. The Soviet Union survived and won World War II not under the banner of Marxism-Leninism, but mostly on the impulse of *Russian* nationalism. In today's USSR, nationalism is both the main source of strength of the Soviet regime and, from another perspective, it is the most serious long-run threat to Communism.

Behind these convoluted paradoxes lies the involved story of the regime's policy on the nationality issue. Following the war, the Georgian-born dictator sponsored Russian chauvinism. Anything smacking of a suspicious idealization of a non-Russian nationality's independent past or existence, whether an ardent ode by a Ukrainian poet, a historian's denunciation of *tsarist* imperialism in Central Asia, or an excessive glorification of a nineteenth-century Caucasian leader against his country's absorption into the empire, was condemned. "Cosmopolitanism," i.e., acknowledgment of foreign sources and influences on Russian culture and admission that there was much to be admired in other countries' cultural and scientific achievements, was considered a transgression next to treason—ironic for a regime tracing its descent from Karl Marx and Friedrich Engels. Toward the end of Stalin's life the campaign against "the rootless cosmopolites" demeaning the achievements of Soviet culture and of the Russian nation took on clearly anti-Semitic undertones. The Jews, once so numerous in higher state and party positions in the Soviet Union, were now, with the exception of a privileged handful, removed, some of them slated for a worse fate.

One could believe at first that this xenophobia and Russian chauvinism were principally an outgrowth of the war, when patriotism proved to be the bulwark of the regime, while many other ethnic groups behaved in a less exemplary fashion. One might also speculate that Stalin's death would bring an improvement in the nationality problem, as it did with many other repressive policies. And, to be sure, after March 1953 some of the most glaring aspects of Russification policies were discarded. The national groups in the Northern Caucasus region which in 1944 were decreed to have been disloyal and deported *en masse* from their homelands were now rehabilitated, and the survivors among them allowed to return to their native lands.[3] Official anti-Semitism was muted. The Stalinist pattern of running the non-Russian Union Republics, under which the holder of the most important posts, such as the ministry of security, used to be a nonnative (usually a Russian), was changed to conform with the theory of equality of all the nationalities. From 1953 the first secretary of the Ukrainian party would be a native.

Yet from the perspective of more than a generation since the demise of Stalin, it is possible to say that, as in many other things, changes in the nationality policies have been more apparent than real. Russian nationalism remains the main source of support for the regime, and the latter, well conscious of this fact, stresses, though not as explicitly as before 1953, the dominant role of the Great Russian element in the state. It views with suspicion any "excessive" attachment by the non-Russians to their own cultural ways and responds with repression to any plea or agitation for greater local autonomy for the other ethnic areas or groups.

The official view clings to the ritual formula that Communism has solved the nationality problem. What we have in the Soviet Union is fraternal coexistence of all large and small national groups. The Soviet constitution, both in its 1936 and 1978 versions, postulates absolute equality of the fifteen Union Republics, which on paper enjoy rights not found in other federal systems, including that of secession. In fact the principle of centralization inherent in Communism has always, even in the earliest days of the Communist state, made any idea of genuine political or economic autonomy of the national areas completely unreal. The official dogma extols *Soviet* patriotism, i.e., the Soviet citizen's feeling of loyalty and devotion to his state, in which are blended harmoniously his overweening attachment and allegiance to his Socialist fatherland, his pride in his particular nationality, and his faith in the ideals of Communism. Yet in fact, upon a closer examination, Soviet patriotism turns out to be *Russian* nationalism with a specific political coloring. A Ukrainian or Uzbek is expected to acknowledge the Russian nation as the "elder brother" within the Soviet family and to accept the fact that his own country's destiny is regulated by a body—the Politburo of the Central Committee of the Communist Party—dominated by the Russian element. To be sure, he is no longer expected or pressed as he had been in the tsarist time, and came close to being during the last phase of Stalinism, to become Russified in his culture or even language. But what the regime still demands is what might be called political assimilation of its subjects: their acquiescence in the essentially Russian character of the state, their abandonment of any aspiration that the decisions regulating social and economic policies of their native lands be made there, rather than in Moscow. Communism in the USSR has not solved the national problem nor, as Lenin once fondly imagined it would, made national differences irrelevant in politics. What he had said in 1919, "scratch some Russian Communists and you will find Great Russian chauvinists," is much truer today than then, when the Communists were filled by a genuine internationalist spirit. The Soviet state lives in a symbiotic relationship with Russian nationalism, and this relationship, while the source of its strength, poses increasing problems and dangers for the regime.

The element of strength comes from the fact that Communism has become a seemingly indispensable servant of Russian nationalism. Would any other but a Communist regime be able to preserve Soviet Russia's power, and, even more important, territorial integrity? Even a dissenter is taken aback when he imagines what a genuine liberalization of the political system under which he lives would imply in the non-Russian areas. Wouldn't a democratic Russia be eventually constrained to grant independence to the Ukraine, and at least far-reaching autonomy to the Central Asian, Caucasian, and Baltic nationalities? This dilemma is especially acute for those who, like Solzhenitsyn, combine anti-Communism with fervent

Russian nationalism. And when we consider the bulk of Soviet citizens, many of whom must resent even if in silence various features of the system under which they live, we can be sure that their acquiescence in it is largely based on the premise, whether articulated or not, that any alternatives would mean the breakup of the state and a catastrophic decline in their country's power and standing in the world.

By the same token industrialization and modernization have undoubtedly strengthened particularistic feelings among the non-Russian nationalities. Ironically, it was also the policy of the Soviet regime in the first decade after the revolution—even more ironically in its earliest phase sponsored by none other than Stalin in his capacity as commissar of nationalities (1917-1922)—which had contributed to the building of national self-consciousness among the most backward ethnic groups. Once set in motion, the process could not be reversed, but only temporarily repressed. And with the disappearance of terror, the fact that almost half of the population of the USSR is not Russian is felt by the regime to constitute a serious vulnerability accentuated by the recent demographic trends.[4]

To be sure, in an ideal Communist world national differences should not lead to separatist movements or feelings. An Uzbek or Lithuanian ought to be able to combine the pride in his national heritage with a broader Soviet patriotism, and more prosaically with the appreciation of the economic and political advantages of being a citizen of a huge and powerful state. And even in the present nonideal world, the realities of Soviet politics are such that the average non-Russian gives but little thought to the desirability, let alone possibility, of independent national existence. Yet we have had evidence of continuing nationalist stirrings in the Ukraine and Georgia. As with political dissent in general, so with the burgeoning nationalist aspirations in the USSR. Any repression short of mass terror can check their manifestation but cannot eradicate their source.

Here then, to use Marxist semantics, is another of the inherent contradictions of the Communist system: its ideological premises, in this case national equality, clash with the political interests of the regime which require it to stress

Russian domination and to curb national aspirations of the non-Russian groups. The most vivid demonstration of this paradox is seen in the Jewish question. Among the proudest boasts of Communism, and one which for long brought it solid propaganda dividends among liberal circles in the West, was that the Revolution emancipated the Jews from the second-class-citizen status they had suffered in tsarist Russia. With the rise of anti-Semitism in the West during the interwar period, many a progressive tended to turn a blind eye to the Soviet regime's sins of omission precisely because it freed one of the largest Jewish communities in the world from the pattern of discrimination which had been its lot, and because its policy on that issue stood in such glaring contrast to that of dictatorial regimes of the right. Yet it should have been obvious even before there were any explicit signs of anti-Semitism in the Soviet Union that there can be no meaningful social or national equality under a system which does not observe human rights as such. And with the officially sponsored xenophobia and "anti-cosmopolitanism" drive of the post-war years, it became clear that the Jews not only shared in general unfreedom which was the lot of all Soviet people, but were to some extent singled out as *the* national group allegedly most susceptible to the subversive, anti-Soviet sentiments. Stalin's death probably saved the Jewish community in the USSR from mass repression comparable to that which struck the supposedly disloyal nationalities of the Northern Caucasus, the Crimean Tatars, and the Volga Germans. But the pattern of covert discrimination, and its premise—of all Soviet nationalities, the Jews, because of their links with the outside world and because they have an alternative focus of national allegiance, Israel, can be least trusted to give wholehearted allegiance to the Fatherland of Socialism—has continued and become intensified. With mass terror no longer practicable, the Soviet government could have resorted to what on the face of it would have seemed both a logical and humane approach to the problem, to allow emigration of those Jews who found their national or religious feelings incompatible with allegiance to the USSR. And indeed, in a decision which it probably regrets today, in the early 1970's the regime authorized emigration on a moderate scale, hoping no doubt to get rid of the trouble-makers, while scoring points with world public opinion for its humanitarian stance.

However, it became obvious that like any half measure, this one, instead of solving the problem, compounded it. Applications for permission to emigrate, instead of an expected trickle, threatened to become a flood. They came not only from those who felt the stirrings of Jewish nationalism, but also from people who though thoroughly assimilated felt, whether for political or personal reasons, that life under Soviet conditions was unendurable. Although as of the end of 1978 some 150,000 Jews have been permitted to leave the USSR, the regime obviously feels that it cannot accept the principle of free emigration. To do so would deprive it of one of the most effective means of control and of enforcing conformity among its people, and would encourage dissent, not only among the Jews, but among other ethnic groups. Hence the chicanery, intimidation, long delays, and in some cases imprisonment of those who want to leave. Hence the attempt to deny that the Jewish exodus has had any relation to the conditions of Soviet life in general. In the official Kremlin view, there is no Jewish problem in the USSR, and what passes for such in the West is simply a by-product of the ideological war waged by capitalism against the USSR. Zionism in this view is one of the ideological tactics employed by the reactionary forces in their attempt to undermine the ideological cohesion of Soviet society. But the real dimensions and implications of the problem go far beyond Zionism and its alleged anti-Soviet orientation. Marxism taught that in the socialist state of the future, one's national origin would become politically irrelevant. Sixty years after the Revolution, it is Marxism which has become irrelevant when it comes to discussing the national problems of the USSR.

The Economic Side

If ideology has become less and less important in regard to anything which affects political power and organization in the USSR, the same cannot be said in connection with various social and economic elements of the system. But even here the role of ideology has drastically changed. What has once been a religion lingers on in the main as a set of superstitions. The old formulas are being repeated, the ancient practices are being repeated, not because of any ideological fervor or real conviction on the part of the leadership, but simply because of its deep traditionalist and conservative bias. Writing to the queen concerning an ecclesiastical appointment, a Victorian prime minister explained his objections to one of the candidates on the grounds that he was prone to enthusiasm, a quality most inappropriate in a bishop of the established church. Very similar must have been the feelings of the Soviet oligarchs when they decided they could no longer put up with Nikita Khrushchev and his "harebrained" schemes and improvisations, as they cruelly characterized them after his dismissal.

Conservatism and fear of innovations have characterized the attitude of the Communist party during the last twenty-five years on most issues touching on economic and social problems of Soviet society. Its leaders have shown great sensitivity to and eagerness to exploit technological and scientific innovations. Yet they have combined this Marxist awareness of the importance of scientific progress with the unwillingness to heed its social and organizational implications. Hence for all the prodigious economic growth, the Soviet Union remains an economically backward society.

This paradox has been most evident in the field of agriculture. Decades of collectivized farming have not succeeded in turning peasant into worker with the same mentality and responses as the city dweller. No problem claimed greater attention from Stalin's successors than that of the perennially ailing segment of the Soviet economy, that of agriculture. As has already been shown, exploitation of the peasant had been raised to the point where even by the premises of the regime it had become counterproductive and had catastrophic results for the productivity of the countryside. Khrushchev lifted the curtain of propaganda and fraudulent statistics which had concealed the true state of affairs before 1953, and the whole nation could see for the first time how official policies had not only pushed the peasant down to the level of subsistence, and at

times below it, but also how they threatened the whole
economy with a disaster. In 1958 Khrushchev revealed that for
all the vaunted mechanization, Soviet agricultural output in
the early 1950's fell below that of 1913.

The post-Stalin regime proceeded to tackle energetically the
secondary causes of the agricultural crisis. Prices for the
collective farms' compulsory deliveries of foodstuffs and
industrial crops were steeply increased. The peasant was
relieved of much of the burden of "voluntary" loans to the state
and given tax concessions. And with material incentives the
volume of production did in fact materially increase, but
hardly in proportion to the needs of the growing population,
or the ambitious aspirations of the regime not only to narrow
down but to eliminate the food consumption gap between the
USSR and the most advanced capitalist states.

To quicken the pace of advance in agricultural production,
Khrushchev plunged into risky improvisations. He became
personally identified with the vast program of settlement and
cultivation of "virgin land," areas in Kazakhstan and elsewhere
that were previously thought unsuitable for agriculture
because of their climate and soil. Some experts at the time
warned that intense cultivation of those lands would turn them
eventually into a dust bowl, and in the early 1960's their
predictions were largely borne out. Another trick pulled out of
the hat by the ever resourceful First Secretary was the campaign
to grow more corn. In January 1955 it was decided to increase
the area of corn cultivation during the next three years from 3.5
to 28 million hectares. The immediate results were spectacular.
By 1958 the index of the gross agricultural production stood at
151 percent of that of 1953. Still, this was impressive only by
comparison to the Stalinist times. The sum total of the advance
fell short of the promise to catch up with the United States in
the production of meat, milk, and butter, or of satisfying the
growing needs of the Soviet consumers. By the early 1960's the
coincidence of some bad harvests and failures with the virgin
lands plunged Soviet agriculture into a new crisis and
undoubtedly contributed to Khrushchev's downfall.

His successors proposed to deal with agriculture in a more
sober and fundamental way. Investments were doubled, prices

for state purchases from the collective farms increased. The Brezhnev-Kosygin regime seemed at first to recognize the crux of the problem, the depressed and unfree situation of the Russian peasant who needed more than just material incentives to become more productive. The Stalin reforms had turned the peasant into a virtual serf. Tied down to his farm,[5] his remuneration subject to yearly fluctuations, dependent on the harvest, deprived of social security benefits open to all other citizens, he had been the veritable beast of burden of society. After 1966 most of those disabilities were removed. The *kolkhoz* member, instead of being paid according to the so-called labor day formula, was given a regular wage. And he now became eligible for old-age pensions and other social benefits, like the industrial worker.

Yet by the Soviets' own admission, the sum total of these reforms and ameliorations has failed to solve the problem. The bad harvest of the 1970's and the massive grain purchases from the United States and Canada have highlighted once again the fact that the agricultural sector lags far behind the industrial one. For all the mechanization of farm work and urbanization of the country, the Soviet Union still employs an unduly large proportion of its labor force in agriculture. As in other aspects of Soviet life, the disappearance of mass terror has added another dimension to the problem. The Soviet consumer, though more patient than most, cannot be expected to put up with conditions like those experienced under the Stalin regime, when a bad harvest would bring large-scale regional famines but the power and standing of the regime would remain unaffected. The Kremlin must heed the lesson of 1970 in Poland, where food shortages and the rise in prices led to the workers' riots, which came close to turning into a revolution, and toppled the then leadership of the Communist Party of Poland.

The key to the problem remains the low productivity of the collective and state farm peasant. By the official Soviet statistics, one Russian working on the land produces one-fourth of what his American counterpart does, but in reality this proportion is more likely to be one to seven or eight. Granted the climatic advantages enjoyed by American agriculture, one must still conclude that the major cause of the disparity in the performance of the systems must lie in the social and political systems under which they operate. Or to put it differently, the kind of Marxist solution Stalin forced upon Russian agriculture has not worked. Yet though they have dealt with the peasant in much more humane and rational ways, his successors have stubbornly clung to the essence of that solution: the herding of agricultural workers onto collective and state farms, refusing to allow for any dilution of what in fact is state ownership and management in favor of individual initiative of the land cultivator. In fact the thrust of their policy is toward the opposite: the merging of collective farms into greater and greater units, and the progressive shift from the *kolkhoz* into the "higher" form of socialist agriculture, the *sovkhoz*—the state farm. They have before their eyes a palpable proof that when left to work on his own and for himself, the peasant can be much more productive than as an indentured laborer. Those tiny areas left under collectivization to individual rural households accounted in 1970, though comprising but three percent of the total area under cultivation, for more than one-third of the total output of meat, forty percent of milk, and fifty-five percent of eggs. But it is the regime's conscious policy to liquidate eventually those last relics of private property in the countryside.

None of Russia's leaders during the past fifty years could be described as an ideological fanatic. The present ruling team is composed of pragmatically minded bureaucrats. Why then do they stick to policies which clearly hamper the economic development of their country? The reason lies in what might be called ideological inertia of the elderly rulers. To tamper with one of the fundamental features of the authoritarian edifice which they inherited would mean in their view to court danger. Witness the harm done by Khrushchev's garrulity about Stalin's crimes. The present system of management of agriculture, if it does not make the peasant happy or productive, still has kept him quiet and obedient. Who knows what ideas the rural population might get if the present methods of controls were loosened? Wouldn't other groups, say the industrial workers, feel in turn they could exact concessions by exerting economic pressures on the government? There are many unbelieving people who still feel constrained to observe the outward forms of their creeds for fear there might be something to this business of posthumous rewards and punishments. And by the same token, the Communists carry on with their Marxist rites and incantations because they are afraid that their cessation might bring damnation: loss of power.

The tendency toward doctrinal inertia and bureaucratic ossification has not been absent from the field of industrial relations. To be sure, here, in contrast to agriculture, the ideological and power imperatives have joined in urging an innovative course and a veritable cult of productivity and of technological progress. And it can be argued that for a long time Marxism helped with the industrial development and growth of the Soviet economy. It did so through Communism imitating and surpassing the practices and exactions of the earliest, most exploitive phase of capitalism: by imposing a draconic labor discipline, by neglecting the consumer in favor of rapid capital formation, in brief by the state becoming the collective capitalist and expropriating in the early nineteenth-century fashion the surplus value produced by the entire people. But as with the early capitalist practices, so with the Communist one: a moment had to come when they became not only politically dangerous, but economically counterproductive. The strict code of industrial relations which bound the industrial worker to his place of employment had to be given up in the wake of the events of March 1953. The worker could now move from one factory to another without necessarily securing his boss's permission and would no longer be subject to criminal sanctions for lateness or for missing a day's work. His needs as a consumer would no longer be among the lowest priorities of the government. Ruthless exploitation of the working force, labor passports, fantastically crowded living conditions could have had some, even if perverse, logic during the period of the most intensive industrialization and while the war lasted, but the same logic was obviously lacking, even to the most indoctrinated Communist, in the continuation of the same system into the more advanced industrial period when improvements in productivity must also reflect and depend on rising living standards.

The new policies proved their merit. Throughout the 1950's and early 1960's indices of the Soviet industrial growth continued to impress and cause concern to some of the West, while to others they held out a comforting promise that the Soviet regime, now that its energies had to be largely absorbed in satisfying the consumers' needs, would have less time and inclination for adventurous foreign policies.

Yet it soon became apparent that even on the industrial front, the ideologico-political premises of Communism stood in the way of reform. Overcentralization and the bureaucratic mentality pervading every nook and cranny of the Soviet system have become an increasing encumbrance on the Soviet economy as a whole. The industrial growth has slowed down considerably. The quantitative growth in consumers' goods has not been paralleled by an improvement in their quality; if anything, the opposite has been true.

Complaints that the Soviet industrial system is rigid and overcentralized, discouraging initiative and innovation in individual enterprises, have been a constant theme in Soviet economic literature and in the leaders' speeches. But equally insistent and usually victorious has been the counterargument that socialist planning requires centralized direction and detailed supervision of all branches of industry. Denunciation of the evils of bureaucratism is the favorite topic of official oratory, of what passes in the Soviet Union for investigative journalism, and of satirical literature. But how can one curtail the bureaucratic evil without curbing the power of the bureaucrats, beginning with those who constitute the Politburo and the Central Committee of the CPSU?

Hence the antibureaucratic crusades in the Soviet Union have always involved shadowboxing. Khrushchev believed that he struck a blow for decentralization and innovation when in 1957 he abolished most of the ministries dealing with the economy and transferred their competence to the network of regional economic councils (*sovnarkhozy*) paralleling the Union Republics' boundaries. Soon there were complaints that the new system, far from eliminating the old ills, created new ones, such as the swollen local bureaucracy concentrating excessively on the needs of the given region rather than keeping the overall economic problems in sight. And so in 1965 the once much trumpeted-about local economic councils were abolished and the old industrial ministries restored in their full bureaucratic splendor.

It was to be expected that the Brezhnev-Kosygin team would come up with its own panaceas for Soviet industry. And indeed early in their rule they embraced an idea advocated by a number of Soviet economists, the best known of whom was Evsey Liberman, which called for reforms at the factory level, rather than in the overall network of industrial administration and planning. Stalin had discovered that managerial authority and labor discipline were necessary for economic development; Liberman followed with the equally unsensational finding that profit and competition were essential ingredients of successful industrial management. "We should consider the use of profit as a yardstick or indicator of the effectiveness of the production of our enterprises."[6] Let the latter compete for the market and thus have the incentive to reduce costs of production and to improve quality, two respects in which Soviet industry has for long been under a great disadvantage when compared with that of the West.

The mere word "profit," when applied to the Soviet economy, stuck in the throats of the more orthodox Marxist theorists, but nevertheless the regime bravely launched still another effort to cure the ills of socialism with capitalist remedies. In 1965 Kosygin announced a series of measures which beginning with some selective enterprises were supposed by 1970 to be introduced in all nonagricultural enterprises. Their central feature was to be the enhancement of the individual firm's autonomy. Instead of the approximately thirty sets of directives from above which the firm's manager used to receive, he would now get "only" eight. The central authority would still prescribe how much the firm must produce and how much money it would have in its wage fund, but it would now be up to the manager to decide how many workers he should employ, what labor-saving devices to use, etc. The given firm's success in meeting and surpassing not only quantitative but also qualitative targets for production would be rewarded by bonuses for the director, technical personnel, and the workers.

The reforms encountered considerable resistance among the more conservatively minded economic bureaucrats, who were scandalized by what to us would appear a very modest degree of decentralization inherent in the new plan. It was pointed out that one of the undesirable by-products would be an increased fluidity of the labor market; and since the managers could now fire superfluous workers, this could bring new strains and stresses on the economy, which according to the official creed is not supposed to have even short-term unemployment. But what mostly worried the die-hard bureaucrats was the prospect of unemployment in their own ranks, since the logical corollary of the scheme should have been a considerable reduction in the personnel of the central agencies. And eventually the reforms, while not formally abrogated, were allowed to wither away. Since 1971 the pendulum has swung again in the direction of centralization of economic adminis- tration. The political structure of the Soviet regime, one must conclude, will always stand in the way of any meaningful decentralization of economic decision making.

One may pose a more fundamental question: In what way can the Soviet economic system be classified as socialist? True, it has eliminated almost completely (except for the peasants' individual plots) private ownership of the means of produc- tion, vesting their control in the state.[7] What of those other features which, in the opinion of the fathers of socialism, beginning with Marx, would characterize the socialist mode of production? This system, they believed, would soon establish its superiority over capitalism in its ability to absorb and ex- ploit technological and scientific innovations, in its sensitiv- ity to the consumer's needs, and in giving the worker the feeling of real participation in the creation of communal wealth, rather than being a mere soldier of the industrial army and an adjunct of the machinery. Yet on none of these counts has Communism passed the test. Sixty years after the Revolution, it is in the capitalist West that the Soviets seek the source of technological innovations and of managerial and production techniques which might enable them to improve the performance of their economy. The worker, far from having acquired a new status and a new attitude toward the industrial system, remains very much a private of the industrial army, his ability to influence his conditions of work and remuneration much smaller than that of the worker under what is still called capitalism. The capitalist has disappeared but the boss remains, much more so in the USSR than in the West. Until very recently no regime anywhere has been as neglectful of the consumer's needs. Communism in Russia, to paraphrase what Karl Marx wrote about capitalism, has ruthlessly forced the Soviet people to produce for production's sake, but even in the economic sphere it has utterly failed to create "those material conditions, which alone can form the basis of a higher form of society, a society in which the full and free development of each individual forms the ruling principle."

Soviet Domination and International Communism

Soviet victories, geography, and the deplorable policies of the Western powers combined to give Eastern Europe to the USSR. One of the most startling developments of the post-war era has been the end of what during 1917-1939 was called in Communist semantics "capitalist encirclement." By 1947-1948 there was in existence the "socialist camp"—the Soviet Union was no longer the only Communist state in the world, but the head of a bloc composed of its Eastern European satellites and its sole Asian one, Mongolia, which though under Soviet influence since the early 1920's was not formally declared independent of (the then Kuomintang) China until 1945. The number of Communist states has continued to grow, and as of this writing the process continues.

We cannot here discuss in depth the question of how far this process has reflected the West's sins of commission and omission, the Soviet Union's military strength and political skills, or the proverbial ineluctable forces of history. Our main concern is to try to analyze the impact of the expansion of Communism on the ideological and political dilemmas of the Soviet state, and to assess what this expansion portends for the current and future fortunes of Marxism.

In the heyday of Stalinism, roughly 1930-1948, the interrelationship Marxism/international Communism/the Soviet Union was very simple. Marxism meant whatever was proclaimed as such by the Kremlin; international Communism was an extension of Soviet power and the world's Communist parties were its docile servants. The enormous bulk and prestige of the only Communist state precluded any effective challenge of Moscow's hegemony by any Communist party, and stood in the way of any definition of the goals of Communism that would put them at variance with the interests of the Soviet Union. When the Comintern was dissolved in 1943 to reassure Russia's allies, the gesture in fact was quite meaningless. Foreign Communists' habit of obedience and the Soviet ability to command them were so well ingrained that the Third International had become a fifth wheel.

Superficially, the appearance on the scene after 1945 of other Communist states should not have brought any alteration in the now traditional relationship. In most cases the new Communist regimes had been installed by the Red Army, and their ability to stay in power depended in the last analysis on the Soviet Union. For all the techniques of repression they soon employed it is fair to say that with the exception of the Yugoslavs, none of the Eastern European Communist regimes of 1945-1948 could have held on to power for one week, were the Soviet Union to declare its disinterest in its survival.[8]

But almost immediately it became clear that a foreign Communist leader in power was a different animal than he had been when he was a conspirator fighting for power. Much as they loved the Fatherland of Socialism, declared the Yugoslav Communists when Stalin first began to press them to get rid of Tito, they could not love their own country less. In more prosaic terms, all those erstwhile agents of Moscow now had their own garden to cultivate. They had not become anti-Soviet. Far from it. As much as the Russians lorded it over them, they would have remained at that stage obedient followers of the USSR and Stalin, had the latter allowed *some* latitude in running their own affairs and relief from the insulting day-to-day supervision of their policies, and had the

Russians observed some moderation in exploiting the satellites' economies, in many cases as cruelly ravaged by the war as had been their own.

Stalin's Russia was, however, incapable of moderation when it came to demanding obedience from its vassals, and the despot himself in his last phase appeared oblivious of the possibility that his slightest whim might be defied by a *Communist*. Thus the brutality and heavy-handedness of the policy toward the satellites turned the Yugoslav Communists, initially the most fervent of the Soviet Union's supporters, into rebels. Even as late as 1948 the rupture might have been avoided had the Soviet Union exercised some diplomacy rather than demanded unconditional submission. During the next five years, Tito's defection was followed by a thorough purge of the satellite regimes of anyone who in Moscow's opinion might be tempted to try to follow in the Yugoslav leader's footsteps. The conditions which enabled the Yugoslav Communists to mount their successful defiance did not as yet exist in other Communist states: in none of them was the leadership as united nor as confident that it could stay in power without the shadow of the Soviet army behind it.

As in the case of their own country, so in regard to world Communism, Stalin's successors realized that they could not carry on with his methods. To continue with them risked the satellites becoming liabilities rather than assets to Soviet imperialism: their economies damaged by Soviet exactions, their Communist parties demoralized and terrorized, they would present an additional danger in case of an emergency. And in the long run the policy of complete control or of subversion of internal Communist leadership by Moscow would inevitably lead to a vaster case of Titoism in China, which even Stalin had realized could not be dealt with *exactly* the way he had treated Poland or Bulgaria. The satellites had to be accorded a degree of internal autonomy, and the Great People's Republic of China, as it was now increasingly referred to in the Soviet press, had to be accorded a special status as the Soviet Union's junior partner and to be propitiated by economic and technological help. In the same vein, the Khrushchev regime embarked on a policy of *détente* with

Belgrade, followed by a strenuous if rather clumsy courtship of the Yugoslav leaders designed to bring them back into the fold. The Cominform, that misbegotten child of late Stalinism, was now found to be incompatible with the spirit which was to prevail in relations among Communist states, and it was dissolved.

Inherent in the new course was the hope that the ideological bond would prove strong enough to compensate for the elimination of the more crude forms of control over the Communist bloc. But, alas, things were to turn out differently. The result of the new policies was not to make the Soviet Union and Communism more popular in Eastern Europe, but only less feared! And so, with the crushing of the Hungarian revolt in the fall of 1956, the course had to be altered again. With the ideological links proving too weak, the Red Army and internal repression reverted to being the principal guarantors of the Soviet-Communist domination of East Europe.

Yet as in domestic politics, so in intra-Communist relations, there could be no question of returning to the old Stalinist pattern. Military force could not, without incurring incalculable risks, be used to prevent China from assuming an increasingly defiant attitude *vis-à-vis* the USSR. And with the Sino-Soviet conflict bursting into the open in 1960, some other Communist states were given an opportunity to secure greater freedom by maneuvering between the two giants. Little Albania slipped the Soviet leash entirely. The Rumanian Communists, while not going that far, still were defying Moscow on a number of foreign policy and economic issues.

The Chinese in their attacks not only stressed the imperialist role of the USSR, but accused its leaders of betraying Marxism-Leninism and contributing to the bureaucratic and bourgeois degeneration of Soviet society, and of being in secret collusion with the American capitalists. Yet at the same time Peking warmly endorsed the Rumanians, though they for their part sought and obtained closer relations with the West—a telling proof that the ideological issue was not the prime cause of the Sino-Soviet dispute, and that for Mao defiance of the USSR more than compensated any ideological peccadilloes by a Communist regime. Scratch a Russian Communist, Lenin once said, and you will find a Great Russian chauvinist. Scratch any ideological dispute among the Communists and you will find a national and power conflict.

But while not ideological in its essence, the great Communist schism still carries the most profound implications for the ideology. Neither the Russians nor the Chinese can admit to the world, nor fully to themselves, that their quarrel is grounded in a clash of national interests and in mutual fears. To do so would be to admit that Communism is incapable of solving national conflicts and securing peace, that on the contrary the passion for power which is its outstanding characteristic makes a conflict between the two Communist superpowers much more intractable than is any clash between either of them and a capitalist state. And in turn such an admission would go far in undermining the universalistic claims of the doctrine, would make nonsense of the effort to propagate it in the non-Communist world, and would thus threaten the rationale of both the Soviet and the Chinese regimes. Instead of saying "we are afraid of you because you're 800 million strong and threaten our territories in Asia," Moscow persists in blaming the dispute on the "dogmatism and left sectarianism" of the "Maoist clique" and in asserting that eventually the Chinese comrades would see the light, return to the true path of "proletarian internationalism," and ever after live happily in amity with the USSR. Instead of saying explicitly that it is largely Communism which makes the Soviet Union an imperialist state and a threat to them, the Chinese both under Mao and his successors have seen the root cause of the dispute in the betrayal of Marxism by "Khrushchev and his heirs" and express confidence that once the Russian Communists mend their ways, all will go well between the fraternal Soviet and Chinese people. Yet, how convincing are such ideological sophistries to the Soviet, or for that matter, the Chinese man in the street?

It is then the international dimension of Communism which illustrates best its strengths and weaknesses. Since World War II Communism has vastly expanded its area of rule and influence. It bids today, with the power of the Soviet Union behind it, to score further successes and to bring new countries into the Communist camp, seemingly justifying the boast that "in our century all the roads lead to socialism." Yet socialism in its Communist version has failed to fulfill its most enticing promise: to demonstrate its ability to strip nationalism of its distinctive character and to lay the foundations of a peaceful world community which would dispense with war, armaments, and national oppression. The example of the Soviet Union strongly suggests the opposite: Communism there has been able to survive, and in a way thrive, only because of its symbiosis with Russian nationalism; the mainstay of its leading position within the international Communist movement has been its military power, and the camp of socialism is held together not by any ideological links, but by that power as demonstrated in Hungary in 1956 and Czechoslovakia in 1968. When military power cannot readily be applied, national conflicts between states, far from being assuaged by their sharing in the cult of Marx and Lenin, become in fact aggravated. The Sino-Soviet conflict is not the only illustration of this. The *inherent* tendency of most Communist systems to grow bellicose and expansionist can be observed in the recent developments between Vietnam and Cambodia, and between what might be called the semi-Communist regimes of Ethiopia and Somalia. It is within the body of Communism that the virus of nationalism is today bound to become especially virulent. Among the many compliments that Marx paid to capitalism in the *Communist Manifesto*, the most startling (but alas disproved by the early twentieth century) was his praise of it as a factor for peace: "National differences and antagonisms between peoples are daily more and more vanishing, owing mainly to the development of the bourgeoisie, to freedom of commerce." But he was a much worse prophet in postulating that socialism would entirely eliminate international conflicts and wars: "The supremacy of the proletariat will cause them to vanish still faster."[9]

Marxism under Glass

Many would object to the concluding passage of the preceding paragraph on the grounds that Communism as currently practiced has very little to do with "the supremacy of the proletariat." In the same vein, haven't we really been talking about the crisis of the Soviet system rather than a crisis of Marxism? To paraphrase a famous statement about Christianity, many of the latter-day defenders of socialism would argue that the trouble with Marxism is that it has never been practiced. There are many variations on this theme: scientific socialism could not develop properly in a predominantly agrarian society. Stalin perverted the true meaning of the ideology; we must not preclude the possibility of the USSR eventually evolving in a direction which would not displease the ghosts of Karl Marx and Friedrich Engels. Within the past few years several Communist parties in Western Europe proclaimed their determination to depart from the Soviet model insofar as their policies, whether currently in opposition or in power, are concerned (and in Italy, the Communists are to some extent a government party, if that country can be said to have a government in the real sense of the word). Even within the Communist bloc we had in 1968 a brief experiment in "socialism with a human face" in Czechoslovakia, and its tragic termination was due to a military intervention by the Soviets rather than to any inherent incongruity of the idea.[10] In brief, many would argue that it is a considerable oversimplification to discuss Marxism in terms of Communism or to judge the latter solely or mainly on the basis of the Soviet experience.

But it has not been argued here that Soviet Communism has been an *inevitable* outgrowth of Marxism or that it represents the *only* true application of the ideology to practical politics and economics. Still, it would be quibbling to deny that what has been happening in the Soviet Union is central to our understanding of the current status and prospects of Marxism. That Marxism was at one time a vital force in Soviet life is admitted even by as categorical an enemy of everything Communism stands for as Solzhenitsyn: "This ideology which is driving us into a situation of acute conflict abroad has long ceased to be helpful to us here at home, as it was *in the twenties and thirties.*" The author follows this undoubtedly unwitting (for it is the only hint in his voluminous writings that he has something positive to say about Marxism) admission with a more typical scathing attack on the current role of ideology: "In our country today, *nothing constructive rests upon it*, it is a sham, cardboard, theatrical prop—take it away and nothing will collapse, nothing will even wobble."[11] But here one cannot agree with the great writer: *something* would wobble and might collapse if you removed the rites and incantations of Marxism-Leninism—the Soviet regime. The official cult has become a screen designed to filter out the truth about Soviet society, to conceal the reality of an oligarcho-bureaucratic system practicing repression at home and imperialism abroad and to project instead an illusory one of democracy, social progress, and adherence to the principles of "proletarian internationalism." To the degree that the regime has reduced its dependence on terror, it has felt constrained to increase its emphasis on the other major prop of its power, ideological illusion-making. It is thus unlikely to heed Solzhenitsyn's advice and to "cast off this cracked ideology." Cracked though it may be, it is in the rulers' eyes probably more important as a safeguard of their regime's legitimacy than it was under Stalin.

But how effective is the ideology in filtering out the truth about Soviet society and in shielding the ruling elite from a challenge to its powers? It would be a mistake to assume that the average member of the party is no longer a believer. To be sure, it is unlikely that he is driven by the ideological fervor of an early Bolshevik or of a Communist participant in the great economic transformations of the 1920's and '30's. Nowadays his ideological allegiance is likely to be of a more passive and prosaic variety: self-interest as well as indoctrination urging acceptance of the dogma and ideological apathy, rather than zeal inhibiting any questioning of its premises. *Up to a point* this ideological secularization of the party membership has been a factor of stability for the system and a source of comfort to the rulers. They prefer regular, even if tepid, observance of the cult to a passionate zeal, which if triggered off by an intraparty dispute might, as it did with the young Chinese fanatics during the Cultural Revolution, threaten the very foundations of the regime. But a *complete* ideological secularization is something the ruling oligarchy dreads and a totalitarian system can ill afford. Ideological agnosticism must in the long run lead to one thing: a Soviet man, even if he is externally a good Communist and thinks of himself as such, will view his interests and aspirations through the prism of his trade union, level of officialdom, or economic class rather than through that of the party of Lenin. The latter would cease to be an efficacious instrument of government.

Thus even within the party, allegiance to the official doctrine is of a synthetic and strained nature. But outside the ranks of (let us call them) the semi-faithful, the attitude towards the ideology ranges from complete indifference to exasperation and boredom. The intellectual discourse about Marxism has atrophied into the most lifeless kind of scholasticism. And the attempt to saturate all spheres of thought and social activity by what passes for the Marxist ethos has, without ceasing to be oppressive, reached the stage of preposterousness. Again Solzhenitsyn: "This ideology does nothing now but sap our strength and bind us. . . . Everything is steeped in lies and *everybody knows* and says so openly in private conversation, and jokes and moans about it, but in their official speeches they go on, hypocritically parroting what 'they are supposed to say'."[12] What the regime beats into the heads of its hopeless subjects cannot even be called ideological propaganda in the proper sense of the term. Rather, it might be described as ideological noise, intended to crowd out any voices of protest or doubt and to stultify minds into conformity.

As of late this din has been failing to do the job it is supposed to do. How imperfectly the official themes impose themselves even on the minds of the group usually most susceptible to indoctrination is illustrated by the testimony of the Soviets themselves. A poll of young workers in a factory revealed that seventy percent of them hope to advance to engineer or technician. The investigator then writes plaintively: "This is true despite the fact that average earnings for technicians and engineers at the plant are lower than workers' earnings. Certainly one can welcome the young people's thirst for knowledge, but the desire to become an engineer or technician is becoming so widespread that one automatically asks: Who will be left in the workers' jobs?"[13] How few in what is officially the "workers' state" desire to become workers comes out even more vividly from a poll of some three thousand school children in Kiev. Hundreds named as their preferred goals and professions medicine, engineering, and teaching, with only eighty expressing a preference for industrial labor.[14] And all the participants in the polls must have read and discussed in the course of schooling the famous phrase of Engels: "The proletariat seizes political power and turns the means of production into state property. . . . In doing this it abolishes itself as the proletariat, abolishes all class distinctions and class antagonisms."[15]

It is not that Soviet leaders have been ineffective as educators and propagandists; on the contrary. Their skills in these respects contributed greatly to their victory in the Revolution and the Civil War. It took a prodigious ability at illusion-making to persuade many in Russia and abroad that the sufferings of collectivization were justified by the grandiose feat of social engineering, that the horrors of collectivization were necessitated by real treason and foreign danger, and that the crimes of Stalinism were due entirely to the "cult of personality" of one man and a small group of his henchmen. But increasingly of late, propaganda and indoctrination have been unable to duplicate their previous magic feats. In a sense this is a tribute to the father of it all: in refusing to think in Marxist categories, the Soviet citizen affirms the truth of Karl Marx's dictum that human consciousness must ultimately reflect the economic and social conditions of the given society, rather than its ideological or religious veneer. And so, quite independently of his or her feelings about Marxism as such, the average Soviet man or woman has no reason to give thought to something which lies entirely outside his or her everyday concerns and problems. It is only an occasional dissenter, such as Solzhenitsyn, who has the insight that this ideology does not work; yet like the noise one has grown accustomed to, barely noticed by the mass of the people, it still weighs heavily on Soviet society, crippling its moral and intellectual forces.

Although the Soviet Union has not been at war for some

thirty-five years, and a whole generation separates it now from the excesses of the "cult of personality," few of the Marxist prophecies about what the new and brave world of socialism would be like have come to pass. The virtues its apologists claim for the Soviet system and its alleged points of superiority over the West turn out, upon a closer examination, to be the traditional values of *old* capitalism. The Soviet citizen is congratulated on living in a society where education is structured and the young are free of that ailment so general among their Western peers—alienation. Since under socialism economic and social causes of crime have been eliminated, its infrequent perpetrators cannot expect any leniency at the hands of the state. Socialist morality, unlike that of decadent capitalism, does not take a tolerant view of sexual deviation, drug addiction, or pornography. Having solved the principal social problems, the Communist state is spared the turbulence occasioned in the West by movements like women's liberation, racial conflicts, anti-industrialism masked as environmentalism, etc.

Many who nostalgically treasure the old Victorian bourgeois values will find the attitudes described above quite attractive. But alas, insofar as actual Soviet society is concerned, they bear as little relation to it as does "socialist realism" to reality. The total picture is composed of propaganda, wishful thinking, *some* facts, and many outright falsehoods. Even by reading the Soviet press, not dedicated to exposing official myths, one can observe that the USSR has not escaped the problems and traumas which seem to affect all advanced industrial societies in today's world. One finds there complaints about social parasitism among the young, crime and corruption, sexual permissiveness, and the consequent threat to the Soviet family. The blight of alcoholism parallels, but in its seriousness probably surpasses, the scourge of drug addiction in America. It is official statistics which attest that between 1940 and 1973, the period during which the population of the USSR grew by twenty-eight percent, sales of alcohol increased by 534 percent.[16] The birthrate in the industrialized areas is steadily declining. There has evidently been a steep rise in the number of abortions, and few urban families nowadays seem to plan on having more than one child. In brief, despite its enormous power, the Communist state appears unable to enforce the traditional bourgeois standard of values, not to mention ushering in a new socialist one.

The present state of Soviet society is thus deeply disappointing to ideologists, whether of the Marxist or non-Marxist variety. For the former, its actual condition mocks the vision of socialism releasing the full creative potentialities of men, leading them to a new and higher form of freedom. For some time it was possible to believe that it was an accidental perversion of Communism which inhibited the consummation of its ideals. After Stalin's death, Isaac Deutscher, who represents this point of view, wrote:

> Within the Communist Party there already exist various potential trends which will become actual and will crystallize in the process of inner party discussion. Diverse shades of internationalism and nationalism will come to life. Divergent attitudes toward the peasantry will be expressed, conflicting views will arise about the tempo of further industrialization, consumer interests. . . . Once the ruling party begins to discuss its affairs, it cannot monopolize freedom of discussion for long.[17]

Well, though twenty-five years have passed and the country has been released from the vise of terror, we still have not witnessed this promised outburst of creative Marxism, whether within the Communist party or in society at large. On the contrary, what little there was in the way of an ideological stir under Khrushchev was quite effectively suppressed by his successors.

But almost equally disheartening has been the experience of an anti-Marxist who might have expected that once the scales had fallen from the eyes of the people and they could see Stalinism for what it was, there would be a widespread and sustained revulsion against the system as a whole. Instead, as one who stands for the most uncompromising opposition to Communism admits:

> The majority of young people could not care less whether we have been rehabilitated or not, whether twelve million people are inside [the camps] or are inside no longer. . . . Just so long as

they themselves are at liberty with their tape recorders and their disheveled girl friends. A fish does not campaign against fisheries—it only tries to slip through the mesh.[18]

What seemingly has withered away in the Soviet Union has been an interest in politics.

Even most of what goes on under the name of dissent cannot be described as political in its nature, since it does not, and because of the nature of things (or, less euphemistically, repression) cannot, represent an *organized* and systematic effort to change the governing system. With few exceptions, the dissidents *protest* against various features of Soviet politics and society, and specific actions of the government, *assert* ideas and values which clash with the official ones, or *plead* with the regime to change its policies—rather than *fight* it the way a pre-1917 revolutionary or even reformer did. But what is striking, even granting the impossibility of organized political opposition in the USSR (not to speak of an open or clandestine effort to overthrow or force the regime to change), is what might be called the fatalistic attitude of most dissenters. Practically none of them see the possibility of a basic alteration of the system, except as a consequence of external events, such as war, either with the West or China. Short of such a calamity, a meaningful change is predicated on the eventuality of a sharp struggle within the ruling oligarchy, which, as by the analogy to the period 1953-1957, might enable more liberal ideas and practices, so to speak, to sneak in. That faith in the people, the conviction that even the most efficient machine of repression cannot indefinitely suppress its craving for freedom, which characterized the Russian revolutionary thought before 1917, is now conspicuous by its absence.

Historically, dissent is a child of de-Stalinization, rather than of any ideological cravings. "One does not have to be as much afraid as before" was the point of departure for most future dissidents, when after March 5, 1953, civic courage became again a meaningful concept, rather than a synonym for a suicidal impulse. At first practically all of them shared the hope that the system could reform itself, not out of their attachment to Marxism-Leninism, but simply because this appeared the only practical hope for improvement.

The next stage was reached with the realization that the victory of the conservative elements within the party and the fall of Khrushchev barred for the immediate future any hope of reform from above. It was then that dissent became differentiated. Some dissidents switched to a position where they uncompromisingly rejected the Soviet system and its ideological underpinning. A group of dissidents, with not much hope of success one should think, have based their protest against the system on, and demand change in the name of, its ideological and constitutional rhetoric: some call on the regime to observe the constitutional "guarantees" of individual rights, others denounce the actual nationality policy by pointing out its jarring departures from Lenin's teachings, etc. There have been but few dissenters who are genuinely Marxist in their professions and who fault the system for its alleged failure to live up to its *ideological* premises. The inherent weakness of this approach is best seen in the writings of its main if indeed not its only articulate spokesman, Roy Medvedev. The present stage of Marxism in the Soviet Union requires, according to Medvedev, "a gradual and systematic development of socialist and party democracy." He then argues that toleration of dissent and/or outright opposition to the regime would not mean an end of the Communist party's monopoly of power.

> In conditions of real socialist democracy, all these non-Marxist movements, parties, and groups [the neo-Stalinists may be included among them] will be deprived of a mass basis and therefore would present no threat to the future of socialist society. Allowed into the open, their activity can be kept within reasonable bounds by democratic methods.[19]

Medvedev's arguments have aroused considerable interest in the West, since in some ways they parallel certain theses of Euro-Communism. But they cannot find any significant following in the USSR. Most Russians could not take seriously the vision of the leadership of the Communist party presiding cheerfully over the liquidation of the system and thus giving the lie to one of the most perceptive observations of Marxism: to wit, that no ruling class is likely to surrender voluntarily its power. And what Medvedev means by "socialist democracy" is at best ambiguous: "genuine socialist democracy allows opposition within the framework of socialist and communist doctrine (which under socialism will *always* be the ideology of the overwhelming majority)."[20] What if it isn't? In any case, it is safe to say that the overwhelming majority of Soviet citizens find both democracy and socialist or Communist doctrine quite remote from their immediate concerns and needs.

The fate of Marxism in today's USSR is in many ways reminiscent of that of Lenin's earthly remains. The latter, under glass, are on public exhibition in the Kremlin Mausoleum. They are guarded by soldiers whose duty is to see to it that those who file by the coffin stay silent and reverent and that no one lingers by the bier, slowing the movement of the line, and perhaps examining the relics to see if they are genuine or made out of wax. Once in a while the mausoleum is shut down for repairs, but as long as the Soviet system continues, it will never be closed permanently, nor will Lenin be given a proper burial. The ceremony has nothing to do with the rate of growth of the Soviet GNP nor with the number of ICBM's at the disposal of the armed forces, but for the rulers it is obviously an equally important element of the security of the Soviet system. What would be the people's reaction if it were stopped?

There is an added symbolism in the fact that it is from the top of Lenin's tomb that the leaders review those gigantic parades celebrating the anniversaries of the Revolution and other festive days of Communism. Tanks, missiles, the serried ranks of soldiers and crowds of athletes, tangible proofs of the might and vitality of the Soviets, pass in review and pay homage not only to the living rulers, but also to a corpse, to the past. In itself comatose, the ideology takes on a real meaning and importance when engrafted onto what is the real source of the regime's strength: national power and pride. For what other regime, runs its unspoken message to its subjects, could preserve the vast multi-national country's unity and greatness? And cumbersome and irrelevant as the doctrine seems, hasn't the Soviet Union under its banner reached unprecedented power and influence in the world, while the West for all of its vaunted freedom and riches has been declining? "The Western world, as a single clearly united force, no longer counterbalances the Soviet Union, indeed has almost ceased to exist," writes one who cannot be accused of being influenced by Soviet propaganda.[21]

And so, as the most perceptive among the dissidents recognize, to undermine the regime's claim to legitimacy, to shake off the people's acquiescence in the repression which masquerades as socialism, one must first of all dissolve the symbiosis between Russian nationalism and Marxism, and point out the illusory character of the argument that Communism is necessary to Russia's greatness, that the two are inextricably connected. Communism, runs the counterargument, is inimical to Russia's national interest. What capitalist power poses as much of a threat to the country's territorial integrity as does Communist China, and primarily because both it and the USSR are Communist? And so the ideology has become not only useless, but a clear danger to national security.

By the same token the regime, since it sees any challenge to the ideology as a threat to its survival, must continue to demonstrate that Marxism-Leninism is the wave of the future. And what more effective way of doing it than by scoring repeated successes at the expense of the West in its current state of disarray and indecision? It is this restless search for a justification of the faith which provides the rationale of its autocratic power, that pushes the Kremlin into policies which pose incalculable dangers to peace. Being intelligent men, genuinely interested in improving their people's lot, the Soviet leaders cannot desire a nuclear holocaust. But at the same time they are driven, by an ideological compulsion much more complex than the now obsolete dream of world revolution, into adventurous and aggressive foreign policies.

— 7 —
Conclusion

He had seen the future, and it worked, wrote an American visitor to Russia in the 1930's, the Russia of famines and terror. Our discussion has reached the point where one might ponder whether Marxism still represents the future, though it does not work.

It certainly does not work in terms of the traditional, including Marx's own, criteria of what constitutes the viability of a social system.

Economically, the performance of the Communist states, though at times impressive in terms of the speed with which industrialization and economic growth were or are being achieved, still falls short in comparison with those societies which retain a considerable element of private enterprise. The standard of living (consumption per head), even in the countries of the "socialist bloc" that are the most advanced in this respect, such as East Germany and Czechoslovakia, lags far behind that of the industrialized countries of the West. Even measured by the capacity to effect rapid industrialization and modernization, its strong point, Communism does not always score against alternative models of economic development. Witness the record of Taiwan and South Korea against that of Communist China and North Korea, not to speak of post-war Japan.

To put it temperately, Communism has not enlarged the area of individual freedom. This statement, though obvious to an unprejudiced mind, will still run into a number of by now classical Marxist objections and qualifications: Marxism, some will protest, has not been tried in a society with a strong tradition of the rule of law; hence it is unfair to judge its potentiality in this respect by what has been happening in Russia or China. How meaningful is it to speak of political freedom in a society which tolerates a high level of unemployment and economic insecurity? For all the necessary limitations it places on various freedoms during the period of revolutionary transition, Communism is explicitly committed to the elimination of racial, ethnic, and sex discrimination.

But all such arguments add up at most to a critique of various non-Communist societies, rather than constituting a viable rebuttal of the charge that as it has been practiced, Communism has invariably restricted and repressed the area of individual freedom. Take Tito's Yugoslavia during the last twenty years, undoubtedly the most tolerant Communist regime insofar as the individual's rights and the treatment of political dissent are concerned. Yet it is at least open to question whether Yugoslavia's record in these respects compares favorably with, never mind a Western democracy, even an old-fashioned authoritarianism, as in Franco's Spain.

Some would claim that a Communist citizen does not miss "bourgeois freedoms," since his sharing in the task of socialist construction gives him a feeling of social solidarity and equality which more than compensate for their absence. Let us note that this phrasing of the question would not have appealed to Karl Marx and his disciples, for whom socialism meant not a rejection of "bourgeois freedoms" but their implementation and expansion, and whose critique hinged not on the undesirability or irrelevance of the freedom of speech, press, etc., but on the allegation that under capitalism only the elite enjoys them. But, more fundamentally, to say as some Western intellectuals do that under Communism the individual does not care for or need those liberal shibboleths, since he has something much better—a wonderful sense of participation and comradeship—reflects both ignorance and condescension. Whenever a Communist regime allows some light to be shed on its internal conditions, as did the USSR after 1953 and as China and Vietnam have begun to do in recent years, such facile generalizations are exposed as myths.

There are those who, observing that excesses of democracy have aggravated certain social problems in the West, are too ready to jump to the conclusion that absence of democracy must be conducive to social tranquility, law and order, labor discipline, etc., in the East. Communism, this view holds, secures its people's allegiance neither through repression nor by giving them a "higher" form of freedom, but by *conditioning* them to obedience. Thus an eminent scholar could write: "The socialist order presumably will command that moral allegiance which is being increasingly refused to capitalism. This, it need hardly be emphasized, will give the workman a healthier attitude toward his duties than he possibly can have under a system he has come to disapprove.... He disapproves because he is told to do so."[1] The clear implication of this argument, hardly flattering to socialism or the working class, is that the masses will obey as long as they are not stirred up by some unruly intellectuals. Yet the notion that the Soviet worker because he lives under Communism has a "healthier attitude toward his duties" than his American or Japanese counterparts is not borne out by statistics on labor productivity in the respective countries, nor by what the Soviets have to say concerning the high incidence of alcoholism and other disrupting phenomena among the labor force. As the Russians have grown more candid about their social problems, it has become fashionable in certain circles in the West to point to China as the home of the true Communist spirit. There, it is asserted, the masses toil selflessly and cheerfully for the common goal of socialism, having submerged their individual desires and preferences in its service. Well, by Peking's own testimony since Mao's death, this image appears as fanciful as was its earlier Russian version.

Marxism, as we have observed, endows the revolutionary elite with the passion not only for power but for modernization and industrialization. But once the decisive break toward industrialization has been accomplished, the given society is bound to develop needs and aspirations, including those for "bourgeois freedoms," which clash with the monopoly of power by the revolutionary elite. What Marx believed to be true about the bourgeoisie in the nineteenth century is certainly much truer of Communism in the second half of the twentieth century: "objectively" it has become superfluous, a drag on the social, economic, and intellectual development of societies in which it has been in power. The bourgeoisie, Marx observed, "supplies the proletariat with its own elements of political and general education. . . . It furnishes the proletariat with weapons for fighting the bourgeoisie."[2] Or, to put it more plainly, the bourgeoisie has conceded democracy. This is something Communism has emphatically refused to do.

To get a perspective on the role of Communism after more than sixty years of its existence, we might quote certain passages in the *Communist Manifesto*, taking the liberty of inserting "liberalism" for Marx's "bourgeoisie." If so, liberalism

> during its rule of scarce one hundred years, has created more massive and more colossal productive forces than have all preceding generations together . . . has through its exploitation of the world market given a cosmopolitan character to production and consumption in every country. . . . [It] draws all, even the most barbarian nations, into civilization. . . . National one-sidedness and narrow mindedness become more and more impossible.[3]

It is on the last count that the comparison of the achievement of nineteenth-century liberalism with that of Marxism as manifested in Communism is most shattering for the latter.

Yet the fact remains that today the philosophies which can claim descent from nineteenth-century liberalism are almost everywhere in retreat, while those purporting to represent Marxism, notably Communism, are advancing. Or to put it in more concrete terms, the number of countries under Communist rule and influence is increasing, whereas the number of countries under what people continue to call (though neither Karl Marx nor a nineteenth-century liberal would recognize it as such) capitalism is decreasing. Why?

Of the tentative explanations, we must first consider those which, because of their lack of theoretical sophistication and reliance on what they claim is merely common sense, can seldom find favor with an academic analyst. The successes of Communism, one such inelegant argument would claim, have but little to do with the virtues of Marxism, just as the disarray of the West has not primarily or mainly been caused by real or alleged deficiencies of the liberal creed. Countries and societies are not conquered and kept in subjection by ideologies, but by men and arms. Whatever the theoretical defects of Communism, its leaders have shown themselves superior to their Western counterparts in understanding the meaning and uses of political and military power. Following World War II the West, most notably the United States, was not able to translate its enormous economic and military strength into political power; the USSR, for all of its enormous human losses and economic devastation, conquered Eastern Europe for Communism and imparted a momentum to the movement. Thus, ironically it has been Russia which was able first to "contain" the West and then to "roll back" its sphere of influence. And of late the enormous growth of Soviet power, its feat of "catching up and surpassing the West," not, to be sure, in the economic sphere, but in nuclear and conventional weapons, has accelerated the process. The Soviet Union, your more reasonable "realist" will grant, would not be able to achieve world mastery because of the growing conflicts within the body of international Communism itself, but it has already made it almost impossible to restore a viable world order under which liberal values and nonauthoritarian politics can flourish.

A variant of the preceding would stress the spiritual and moral weakness of the West as the master cause of the decline of liberalism and of the advance of Communism and kindred forms of authoritarianism. Originally liberalism thought of politics and religion as two separate spheres, but never disparaged the latter. In fact the notion of spiritual autonomy of the individual was central to the liberal vision of society and its assertion of the supreme value of freedom. It is thus easy to see how the catastrophic decline of religion in the traditional meaning of the term has damaged the rationale and attractiveness of liberalism. In trying to fill the void once occupied in his mind by religious belief, modern man has turned to nation, class, and party as the object of his worship and the source of spiritual satisfaction. He seeks in politics a surrogate for religion. Hence the weakened appeal of the liberal state which gives the individual "just" political freedom and participation. Hence also the threat to the democratic process where it still exists. Many seek in it something which by definition it cannot provide; religious experience—and then, frustrated, turn to esoteric and authoritarian cults masquerading as politics. In addition, democratic society as a whole no longer has that self-assurance and hope in the future which was once a striking characteristic of nineteenth-century liberalism. It has become intellectually respectable, indeed fashionable, to inject into a discussion of East-West relations moralistic litanies calling upon Western civilization to repent of its affluence, its past and present sins of capitalism and imperialism, of being Western. Well, civilizations are incapable of expressing guilt, but the average middle-class Englishman or American is occasionally made to feel guilty for his unsophisticated and self-righteous distaste for Communism, as well as uncertain whether what goes on in Russia, and especially China, may not, for all its apparent brutality and irrationality, be a sign of vitality and idealism. Does not one by opposing the encroachments of Communism oppose in fact History? Or, isn't the only effective way for the West to compete with Communism to offer repeated and convincing proofs of its democratic virtue by removing what is left of the selfish, ethnocentric, and inegalitarian in its own society and policies?

Another view of the current travails of the West and its inability to check the advance of Communism emerges from that heterogeneous collection of movements and writings which goes under the name of New Left. Insofar as it has any serious intellectual content, rather than being incoherent activism ranging from student demonstrations to individual terrorism, the New Left merges with what has been called neo-Marxism. The latter in turn retains Marxism as its philosophical framework and basis for political activism, but rejects, or rather is uninterested in, Marx's strict determinism and his economic theory. Not "exploitation" but "alienation" is the battle cry of the New Left; not the worker, but the student, in general the young, is the target of its message.

Upon a closer examination, the New Left then begins to remind one of the Old Left, that variety of anarchist and utopian socialist theories which had preceded and then battled Marxism, were reduced to relative insignificance by the latter, but never quite disappeared. And as suggested above, the revival of the older variety of socialism is not entirely fortuitous. Anarchism was born as a response to the bewildering phenomenon of the Industrial Revolution; the New Left has been generated by the post–World War II social turbulence, as bewildering and corrosive of the traditional values as had been that of the first half of the nineteenth century.

The old anti-industrialism had eventually spawned scientific socialism. But its current variety is unlikely to produce such a distinguished progeny. Rather, like anarchism, the New Left is bound eventually to disappear, its partisans, except for a few diehard eccentrics, being absorbed either by democratic socialism or Communism. No philosophy, or quasi-philosophy, based *purely* on protest and rejection of all forms of authority can give rise to a serious political movement.

But our interest in the New Left lies mainly in the light it throws on the current dilemmas of both Western and Communist societies. What is very instructive in this connection is its use of the term "alienation." In Marx the term had a very specific meaning: the worker's feeling that his labor is not voluntary and creative, since he is merely an adjunct of the machine. In the New Left's parlance, alienation has become a catchall term standing for all kinds of resentment and frustration which the citizen of an affluent democracy should feel; oppressed as he is by the glut of material goods, boring work, the intolerable din of the media, and the meaninglessness of it all, to mention only a few. The realm of capitalism, with alienation the king, is a topsy-turvy world where words and concepts have had their usual meanings reversed and the reality is made to appear as a hallucination:

The distinguishing feature of advanced industrial society is its effective suffocation of those needs which demand liberation—liberation also from that which is tolerable and rewarding and comfortable—while it sustains and absolves the destructive power and repressive function of the affluent society. . . . Liberty can be made into a powerful instrument of domination. . . . Free election of masters does not abolish the masters or the slaves.[4]

The terrified reader might well recall Gertrude Stein's deathbed monologue: "What is the answer?" and then, after a while, "What is the question?" Certainly the message of the New Left neither asks the question nor provides the answer. Rather it is intended to create a mood of exasperation with, if not outright hostility to, liberal values: possessed by this mood, one may "drop out" and eschew the empty rituals of earning one's living and voting in elections. But there is also an existentialist response to the call of the New Left: its young followers have occasionally followed the injunction of a Russian radical of the 1860's who wrote: "Here is the message of our camp: everything which can be destroyed must be destroyed. . . . What falls into pieces is nothing but rubbish; in any case, hack out right and left." It is thus easy to see how the convoluted language of the New Left can be deciphered by some as a justification for terrorism. For all its limited and waning appeal, the phenomenon of the New Left illuminates the vulnerability of democratic society in an age in which the rationalist foundations of its creed are increasingly being challenged. Activities of even a small minority can cripple the functioning of the democratic state, e.g., the case of the Red Brigades in Italy.

While Communist society is not invulnerable to similar disruptive forces, the Communist *state* has traditionally been able to deal with them with none of the hesitations and inhibitions which attend democracy's struggle with dissent. The ghost of its anarchist past has occasionally haunted Communism. What could be a clearer statement of counterculture than the verses of a young Soviet writer in the early 1920's: "We have been seized by a rebellious passionate intoxication. Let them shout about, 'You are destroyers of beauty.' In the name of our Tomorrow we shall burn Raphael, demolish museums, melt down the masterpieces of art." That nonsense went under the name of Proletarian Culture (or, in brief, *Proletkult*) and was put a stop to even before the onset of Stalinism. The Chinese Cultural Revolution partook of the same rage against the traditional and rational—hence the brief infatuation of the New Left in the West with Maoism. But in its inception, the Cultural Revolution was a contrived affair, stage-managed by one faction of the ruling oligarchy which unleashed millions of young fanatics against its rivals. And when it threatened the very foundation of the Communist state, those who had started it quickly put an end to the whole business. Since Mao's death, Chinese Communism seems to have forsaken its penchant for such risky experiments, and threatens to become as "square" as its Soviet counterpart.[5]

Communism enjoys several advantages over liberalism when it comes to their competition in the Third World. On the ideological side, Marxism appeals both to the grievances and the aspirations of a society in the process of transition, while liberalism is the mood of maturity and hence has a certain middle-aged quality about it—its appeal is strongest in a society that has forgotten both nostalgia for the past and excessively utopian visions of the industrial and egalitarian future. At a different level, association with Communism, if not outright identification with it, offers certain tangible advantages for the ruling elites in the new nations. The idiom of Marxism provides a more convincing rationalization of political repression in the name of progress than does that of more traditional forms of authoritarianism. The Soviet Union, or in special cases China, is likely to be a more dependable and indulgent ally of an up-to-date Third World regime or "national liberation" movement than a Western power, subject to the vagaries of democratic politics and with its school-masterish attitude concerning political freedom, the use of terror, etc. To be sure, many of the new states find their flirtation with Communism brings unexpected results, and some may free themselves from Soviet influence, but the general momentum of political developments in the vast area which has been emancipated since World War II certainly does not favor the cause of democracy and the world order. In the nineteenth century, democracy and constitutionalism gained a worldwide currency, and became embodied into the law, even in countries whose level of social and economic development did not favor their successful functioning. This was not only a tribute to the inherent attractiveness of those ideas, but also to the power and prestige of their carriers—the leading countries of the West. And so today Marxism and Communism are also the beneficiaries of the massive presence of the USSR and the People's Republic.

But if most roads in this century seem to lead to socialism, it is far from certain where in turn Marxian socialism will lead. Certainly not to a world order which would secure peace. Certainly not to Communism as Marx and Engels understood it, i.e., material abundance and "real" freedom—progressive elimination of the coercive aspect of political power. In the two largest Communist states it is nationalism rather than ideology which assures social cohesion, and it is the centralization and repressive character of political authority which are its most prominent characteristics. Marxism, which plays such a prominent part on the world scene, has become but an ideological façade in the country where it originally triumphed. But perhaps even there its historical role has not been completed. It would be in accordance with the sardonic spirit of Karl Marx's philosophy of history, if not with its letter, if the Soviet regime, its internationalist premises grown irreconcilable with the nationalist ones, found that it is Marxism as well as the bourgeoisie that produces its own gravediggers.

Notes

Chapter 2

1. Joseph A. Schumpeter, *Capitalism, Socialism and Democracy,* New York, 1950, p. 11.

2. *The Theory of Capitalist Development,* New York, 1942.

3. *Capital,* Volume I [1867], edited by Ernest Untermann after the fourth German edition by Friedrich Engels (New York: The Modern Library, 1932), pp. 648-649. All subsequent page references to *Capital* in this book are to the Modern Library edition.

4. Karl Marx and Friedrich Engels, "Manifesto of the Communist Party," in *Capital and Other Writings by Karl Marx,* tr. by Samuel Moore, ed. by Max Eastman (New York: The Modern Library, 1936), p. 321. Page numbers given in all subsequent quotations from the *Manifesto* refer to this edition.

5. *Capital,* p. 649. (Italics mine)

6. Maximilien Rubel, *Karl Marx: Essai de biographie intellectuelle,* Paris, 1957.

7. "The Civil War in France," *Capital and Other Writings,* op. cit., p. 421.

8. Karl Marx, *Critique of the Gotha Program,* New York, 1938, p. 10.

9. Ibid, p. 10.

10. Karl Marx, "Address to the Communist League," in *A Handbook of Marxism,* edited by Emile Burns, New York, 1935, p. 70.

Chapter 3

1. *Manifesto,* p. 343.

2. *Economic Problems of Socialism in the U.S.S.R.,* quoted in

277

Current Digest of the Soviet Press: Current Soviet Policies, ed. Leo Gruliow, New York, 1953, I, 4-5.

3. J. H. Clapham, *An Economic History of Modern Britain,* Cambridge, England, 1926, II, 477.

4. Arthur Redford, *Labour Migration in England 1800-1850,* Manchester, 1926, p. 18. (Italics mine)

5. *Boswell's London Journal,* ed. Frederick Pottle, New York, 1956, p. 106.

6. "Again, the legend that everything was getting worse for the working man, down to some unspecified date between the drafting of the People's Charter and the Great Exhibition, dies hard. The fact that, after the price fall of 1820-21, the purchasing power of wages in general—not, of course, of everyone's wages—was definitely greater than it had been just before the revolutionary and Napoleonic wars, fits so ill with the tradition that it is very seldom mentioned, the work of statisticians on wages and prices being constantly ignored by social historians. It is symbolic of the divorce of much social and economic history from figures that, in a recent inquiry into the fortunes of one group of trades, the tradition of decline appears in the text, some corrective wage figures in an appendix and the correlation nowhere." J. H. Clapham, *An Economic History of Modern Britain,* Cambridge, England, 1930, I, vii.

7. *The Autobiography of William Cobbett,* London, 1948, p. 179.

8. Ibid., p. 218.

9. *Rural Rides,* ed. G. D. H. and Margaret Cole, London, 1930, II, 665.

10. Ibid., II, 512.

11. *Industry and Trade,* London, 1920, p. 48.

12. William Cobbett, *A History of the Reformation in England and Ireland,* Philadelphia, 1843, p. 26.

13. G. D. H. Cole, *The Life of William Cobbett,* London, 1947, p. 269.

14. "The Condition of the Working Class in England in 1844," in *Karl Marx and Frederick Engels on Britain,* Moscow, 1953, p. 52.

15. *Sybil, or the Two Nations,* London, 1927, p. 134.

16. Engels, *The Condition of the Working Class,* op. cit., p. 52.

17. Quoted in *The Chartist Movement in Its Social and Economic Aspects,* by F. F. Rosenblatt, Columbia University Studies in History, Economics, and Public Law, New York, 1916, LXXIII, 51.

18. William Lovett, *Life and Struggles of William Lovett in His Pursuit of Bread, Knowledge and Freedom,* London, 1820, I, 134.

19. Ibid., I, 59.

20. Quoted in Graham Wallas, *The Life of Francis Place,* New York, 1919, pp. 383-384.

21. Karl Polanyi, *Origins of Our Times: The Great Transformation,* London, 1945.

22. *Letters of David Ricardo to Thomas Robert Malthus,* ed. James Bonaro, Oxford, 1887, p. 138.

23. Sir Robert Peel to William Croker, quoted in *Croker Papers,* London, 1887, II, 383.

24. *Capital,* p. 649.

25. John Morley, *The Life of Richard Cobden,* London, 1918, I, 209.

26. Ibid., II, 20.

27. Ibid., II, 26.

28. Place, quoted in Wallas, op. cit., p. 384.

29. *Capital,* p. 649.

30. *Nouveau Christianisme,* Paris, 1832, p. 68.

31. Robert Owen, *The Book of the New Moral World,* London, 1842, p. 39.

32. Charles Fourier, *La Fausse Industrie,* Paris, 1836, p. 17.

33. Proudhon, *Systeme des Contradictions Économiques, ou Philosophie de la misère,* Paris, 1850, II, 146.

34. Ibid., I, 382.

35. P. J. Proudhon, *De La Justice, Dans la Révolution et Dans L'Église,* Paris, 1858, III, 542.

36. Edouard Dolleans, *Proudhon,* Paris, 1948, p. 218.

37. J. V. Stalin, *Economic Problems of Socialism in the U.S.S.R.,* in *Current Digest of the Soviet Press: Current Soviet Policies,* ed. Leo Gruliow, New York, 1953, I, 3.

38. Louis Blanc, *Organisation du Travail,* Paris, 1850, p. 27.

39. Ibid., p. 77.

Chapter 4

1. *Fabian Essays in Socialism,* London, 1931, pp. 31-32.

2. *National Guilds and the State,* New York, 1920, p. 143.

3. *The World of Labour,* London, 1920, p. 28.

4. Thorstein Veblen, *Imperial Germany and the Industrial Revolution* [1915], New York, 1957, p. 190.

5. Ibid., p. 236.

6. G. Sorel, *Reflections on Violence* [1908], New York, 1941, p. 87. I have substituted "bargaining between employers and labour" for the translator's "corporative particularism" as the former is obviously Sorel's meaning.

7. Eduard Bernstein, *Evolutionary Socialism*, London, 1909, p. xv.

8. Sorel, op. cit., p. 123

9. Bernstein, op. cit., p. 218.

10. Sorel, op. cit., p. 130.

11. Bernstein, op. cit., p. x.

12. Ibid, p. 166.

13. Paul Louis, *Histoire du Socialisme en France*, Paris, 1950, p. 287.

14. Val R. Lorwin, *The French Labor Movement*, Cambridge, Mass., 1954, pp. 36-37.

15. Carl E. Schorske, *German Social Democracy, 1905-17: The Development of the Great Schism*, Cambridge, Mass., 1955, p. 115.

16. Werner Sombart, *Die Deutsche Volkwirtshaft im Neunzehnten und im Anfang des 20 Jahrhunderts*, Berlin, 1921, p. 455.

17. P. 340.

18. V. I. Lenin, *What Is to Be Done* [1902], New York, 1929, p. 32.

19. Ibid., p. 39.

20. Ibid., p. 41.

21. Ibid., p. 79.

22. V. I. Lenin, *Sochinenya*, Moscow, 1946, III, 527.

23. Oliver Radkey, *The Agrarian Foes of Bolshevism*, New York, 1958.

24. Op. cit., pp. 76, 79.

25. *The Fourth (Unity) Congress of the Russian Social Democratic Workers' Party in 1906* (in Russian), Moscow, 1934, p. 501.

26. V. I. Lenin, *Imperialism*, Detroit, 1924, p. 128.

27. *Russia in Flux*, New York, 1948, p. 182.

28. V. I. Lenin, *The State and Revolution* [1917] New York, 1932, p. 38.

29. Ibid., p. 83.

30. *The Protocols of the Eighth Congress of the Russian Communist Party in 1919* (in Russian), Moscow, 1933, p. 21.

31. Ibid., p. 292.

Chapter 5

1. *Capital*, p. 649.

2. *The Sixteenth Congress of the All Union Communist Party, 1930*, in Russian, Moscow, 1930, p. 56.

3. Alexandra Kollontay, *The Workers' Opposition in Russia*,

Chicago, 1921, p. 33. The Russian text was unavailable to me. The English translation is unauthorized and obviously inexact.

4. Ibid., p. 40.

5. Leonard Schapiro, *The Origin of the Communist Autocracy,* Cambridge, Mass., 1955, p. 294.

6. Ibid., p. 301.

7. V. I. Lenin, *State and Revolution* [1917], New York, 1932, p. 83.

8. Ibid., p. 46.

9. J. V. Stalin, *Economic Problems of Socialism in the U.S.S.R.,* in *Current Digest of the Soviet Press: Current Soviet Policies,* ed. Leo Gruliow, New York, 1953, I, 3.

10. Quoted in Merle Fainsod, *How Russia is Ruled,* Cambridge, Mass., 1953, p. 443.

11. *The Fifteenth Conference of the All Union Communist Party* (in Russian), Moscow, 1927, p. 721.

12. J. V. Stalin, *Leninism,* New York, 1933, II, 431.

13. John Maynard Keynes, *The Economic Consequences of the Peace,* New York, 1920, pp. 11-12.

14. Ibid., p. 20.

15. Ibid., p. 22.

16. *The Fifteenth Conference of the All Union Communist Party, 1926* (in Russian), Moscow, 1927, p. 456.

17. *Manifesto,* p. 327.

18. Quoted in Benjamin Schwartz, *Chinese Communism and the Rise of Mao,* Cambridge, Mass., 1951, p. 37.

19. *A Documentary History of Chinese Communism,* cit. Conrad Brandt, Benjamin Schwartz, and John K. Fairbank, Cambridge, Mass., 1952, pp. 80, 82.

Chapter 6

1. Alec Nove, *An Economic History of the USSR,* London, 1969, p. 299.

2. *Khrushchev Remembers,* New York, 1974, p. 189.

3. But the Crimean Tatars and the Volga Germans who had shared the same fate were not accorded the same indulgence.

4. The statistics for the last decade indicate clearly that the non-Russian groups in the population, most notably the Turkic speaking ones in Central Asia, are reproducing at a much faster rate than the Russians.

5. In order to leave his *kolkhoz* for another one or for the city, the peasant had to secure his farm's chairman's authorization.

6. E. G. Liberman, *Economic Methods and the Effectiveness of Production*, New York, 1971, p. 60.

7. Technically, collective farms represent cooperative ownership, but as we have seen, it is a distinction of little practical importance.

8. Today perhaps we would have to give them a few months.

9. Lewis Feuer, ed., *Marx and Engels, Basic Writings on Politics and Philosophy*, New York, 1959, p. 26.

10. Still it is difficult to believe that had the Soviets allowed Dubcek's policies to continue, the Czechoslovak Communist Party could have maintained itself in power for very long.

11. A. I. Solzhenitsyn, *Letter to Soviet Leaders*, London, 1974, p. 46. (My italics)

12. Ibid.

13. "The Young Age Group," in *Izvestia*, October 25, 1973.

14. "And Here We Are on the Island," *Komsomolskaya Pravda*, September 21, 1972.

15. Lewis Feuer, ed., op. cit., p. 106.

16. *Literaturnaya gazeta* (The Literary Journal), Moscow, July 10, 1974, p. 11.

17. I. Deutscher, *Russia What Next*, New York, 1953, p. 223.

18. Alexander Solzhenitsyn, *The Gulag Archipelago, Three*, New York, 1978, p. 449.

19. Roy Medvedev, *On Socialist Democracy*, New York, 1975, p. 106.

20. Ibid., p. 46.

21. Solzhenitsyn, *Letter to the Soviet Leaders*, p. 11.

Chapter 7

1. Joseph Schumpeter, *Capitalism, Socialism and Democracy*, 3rd ed., New York, 1950, p. 211.

2. Lewis Feuer, ed., op. cit., p. 17.

3. Ibid., pp. 10-12.

4. Herbert Marcuse, *One Dimensional Man: Studies in the Ideology of Advanced Industrial Society*, Boston, 1964, p. 7.

5. The turbulence between 1966 and 1969 served Mao the same purpose as did massive terror for Stalin: the means of getting rid of his real and potential opponents. But the Great Helmsman also came close to postulating a new theory for revolutionary Marxism—a periodic cultural revolution must be a necessary feature of Communist society; it shakes it up and prevents bureaucratic ossification. But this is unlikely to become popular with Communist elites.

Index